sixth edition

STATE AND LOCAL POLITICS

Government By The People

James MacGregor Burns
Williams College

J. W. Peltason
University of California, Irvine

Thomas E. Cronin
The Colorado College

Prentice Hall, Englewood Cliffs, New Jersey 07632

Library of Congress Cataloging-in-Publication Data

Burns, James MacGregor.
   State and local politics : government by the people / James
MacGregor Burns, J.W. Peltason, Thomas E. Cronin. -- 6th ed.
      p.   cm.
   Includes bibliographical references.
   ISBN 0-13-843434-4
   1. State governments--United States. 2. Local government--United
States.   I. Peltason, J. W. (Jack Walter)   II. Cronin,
Thomas E.   III. Title.
JK2408.B87 1990
320.973--dc20
                                                         89-49436
                                                              CIP

Editorial/production supervision and interior design: Serena Hoffman
Cover design: Lee Cohen
Cover photo: AP/Wide World Photos
Manufacturing buyer: Bob Anderson

 © 1990, 1987, 1984, 1981, 1978, 1976 by Prentice-Hall, Inc.
A Division of Simon & Schuster
Englewood Cliffs, New Jersey 07632
as Chapters 3, 24, 25, 26, 27, 28, 29, 30, 31, and 32
of *Government By The People,* Fourteenth Edition

Printed in the United States of America
10 9 8 7 6 5 4 3

ISBN 0-13-843434-4

PRENTICE-HALL INTERNATIONAL (UK) Limited, *London*
PRENTICE-HALL OF AUSTRALIA PTY. Limited, *Sydney*
PRENTICE-HALL CANADA INC., *Toronto*
PRENTICE-HALL HISPANOAMERICANA, S.A., *Mexico*
PRENTICE-HALL OF INDIA PRIVATE LIMITED, *New Delhi*
PRENTICE-HALL OF JAPAN, INC., *Tokyo*
SIMON & SCHUSTER ASIA PTE. LTD., *Singapore*
EDITORA PRENTICE-HALL DO BRASIL, LTDA., *Rio de Janeiro*

Contents

4 STATE LEGISLATURES   74

5 STATE GOVERNORS   106

6   JUDGES AND JUSTICE IN THE STATES   131

7   GOVERNMENT AT THE GRASS ROOTS   154

Preface

This book is about the political forces that shape policy making and policy outcomes in state and local communities. To those of us who are students of American politics, states and their subdivisions are fascinating political laboratories that allow comparisons among different political systems. State and community governments pose certain problems more sharply than others. The party system is much weaker in some regions of the country than in others. State legislatures in some of the smaller or rural states meet for just a few months a year, whereas in other states they meet all year. The importance of interest groups and the media varies from state to state and from city to city. Generalizations are sometimes difficult, yet we try in this book to summarize what political scientists know about state and local politics.

Those who want better government in their communities and states will not achieve it by sitting around and waiting for it. If government by the people, of the people, and for the people is to be more than just Fourth of July rhetoric, activists must understand state and local politics and must be willing to clarify the issues for debate, form political alliances, respect and protect the rights of those with whom they differ, and be willing to serve as citizen leaders, citizen politicians. We hope this book will motivate students to the view that every person *can* make a difference, and that all of us should work toward that end.

This book consists of the last nine chapters plus a chapter on federalism from the fourteenth edition of *Government By The People*, National, State and Local version (1990). We have had the benefit of useful criticisms and suggestions from Professors Gerald Benjamin, SUNY University at New Paltz; Robert X. Browning, Purdue University; Stephen Percy, University of Virginia; and Craig Rimmerman, Hobart and William Smith Colleges. Pat Denis, Kathy North, David N. Lowland, Ann Armstrong, Marj Billings, David Sandford, and Sean Gallup also provided editorial and proofreading assistance. We also thank the staffs of the Advisory Commission on Intergovernmental Relations and the National Conference of State Legislatures for their valuable assistance. We also express our considerable thanks to Serena Hoffman and Karen Horton at Prentice Hall.

James MacGregor Burns
Williams College
Williamstown, MA 01267

J. W. Peltason
University of California, Irvine
Irvine, CA 92717

Thomas E. Cronin
The Colorado College
Colorado Springs, CO 80903

PS. Please point out errors or send us your reactions and suggestions at our college addresses above or in care of the Political Science Editor, Prentice Hall, Englewood Cliffs, New Jersey 07632. Thanks.

1

Who Governs?
State and
Local Politics

State and local governments flourished before the Constitution; on the East coast, long before. Indeed, the framers of the U.S. Constitution shaped the national government in large part on their practical experiences back home with state, village, or community governments. Today this is still true. What happens in the 83,000 state and local governments still influences the forms and policies of the national government. The reverse, of course, is also true: The national government often has an important impact on local and state government.

The national government's activities—dramatic diplomatic maneuvers, key Supreme Court decisions, major congressional debates—receive most of the publicity, so much that we often overlook the countless ways governments closer at hand affect our lives. The quality of the air we breathe, the purity of the water we drink, the character of our schools and universities, the effectiveness of law enforcement, the decisions about how we will pay for these things—these are just a few examples of policies determined by state and community governments.

"Who really runs things around here?" "Who has the clout?" "Who counts?" These are important questions, especially for a people who dream about self-government and a government by the people.

In 1924 two sociologists from Columbia University, Robert and Helen Lynd, studied a typical American city as though they were anthropologists investigating a tribe in Africa. For two years they lived in Muncie, Indiana—at the time a city of 38,000—asking questions and watching how people made their livings, brought up their children, used their leisure time, and joined in civic and social associations. The Lynds reported that despite the appearance of democratic rule, a social and economic elite was actually running things.[1] This stimulated a series of studies by social scientists and journalists in all kinds of communities to find out how government works and whether power is concentrated in the hands of the few, dispersed among many, or somewhere in between.

Studying American state and local governments to find out how they operate and who governs them in the early 1990s presents major problems. It is one thing to study the national system, vast and complex as it is; it is something else to study fifty separate state governments, each with its own legislature, executive, and judiciary—each with its own intricate politics and political traditions. Moreover, the government of each state is only part of a much larger picture. To discuss the government of Mississippi or the city of Detroit without mentioning white-black relations, the government of New York without noting the politics of ethnic groups, or the government of Texas without referring to cattle and oil would ignore the dynamics of the political process. State governments, just like the national government, cannot be properly analyzed and assessed as organizational charts. And the great variations among the states—in population, economic resources, environment—make comparisons and generalizations difficult.

Any governmental system is part of a larger social system. A government is a device that resolves or at least manages conflicts. Further, it distributes, regulates, and sometimes redistributes those things that are valued. It is also a device to achieve certain goals and to perform services desired both by those who govern and by those who are governed. Many outside factors are often more important than the structure of the governmental system itself or even the nature of its political parties. The economic system, the class structure, and the style of life are sometimes more important in determining the policies adopted by a particular state or municipality than are the governmental structures it has adopted.[2] Obviously, the economic circumstances and objectives of a city influence what is discussed and often what is decided.[3] However, the interrelations among the economic, social, and political systems are so complex that it is often difficult to unscramble them and to decide which is cause and which is effect.

This already complex picture is complicated still further by the more than 83,000 cities, counties, towns, villages, school districts, water-control districts, and other governmental units that are piled one on top of another within the states. If all states or cities or towns were alike, the task might be manageable. But of course they are not. Each city, like each state, is unique. Our states, cities, and counties, then, cannot be fitted into simple categories; we must discover the patterns and search for the uniformities underlying all the variation before we can begin to understand how these governments operate and who most influences their operations and policies.

The Location of Power

How can we understand the operations and problems of state and local government without becoming bogged down in endless detail? We can do so by calling attention to the core problems of democratic governance: citizen participation, liberty, constitutionalism, representation, and responsible leadership. Further, we can emphasize a question that throws light on all these problems—*Who governs?* Does political power in the states and localities tend to gravitate toward a relatively small number of people? If so, who are these people? Do they work closely together, or do they divide among themselves? Do the same people or factions shape the agenda for public debate and dominate all decision making, or do some sets of leaders decide certain questions and leave other questions to other leaders, or simply to chance?

ANALYZING PATTERNS OF POWER

Relying on a mix of research methods, social scientists have studied the patterns of power in communities and have come up with varied findings. Floyd Hunter, a sociologist who analyzed Atlanta, found a relatively small and stable group of top policy makers drawn largely from the business class. This elite operated through shifting groups of secondary leaders who sometimes modified policy, but the power of the elite was almost always there.[4] In contrast, Robert Dahl, a political scientist at Yale, studied New Haven and concluded that although some people had a great deal of influence and most others had little, *there was no permanent hard-core elite*. There were instead shifting coalitions of leaders who sometimes disagreed among themselves and who always had to keep in mind what the public would accept when making their decisions.[5]

Of the two cities, Atlanta and New Haven, which is more typical of the distribution of influence in American communities? Could it be that the differences between Hunter's and Dahl's findings stem from the questions they asked? Clearly, the assumptions of investigators and the techniques they use produce some of the differences in what they find.[6]

RULE BY A FEW OR RULE BY THE MANY?

One group of investigators, chiefly sociologists such as Hunter, is mainly concerned with **social stratification** in the political system; in other words, how politics is affected by the fact that in any community people are divided among socioeconomic groups. Are the upper classes the ruling classes? These social scientists, assuming that political influence is a function of the socioeconomic structure of the community, try to find out who governs a particular community by asking a variety of citizens to identify the persons who are most influential in it. Then they study these influentials to determine their social characteristics, their roles in decision making, and the interrelations both among themselves and between them and the rest of the citizens. Those who use this technique report that the upper socioeconomic groups make up the **power elite,** that elected political leaders are subordinate to this elite, and that the major conflicts within the community are between the upper and the lower socioeconomic classes.

Another group of investigators has questioned these findings, raising objections to the research techniques used. The evidence, they contend (even that contained within the stratification studies themselves), does not support the conclusion that communities are run by a power elite. Rather, the notion of a power elite is merely a reflection of the techniques used and the assumptions made by the stratification theorists. Instead of studying the activities of those who are *thought* to have "clout," one should study public policy to find out how, in fact, decisions are made. Those who conduct community studies in this manner usually find a relatively open **pluralistic power structure.** Some people do have more influence than others, but influence is shared among a rather sizable number and tends to be limited to particular issues and areas. Those who have much to say about how the public schools are run may have little influence over economic policies. And in many communities and for many issues there is no identifiable group of influentials. Policy emerges not from the actions of a small group but from the unanticipated and unplanned consequences of the behavior of a relatively large number of people, and especially from the existence of countless contending groups that form and win access to those making important decisions. According to these theorists, the social structure of the community is certainly one factor, but it is not the determining factor in how goods and services are distributed.

Here we have an example of how the questions we ask influence the answers we find. If we ask highly visible and actively involved citizens for their opinions of who is powerful, we will find they name a relatively small number of people as the *real* holders of power. If we study dozens of local events and decisions, we frequently find a variety of people are involved—different people in different policy areas. If we query still other students of local politics, we may find they suggest that local values, traditions, and the structure of governmental organizations determine which issues get on the local agenda.[7] Thus, tobacco, mining, or steel interests, they say, may be so dominant in an area that tax, regulation, or job safety policies thought to be normal elsewhere will be kept off the local policy agenda for fear of offending the supposed "powers that be." And those interests may indeed go to great lengths to prevent what they deem to be adverse policies. They urge us to weigh carefully the possibility that those who defend the status quo can mobilize power resources in such a way that "nondecisions" may be more important than actual decisions. Study who rules, but also study the procedures and rules of the game that operate to *prevent* issues from arising. Determine which groups or interests gain and which are handicapped by political decisions.[8] This is useful advice, although the task of studying nondecisions is complex.[9]

Studies of communities and states have now produced enough findings that we can begin to see how formal governmental institutions, social structure, economic factors, and other variables interact to create a working political system.

The Stakes of the Political Struggle

Events have given the national government enormous influence over the destiny of the American people. The advent of nuclear weapons has put into the hands of one person, the president, life-and-death control of the future of tens of millions of people. By assuming the responsibility for protecting our civil rights, fighting inflation, regulating great economic power groups such as airlines and insurance companies, and subsidizing economically weaker sectors of the economy, the national government has become the custodian of the nation's economic strength and security. Certainly, state and local governments cannot claim so central a role. Yet the role of the states and localities is increasingly large in domestic policy questions, not only in absolute terms but even in relative terms, as compared with the national government. Since World War II *state and local* governmental activities have increased much faster than the nondefense activities of the federal government. Today two-thirds of the expenditures for domestic functions are carried by the states and their subdivisions. States are likely to have to assume even greater responsibilities for raising taxes and setting economic and social priorities as a result of recent attempts to bring about a "new federalism" by the national government's cutback of federal funding of various state and local services in the past decade.

Moreover, state and local governments generally have more intimate relations with the average person than the national government does, for neighborhood, school, and housing problems of Americans are closely regulated by state and local governments. The points at which we come into contact with government services and officials most often are in schools, on the highways, in playgrounds, at big fires, in hospitals, or in courtrooms. (But even in many of these areas, the mix of national, state, and local programs and responsibilities is such that it is often hard to isolate which level of government does what to whom. Also, there are some national-to-individual relationships that bypass state and local governments altogether, such as the mail service and federal tax collection.)

Some things might seem far removed from any government, for example, having a dog or a cat as a pet. But a dog needs a license and a collar, it must be confined, and it must be inoculated. And if anyone thinks that cats are beyond the reach of the law, one should remember Adlai E. Stevenson's famous veto of the "cat bill" when he was governor of Illinois. The bill would have imposed fines on cat owners who let their pets run off their premises, and it would have allowed cat haters to trap them. The governor said:

> I cannot agree that it should be the declared public policy of Illinois that a cat visiting a neighbor's yard or crossing the highway is a public nuisance. It is in the nature of cats to do a certain amount of unescorted roaming. . . . I am afraid this bill could only create discord, recrimination, and enmity. . . . We are all interested in protecting certain varieties of birds. . . . The problem of the cat versus bird is as old as time. If we attempt to resolve it by legislation who knows but what we may be called upon to take sides as well in the age-old problem of dog versus cat, bird versus bird, or even bird versus worm. . . .[10]

So the governor sided with cat supporters over bird lovers, while staying neutral between bird lovers and worm diggers. Such incidents illustrate how the complex working of modern society can lead to government intervention in or overregulation of our lives.

THE MAZE OF INTERESTS

Special-interest groups are found, in varying forms, in all the states. Even industrial Rhode Island has farm organizations, and rural Wyoming has trade unions. Influential economic pressure groups and political-action committees (organized to raise and disperse campaign funds to candidates for public office) operate in the states much as they do nationally. They try to build up the membership of their organizations; they lobby at the state capitols and at city halls; they educate and organize the voters; and they support their political friends in office and oppose their enemies. They also face the internal problems all groups face: maintaining unity within the group, dealing with subgroups that break off in response to special needs, and maintaining both democracy and discipline.

One great difference, however, is that group interests can be concentrated in states and localities, whereas their strength tends to be diluted in the national government. Big Business does not really run things in Washington, any more than does Wall Street, the Catholic Church, or the American Legion. But in some states and localities certain interests are clearly dominant because they represent the social and economic majorities of the area. Few politicians in Wisconsin will attack dairy farmers; candidates for office in Florida are unlikely to oppose benefits for senior citizens; and few black office holders in Boston are likely to espouse strong Republican positions.

It is the range and variety of these local groupings that give American politics its special flavor and excitement. Such groups include auto unions and manufacturers in Michigan, corn and hog farmers in Iowa, French-Americans in northern New England, gas and oil dealers in Texas, gun owners in New Hampshire and Idaho, tobacco farmers in North Carolina, aircraft employees in southern California, cotton growers in the South, coal miners in West Virginia, and sheep ranchers in Wyoming. However, the power of these groups should not be exaggerated.

Different groups have different needs and aspirations, and we have to be

"Where there's smoke, there's money."

Drawing by Joe Mirachi; © 1985 The New Yorker Magazine, Inc.

cautious about lumping all labor, all business, all teachers, all Chicanos, and all blacks together. Labor unions are sometimes sharply divided among the teamsters, building trades, machinists, auto workers, and so on; the business community is often divided between the big industrial, banking, and commercial firms on the one hand and small merchants on the other.

In New England, Irish and Italian fraternal societies have long expressed the opinions of their respective groups on various public issues; other organizations claim to speak for the French-Canadians and Polish citizens. New England politicians have feared the power of such groups to influence elections, especially primaries. But there are many examples of "Yankees" winning in heavily ethnic areas. Compared to the other considerations affecting the voters' choices, the ethnic factor may be small (although a minute percentage of course, may still be decisive in an election). Much depends on the character of the candidates, and on the appeals they create.[11] Any group, no matter how strong, must cope with a variety of cross-pressures, including a general sense of the rules of the game, which suggest that the voter does not vote for "one of our own" merely on that ground alone.

Now, let us look further at interests that are more specialized and that have a closer relation to local government. Many businesspeople sell to the state or perform services for it, for example, milk dealers, printers, contractors, parking meter manufacturers, makers of playground equipment, and textbook publishers. Such people will often formally or informally organize in order to improve and stabilize their relations with purchasing officials. At the local level developers and home builders together with their lawyers press for zoning and planning commission action. Millions of dollars are often at stake, and the resulting action or inaction frequently shapes both economic growth and the environmental quality of a community.

Another type of group intimately concerned with public policy is the professional association. The states license barbers, beauticians, architects, lawyers, doctors, teachers, accountants, dentists, and many other groups. Associations representing such groups are concerned with the nature of the regulatory laws and with the makeup of the boards that do the regulating. They are especially concerned about the rules of admission to the professions and about the way in which professional misconduct is defined. Bar associations, for example, closely watch the appointment of judges and court officials.

Every state has its own set of lobbyists, but some of the more typical and important interests that are likely to be represented by their own associations at the state capital are manufacturing businesses, banking and insurance industries, public school teachers, chemical companies, dairy farmers, cattle farmers, highway contractors, public employee associations, oil, gas, and mining producers, environmental and consumer interests, and unions. Today other groups of citizens are also likely to organize and send lobbyists to the state capital: those who are pro-life or pro-choice; those who want stiffer sentences for drunken driving and for those who use guns in robberies. Even more specialized interests are not going to let what happens in a state capital go uninfluenced these days, so you are likely to find representatives from the Beautician's Aid Association, the Funeral Directors' and Embalmers' Association, the Institute of Dry Cleaning, and the Association of Private Driver-Training Schools at the state house.

Many businesses, especially larger corporations, are likely to supplement their representation through a chamber of commerce or trade association with their own lobbyists—called public relations political consultants. Or they may be served by a law firm hired to represent their business. One of our growth businesses in state politics is consulting, involving specialized lawyers who for a fee help push desirable bills through the legislature or block unwanted ones.

Many law firms and an increasing number of political consultants offer a range of services—from merely providing information about what is going on, to taking statewide polls on various issues, to overseeing concentrated lobbying efforts and campaigns to change elite and public opinion about a matter to those who are able and willing to pay the right price. This again raises the question of who has clout or who governs. Clearly, those who can hire skilled lobbyists and other experts to shape the public agenda can and often do wield significantly more influence than citizens who only rarely follow state and regional governmental decision making.

LOBBYISTS AT THE STATEHOUSE

There is a widespread conviction that lobbyists have freer rein in state legislatures than they do in the United States Congress and, what is more, that bribery by lobbyists is cruder, more basic, and more obvious in state legislatures. This may be because state lobbying restrictions are often more relaxed than those at the federal level and because there is a less likelihood of press exposure at the state level—at least in several states. Kickbacks from highway contractors or from other firms doing business with the states are exposed often enough to give credence to these claims. Spiro Agnew was forced to resign from the vice-presidency back in 1974 because of kickback payoffs he received while he was governor of Maryland. Florida, Illinois, Louisiana, New York, and Oklahoma have all been plagued by indictments and convictions of public officials in the past generation.

Corruption of legislators and state officials is, of course, hard to prove. Insiders sometimes charge that legislators accept favors for votes. Exposure of scandals in several states, especially in the post-Watergate era, pushed many legislatures to curb election abuses and pass ethics codes with more stringent conflict-of-interest provisions. Several legislatures have enacted comprehensive financial disclosure laws, and today most state governments are more open, professional, and accountable than in the past.[12]

In Washington lobbyists tend to spend more time with legislators who are sympathetic to their points of view, while in the state legislature there appears to be more of an attempt to persuade the opposition or the undecided than to bolster supporters. Former President Jimmy Carter, who served for a few years in the Georgia state senate and then as governor, recalled that only a "tiny portion" of the 259 members of the Georgia legislature were not good or honest people. But Carter found that "it is difficult for the common good to prevail against the intense concentration of those who have a special interest, especially if the decisions are made behind locked doors. . . . In the absence of clear and comprehensive issues, it is simply not possible to marshal the interest of the general public, and under such circumstances legislators often respond to the quiet and professional pressure of lobbyists."[13]

In a few states single corporations or organizations have considerable influence; in others a "big three" or "big four" may dominate politics. But in most states there is open competition among organizations, and no single group or coalition of groups stands out. In no state does any one organization control legislative politics,[14] although the powerful Anaconda Company once came close in Montana. Lobbyists are present in every state capital, and they are there to guide through the legislature a small handfull of bills their organization wants passed or defeated. Legislators are concerned with processing hundreds or even thousands of bills, in addition to doing casework in behalf of constituents and worrying about party, district, and colleagues. The governor? "Governors come and governors go, but the lobbyists [or legislative representatives] stay on forever!"[15] Shrewd lobbyists usually get a chance—or several chances—to influence the fate of their few bills.

In one recent year nearly 400 lobbyists were registered at the Arkansas state capitol. Of these, 125 represented utilities, and more than 200 lobbied on behalf of individual businesses, industry, or professions. Nine lobbyists represented labor interests, eight worked on behalf of senior citizens, and three for environmental concerns. In the absence of strong parties in Arkansas, interest groups and their lobbyists are viewed as the most influential sources of information for state officials. Surveys in that state suggest that the Arkansas Power and Light Company, the railroads, the poultry and trucking industries, the teachers, and the state chamber of commerce are the most effective lobbyists. "It is still true that ordinarily those with greater economic resources, greater numbers, and higher status have far more impact than those who lack these attributes. . . ." writes political scientist Diane Blair. "Nevertheless, an increasingly complex economy has produced many more actors in the political system, and especially when there is division among the economic elite, some of the lesser voices can be heard."[16]

Some groups have a special role both because of their relations with government and because of the size and importance of the work they are doing. Consider public school teachers, for example. They are both employees of the local government and an interest group exerting pressure on it. They must deal with many other organized groups in education; for example, parents in local and state PTAs; principals and superintendents, who often have their own associations; and parents of children attending private and parochial schools. Teachers across the nation are increasingly politically organized, and they now regularly interview and endorse candidates for public office at all levels of government. They are often also a formidable political force in local campaigns. Sometimes, too, they use a strike or the threat of a walkout as a weapon to influence their wages and working conditions.

Participation Patterns in Small and Medium-Sized Cities

Citizens generally take less interest in, vote less for, and are less informed about their local governments than they are about the national government. This might seem strange, for people are closer to city hall and to county administration buildings than they are to remote governmental officials and bureaucracies in Washington, D.C. Nevertheless, there are some reasons for this relatively slight involvement in local government. Most of the time most local governments are preoccupied with relatively noncontroversial routines, such as keeping the roads in shape, providing fire and police service, attracting businesses that can create more jobs, or applying for state and federal financial assistance. Most local communities want to keep their tax rates down and to promote their cities as "nice places" in which to live, work, and raise a family.

Mayors and city officials generally try to avoid controversies and the kind of favoritism that will be divisive in the community. Although they do not always succeed, they go to considerable lengths to appear reasonable and work for the good of the community. Few city authorities aggressively seek to alter the status quo. Cities do not, as a rule, seek to promote equality in the sense of taxing the well-to-do and redistributing various resources to needier citizens. City officials tend to believe this is the job of the national or state authorities, that is, if they think it should be done at all. Typically, too, they will say their cities just do not have the funds for that type of program. They might add, "Go see the governor," or "Go talk to your member of Congress." In fact, this may be good advice, because various state and national programs (health care, educational loans, unemployment compensation and disability assistance, and so on) have often been explicitly designed to help the less fortunate. They may not do so, yet this frequently was their original intent.

One result of this reality—that local governments are less involved in **redistributive policy** politics—is that interest groups are less well developed and lobbying is more sporadic at the local level than at the state and national levels of government.[17] Local officials obviously have to be concerned about the political consequences of the decisions they make, but they are often free to do so with less interference from organized interest groups. Indeed, many mayors and county officials are able to make an impressive range of decisions primarily on the basis of what they think is best for the community—guided mainly by the professional and technical advice they get from city managers, planners, and other community employees who help administer their cities.

Of course, there are exceptions to this generalization. Neighborhood groups sometimes become very involved in protecting their areas and petitioning for improvements. But that kind of involvement usually occurs only once or twice every few years, and it is limited to a minor portion of the city's budget. Or a local school district may seek to close down a community elementary school, almost always a controversial issue. Squeezed by declining enrollments, school board officials often become embroiled in heated community meetings. Still, attendance at local government meetings is usually low.

Those who have major economic stakes in a community actively participate in local campaigns and make it a point to stay in close touch with local officials. In most cities local developers and real estate groups customarily enjoy influence with city officials. Likewise, the local chamber of commerce often has longstanding ties to many members of city and county government. Questions of economic development, the property tax rate, sales tax, and tourist promotion loom large as mutual concerns for local business leaders as well as local officials.

What about local newspapers? Most communities have only one newspaper, and in small communities it is often a weekly. Some newspapers, and some local radio and television stations, do a good job of covering city and county politics. But this is the exception rather than the rule. Most newspapers realize most of their readers are more interested in reading about national news, and especially about sports, than about what takes place at municipal planning meetings or county commissioner sessions. Most of what takes place in local government is rather dull—relatively speaking. It may be important to some people, but it strikes the average person as decidedly less interesting than what goes on at the White House, or whether Congress has really solved the social security problem, or whether the Chicago Bears, the L.A. Dodgers, or the Boston Celtics won last night.

Further, in towns and medium-sized cities many local newspapers develop a rather cozy relationship with elected local officials. Sometimes the owners or editors are social friends or even golfing buddies of local officials. Friendships and mutual interests develop, and close, scrutinizing coverage of what goes on in city hall takes a back seat to city boosterism. In effect, "newspapers boost their hometown, knowing that its prosperity and expansion aid their own. Harping at local faults, investigating dirty politics, revealing unsavory scandals, and stressing governmental inefficiencies only provide readily available documentary material to competing cities. . . ."[18]

Finally, it is expensive to cover community government properly. Most newspapers can afford only a part-time reporter to cover city government, and often this person is relatively new to writing about politics and government. In many instances reporters are intimidated by elected officials, who typically are successful business or professional leaders and are considerably older and more established in the community. Overly irreverent young reporters sometimes find themselves reassigned, perhaps because of the influence some city officials may have with the owners of the local paper. Further, we must remember that the lifeblood of many local newspapers is the ads they sell to local businesses. When these dry up, newspapers have to fold. Thus, some rather basic economic realities partially account for how papers and stations cover, *or fail to cover*, local government.

APATHY IN GRASS-ROOTS AMERICA

One political scientist found that even in New Haven, a relatively active city politically, "political indifference surrounds a great many citizens like impenetrable armor plate and makes them difficult targets for propaganda."[19] He cited as an example a campaign to revise the city charter. City politicians debated the matter vigorously; the newspapers took an outspoken position; a citizens' charter committee ran big advertisements; radio and television programs carried on the debate; fliers were even distributed door-to-door. The result? Only 45 percent of those who voted in the regular election voted on the charter (and most opposed it).

Even New England town meetings have difficulty getting people to participate—even though their decisions have major consequences for the local tax rate and the quality of the schools, the police force, and the parks and recreational areas. Thomas Jefferson once proclaimed the town meeting to be the noblest, wisest instrument yet devised for the conduct of public affairs. Yet most towns find that only about 2 or 3 percent of the population care enough to come.

All these are contributing factors, but the fact is the average person is not fascinated with politics; most people leave politics and political responsibilities to a relatively small number of activists. For most people personal concerns—arthritis, crabgrass, their bowling leagues, their children's Little League or soccer games, or their sons' or daughters' applications to college—all come well ahead of involvement in their city's personnel boards or planning and zoning commissions. Of course, it may be sensible for the many who are satisfied with local governments functioning to sit on the sidelines and leave civic responsibilities to those who are interested and willing to handle them.

Cynicism about the effectiveness of local political processes is sometimes reflected in the occasional use of the politics of protest—mass demonstrations, economic boycotts, even civil disorders—as a way of making demands on the governmental system. As certain issues become more intense, revitalized political activity often occurs. Blacks, Hispanics, gays, and others in the inner city form political organizations in order to present their grievances and organize their votes more effectively. Neighborhood organizations form to work for better housing, enforcement of inspection ordinances, and anti-crime and anti-drug activity. Although community organization work is exacting and the frustrations are many, these efforts have led to active involvement of some of the poor in the politics of the city.

State Parties: A Study in Variety

The major parties—Democrats and Republicans—dominate state and local politics just as they do the nation's politics as a whole. But the state parties are not miniatures of the national parties; each has its own special features. The different social and economic mix in each state today makes the parties different. Moreover,

TABLE 1–1
1988 Voter Turnouts and Change Since 1984

	'88 Turnout Rate (as percentage of voting-age pop.)	Change, '84–'88 (in percentage points)		'88 Turnout Rate (as percentage of voting-age pop.)	Change, '84–'88 (in percentage points)
1. Minnesota	66.3	−1.9	27. Louisiana	51.3	−3.2
2. Montana	62.4	−2.7	28. Delaware	51.0	−4.4
3. Maine	62.2	−2.6	29. Wyoming	50.3	−3.0
4. Wisconsin	62.0	−1.5	30. Pennsylvania	50.1	−3.9
5. North Dakota	61.5	−1.2	31. Mississippi	49.9	−2.3
South Dakota	61.5	−1.0	32. Maryland	49.1	−2.3
7. Utah	60.0	−1.6	33. Oklahoma	48.7	−3.4
8. Iowa	59.3	−2.9	34. Kentucky	48.2	−2.6
9. Vermont	59.1	−0.7	Virginia	48.2	−2.5
10. Oregon	58.6	−3.2	36. New York	48.1	−3.1
11. Idaho	58.3	−1.6	37. California	47.4	−2.2
12. Massachusetts	58.1	+0.5	38. New Mexico	47.3	−4.0
13. Connecticut	57.9	−3.2	39. Arkansas	47.0	−4.8
14. Nebraska	56.8	+1.2	40. West Virginia	46.7	−5.0
15. Colorado	55.1	0.0	41. Alabama	45.8	−4.1
Ohio	55.1	−2.9	42. Arizona	45.0	−0.2
17. Missouri	54.8	−2.5	43. Nevada	44.9	+3.4
18. New Hampshire	54.7	+1.7	44. Florida	44.7	−3.5
19. Washington	54.6	−3.8	Tennessee	44.7	−4.4
20. Kansas	54.3	−2.5	46. Texas	44.2	−3.0
21. Michigan	54.0	−3.9	47. North Carolina	43.4	−4.0
22. Illinois	53.3	−3.8	48. Hawaii	43.0	−1.3
Indiana	53.3	−2.6	49. District of Columbia	39.4	−3.8
24. Rhode Island	53.0	−2.8	50. South Carolina	38.9	−1.8
25. New Jersey	52.1	−4.5	51. Georgia	38.8	−3.2
26. Alaska	51.7	−7.5			

Source: *Congressional Quarterly*, January 21, 1989, p. 136.

the states have also reacted differently to developments in American history, and the parties have reflected their reactions. For example, the Civil War left the South heavily Democratic and portions of the North heavily Republican. And the traumatic experience of the Great Depression, combined with the coming of the New Deal, helped produce a surge of Democratic strength in the big cities that still influences politics. A backlash to the Democratic Party's 1960s programs of affirmative action, busing, and war on poverty helped Republican party fortunes in the 1980s and 1990s.

How difficult is it to generalize about the role of political parties around the country? Consider some recent election results. In Virginia a black Democratic state legislator won election as that conservative commonwealth's lieutenant governor, and in 1989 was elected by a narrow margin as the governor of Virginia. In Houston, Dallas, and San Antonio women candidates have all been elected mayor by comfortable margins. Effective black political leaders are now mayors in Atlanta, Baltimore, Richmond, and New York. At the same time moderate Republicans and Democrats have won the governorships in Illinois, Indiana, and Idaho. As candidates, each campaigned on similar themes, the core of which can be summarized as follows: "The unifying themes for us are individual opportunity, economic growth, and equal opportunity for all, whether we are speaking in a black church, a union hall, or a chamber of commerce meeting." In winning campaigns basic values often become both a bit hazy, as in the preceding statement and in the mainstream message that most Americans want to hear. The centrist message often makes it difficult for us to sift through the influence of party labels and, increasingly, of ethnicity and race as well—all of which once upon a time had a more telling impact on the voters.

THE INTERPLAY OF NATIONAL AND STATE POLITICS

The very structure of national party organizations grows out of the state parties. Not only are national and state party organizations interdependent, but their fortunes are somewhat interrelated (although the great strength of our system of federalism and separation of powers is that it is difficult for any party to gain control over all branches of the national government and all branches or even parts of all the state and local governments.) When the Democratic Party, for example, is in power at the national level, the number of Democratic governors, state legislators, mayors, and local council members tends to increase—though this has been less true in recent decades. The greater the national sweep by a political party, generally speaking, the greater the local party victories.

Many states have acted to avert the influence of national trends. For example, New Jersey and Virginia have *complete* electoral "separation" and elect their governors and all state legislators in years when no presidential or congressional elections are being held. More than two-thirds of the states elect their governors and some legislators in nonpresidential election years. Staggering state elections is usually proposed as a way of concentrating the voters' attention on state issues. But it is

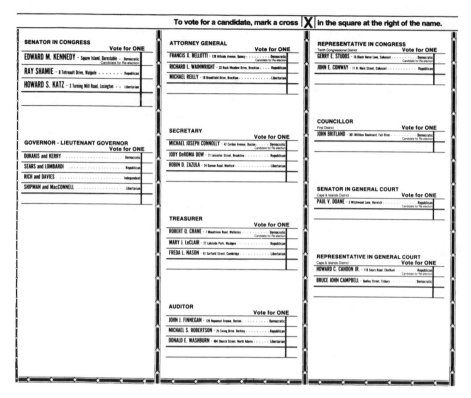

A sample Massachusetts ballot, which lists nominees by office rather than by party.

often a tactical device of party warfare, used by local politicians of one party to prevent the opposition from benefiting from its national popularity.

Not too many years ago voters could enter their polling booths and, by pulling just one party lever, could thereby vote a straight party ticket. Although many states still have more modified ballot arrangements that encourage straight party ticket voting, the trend is to list nominees by office, which is one of the reasons for the rise of **ticket splitting,** or voters' choosing candidates individually, not on party affiliation. The fact that voters see more television ads and television news about candidates also weakens their party loyalties and encourages them to cast votes for attractive or appealing candidates rather than for particular parties.

When presidential and state elections are held simultaneously, the impact of the national contest can be affected by the nature of the ballot. If, for example, the Republicans have a Reagan-type presidential candidate who has great electoral drawing power, it will be to their advantage for the state to have a **party column** or **Indiana ballot.** To reduce the impact of the presidential candidate under such circumstances, the Democrats in this instance would prefer the **office group** or **Massachusetts ballot.** But despite all the ingenious efforts of politicians, national politics still has at least some impact on state and local elections.

PARTY BALANCE AND IMBALANCE

The most important difference among the state party systems is the extent of two-party competition. State politics may be classified by how the parties share public offices: In the *two-party* type, the two parties share public offices rather evenly over the years, and they alternate in winning majorities; in the *modified one-party* type, one party wins all or almost all the offices over the years, but the other party usually receives a substantial percentage of the votes (and surprises everybody—including itself—by sometimes winning); and in the *one-party* type, one party wins all or nearly all the offices, and the second party usually receives only a small proportion of the popular vote. Modified one-party Democratic states are mainly the border states, and a few other states such as Massachusetts, Florida, and Nevada. The one-party states are all in the South, except for Hawaii and Massachusetts. There are no longer any one-party Republican states, because such former stalwarts as Vermont and Kansas have chosen some Democrats for state office in recent elections.

Since the end of World War II there has been an accelerating trend toward two-party politics. In the South Republicans have begun to make a contest of general elections. So far, the Republican resurgence in the South has been mainly in presidential and congressional elections; but Republicans are now regularly elected to the state legislatures in southern states. Arkansas, Tennessee, South and North Carolina, and Louisiana have elected Republican governors, although most of these states have reverted to the Democrats in more recent elections. Republicans still have to make more significant gains in state and local elections before we can call most southern or border states two-party states. But the Solid South is no longer solid, especially within and around the larger cities and in the mountain areas.[20] Outside the South there has also been a gradual spread of two-partyism, with the rise of Democratic strength in the formerly solid Republican states of Iowa, Maine, and New Hampshire. Democrats have lost supporters in the South as more and more white Southerners have moved into the Republican Party. However, Democrats have gained additional party loyalists in the Midwest and Northeast; Democrats have also lost strength in parts of the Rocky Mountain West.

What are the consequences of a fairly even party balance? When parties and their candidates compete on an even basis, each is more likely to be sensitive to slight changes in public opinion, for the loss of even a fraction of the voters might tip the scales to the other side in the next election. Party competition tends to push leaders within each party to work more closely together, at least as elections draw near. Any defection may throw a victory to the opponents, so

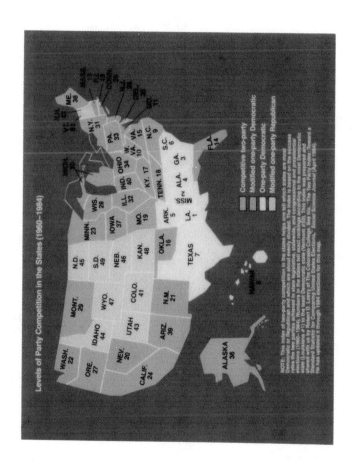

Levels of Party Competition in the States (1960-1984)

Competitive two-party
Modified one-party Democratic
One-party Democratic
Modified one-party Republican

NOTE: This index of two-party competition is the states helps one tell which states are most Democratic or Republican and which are about evenly divided. The index is based on the success rates the two parties witnessed in state legislative, statewide, and congressional and presidential elections (1960-1984). No. 1 is the most Democratic state, and each successive state is less Democratic (Louisiana #1) to the least Democratic state (Vermont #51). This index was prepared and shared with us by Robert D. Loevy of The Colorado College. See his, "The Two Party Index, Toward a Standard Statistic for Comparing Limited United States Elections." *Social Science Journal* (April 1984). He has updated it through 1984 elections for this map.

WASH. 22 / ORE. 27 / IDAHO 44 / MONT. 29 / N.D. 45 / MINN. 23 / WIS. 28 / MICH. 30 / VT. 51 / N.H. 42 / ME. 38 / MASS. 13 / R.I. 2 / CONN. 25 / N.Y. 31 / PA. 33 / N.J. 26 / DEL. 35 / MD. 11 / W. VA. 10 / VA. 15 / N.C. 9 / S.C. 6 / FLA. 14 / GA. 3 / ALA. 4 / MISS. 2 / LA. 1 / ARK. 5 / TENN. 18 / KY. 17 / OHIO 34 / IND. 40 / ILL. 32 / IOWA 37 / MO. 19 / KAN. 48 / NEB. 46 / S.D. 49 / WYO. 47 / COLO. 41 / UTAH 43 / NEV. 20 / CALIF. 24 / ARIZ. 39 / N.M. 21 / OKLA. 16 / TEXAS 7 / ALASKA 36 / HAWAII 8 competition may produce more teamwork and efficiency in government. Doubtless it also produces more constituency work by legislators.

Party imbalance may have a serious effect on the dominant party in a one-party state. Because it is almost guaranteed a victory, no matter how poor its record, the majority party may not keep itself in fighting trim. And the competition that otherwise would occur *between* the major parties often occurs *within* the majority party. Contests in some southern states or in Massachusetts often are not between Democrats and Republicans, but among Democrats—sometimes a handful of them—in the primary. In these intraparty fights, issues may not be clearly drawn. Personalities may dominate the campaign. Voters tend not to participate as much as they do in two-party contests. However, one has to be careful drawing conclusions, for lack of division on major issues within the community may in fact have caused the one-party situation.

If party imbalance disorganizes the dominant party, it pulverizes the minority party. Almost without hope of winning, minority leaders do not put up much of a fight. They find it difficult to raise money for campaigns or to persuade people to become candidates. They have no state or local patronage jobs to give out. Party workers and volunteers are slow to come forward. Young people wishing to succeed in politics tend to drift into the dominant party. And because the dominant party firmly controls the machinery of state and local affairs, the second party is likely to be concerned only with national politics and the patronage that could come its way if the party controlled the White House.[21]

We have been discussing *state* party imbalance, but imbalance can be found in even more extreme form in cities and towns. Republicans hardly ever carry Chicago, Boston, Washington, Baltimore, Albany, Hartford, Pittsburgh, and many other cities throughout the industrial North. Democrats usually do not win in rural towns in the Rocky Mountain states. One result of this imbalance was the rapid growth, during the first half of this century, of nonpartisanship in local elections. Candidates were not able to run on major-party tickets, at least officially. The two parties were, in effect, removed from open influence over local politics. Adopted in the name of good government, nonpartisanship's effect on the major parties was probably to weaken them further as organizations. Nonpartisan elections sometimes help Republican candidates, especially in cities with populations of over 50,000.

PARTY WEAKNESSES

An important fact is that *neither* party is organizationally strong in many states and localities. Just as the national parties tend to break into factions revolving around individual leaders in Congress and the White House, so too, state and local parties tend to fragment into groups following individual candidates and office holders. Most of the stronger leaders have personal organizations that often crowd the regular party organizations out of the picture. In most states the regular party committees are supposed to remain neutral during primary fights and usually do—with the result that candidates have no feeling of obligation to the party organization once they win office. Candidates in the same party tend to run on their own. Each candidate sets up headquarters, puts up posters, sends out publicity, and raises funds. Sometimes a candidate may deliberately keep clear of other candidates on the same ticket and even of the party label. The more offices to be voted on, the more candidates, and hence the greater the fragmentation of the party and the greater the ticket splitting, that is, the greater the chance that voters will vote for a few candidates from both parties. Because most states have the **long ballot** (a ballot with numerous officers to be selected), they have fragmented parties.

What is the result? The late V. O. Key, Jr., a prominent student of state politics, expressed his concern about party organization at the state level. To paraphrase his conclusions:

1. State politics combined with constitutional arrangements, especially the dispersion of power in most of the statehouses, often makes it difficult for the states to act, and thereby contributes to centralization of power in the national government.
2. The rapid growth of state responsibilities makes it even more important to modernize the organization of political forces within the states, which at present is erratic and atomized.
3. The political system places serious obstacles in the path of popular government by sometimes making it impossible for broad popular mandates to be expressed.
4. Over the last half-century party organization has seriously deteriorated. This deterioration has been associated with the rise of the direct primary.[22]

State and local parties are better organized since Key offered his observations two generations ago. Still, the problems presented by party weakness at the state level are the same as those presented at the national level, with this one difference: The national parties are roughly in balance, at least in presidential contests, whereas state and local parties are often noncompetitive, where they exist at all. Critics have suggested changes in the constitutional, legislative, and administrative organization of the states, and many innovations have been put into effect. Yet state political parties have been slow to make changes, and most have stayed the same for years. One reason may be that real reforms in party structure and balance are extremely difficult to bring about. No amount of tinkering with party structure can much alter the fact that most people in Kansas are Republicans and most people in Chicago vote Democratic. As long as strong personal factions exist within a party, preaching about the need for party renewal and unity will have little effect. Attitudes and political behavior change slowly and grow out of basic social, economic, and psychological conditions that reformers can do little to change.[23]

But to recognize that political forces are relatively stable is not to say that they cannot change. If such institutional forces as the long ballot help to make state and local parties what they are, changes such as the short ballot may also affect them; so may changes in legislative representation or in procedures for nominating candidates.

A word about *minor* parties: Whatever their other differences, the Democrats and the Republicans who control state governments agree that minor parties should be discouraged. Although the Supreme Court has struck down as violations of the equal protection clause requirements that made it especially difficult for minor-party candidates to obtain places on the ballot, in most states the laws continue to make it difficult for minor parties to become established and effective. In a few areas, such as in Minnesota, Alaska, Maine, Vermont, and New York City, third or fusion parties have occasionally been successful.

Elections: The Struggle for Office

The framers of the Constitution left the conduct of elections and other political matters largely in the hands of state government. This was one safeguard, they believed, against the accumulation of too much centralized national power. Although the Supreme Court has held Congress may supercede state regulations for the election of presidential electors and members of Congress, nonetheless state control of elections remains the rule, despite greater national supervision of state and local elections to ensure compliance with the Fourteenth and Fifteenth Amendments, and despite the tendency of the Supreme Court in recent years to emphasize the autonomy of political parties in the regulation of their internal affairs.[24] Each state sets up its own way of managing election fraud, and determines who shall be allowed to vote and participate in party affairs—always subject to the limitations of the national Constitution. States also administer the elections of presidential electors, senators, and members of the House of Representatives.

NOMINATIONS

Almost all party nominations—with the exception of the nomination of the president—are made in **party primaries.** These primaries, however, are of different types: closed, open, runoff, and so on. The party primary is a distinct American device that has had a great influence on the nature of state and local politics.

The primaries were not always the chief means of choosing candidates. Once our parties had developed fully in the 1830s and 1840s, candidates for most offices were chosen in **conventions.** (These were like our current national conventions, yet in miniature.) Delegates were called to order in a local hall or hotel; candidates were nominated; speeches were delivered; roll-call votes were taken; and finally candidates were chosen. Statewide candidates, such as the nominee for governor, were not the only ones selected in such local conclaves; candidates for district attorney, state representative, county commissioner, and even for city offices such as mayor were selected as well. Whatever their shortcomings, these conventions provided a vitality at the grass roots that some observers find lacking today.

They also provided opportunities for corruption. In the late nineteenth century, as the rise of big cities provided rich contracts and franchises for politicians, local and state parties fell increasingly under the domination of bosses who used the convention as a means of control. Party leaders or "bosses" often handpicked the delegates and sometimes even used strong-arm methods with those not directly under their control. The great safeguard against such corruption was, of course, the opposition party, which could appeal to the people against bossism. But the creation of one-party states and districts as a result of the Civil War and the polarizing William Jennings Bryan–William McKinley presidential race of 1896 left many American states and localities with one-party systems, especially in the South and Northeast. The great safeguard was gone.

The **direct primary** arose largely as a result of this situation. During the first decade of this century, when reformers were attacking bossism, corruption, and other undesirable conditions, the convention also came under fire. Reformers wanted nominations moved out of these boss-controlled conclaves and put into the hands of the people. Nominations were democratized by means of the direct primary, which was first adopted in the South. Wisconsin enacted the first statewide primary law in 1901, and other states followed. Within a decade and a half, the direct primary had been adopted for most nominations in all but a few states. Today most state laws require political parties to nominate statewide candidates in direct primaries, but in a few southern states parties may choose between primaries and conventions.

How has the direct primary worked out? Like most institutional reforms, it has had mixed results. The primary has probably diminished somewhat the power of the party leaders. It is more difficult for a boss to influence several thousand voters going to the polls than a few delegates going to a convention. But the difference has been one only of degree, and it varies widely from place to place. Some bosses survived the coming of the primary. Participation in the primary is often light, so that some party operatives are still able to control it by advance voter targeting and selective get-out-the-vote efforts. Still, the primaries often encourage—and certainly provide the chance for—people to challenge party bosses.

Some people, however, began to have second thoughts about the effect of primaries on party organization. After all, there were good party bosses as well as bad ones. The primaries have other weaknesses: Primary contests are often disorganized, bewildering, and heavily influenced by local considerations. Primaries make it impossible for the parties to balance their tickets. For example, the Democratic party in Massachusetts, made up of large numbers of people of Irish descent, has sometimes found it difficult to nominate a balanced ticket because the decision was made in the primaries, heavily dominated by the Boston Irish. And primaries are especially hard on the minority party. Up-and-coming politicians naturally run in the major-party primary, and no one may even want the minority-party nomination. In short, primaries sometimes work against competitive, meaningful, and vigorous two-party politics.

Despite these drawbacks, almost every state now uses the primaries for the nomination of statewide office. A few states, such as Connecticut and Colorado, retain some features of the old convention system. A candidate who can win at local caucuses and capture the state convention's nomination does not have to run in a primary unless another candidate wins 25 or more percent of the delegate votes and wishes to challenge in a statewide primary. The adoption of this modified primary system has appeared to strengthen the party systems of these states.

The method of nominating candidates closely affects the organization of the party, and vice versa. The stronger the party, that is, the better led, the more vigorous and competitive and unified, the better its chances of conducting nominating fights through conventions. The weaker the party, the more likely the voters are to want to take nominating decisions out of the hands of party leaders and to entrust them to the people in primaries.

Some people believe parties should play a stronger role in the nominating process in order to select candidates who will be more reflective of the mainstream than the candidates likely to be produced when parties are weak. Parties are playing an increasingly important role. One manifestation of this is that in about a third of the states, party officials attempt to influence the outcomes of primaries by endorsing candidates. They may do this, for example, at their parties' state conventions. Such efforts are designed to unify the party around mainstream and presumably "winning" types of candidates. They are also designed to discourage nonendorsed candidates from running or, if this fails, to help endorsed candidates to win primary voter approval. The record over the past thirty years suggests that party endorsements have a positive impact on both the parties and the candidates they endorse. When endorsements are made, there are fewer contested nomination fights, and if there is a contest, the convention endorsee wins about three-fourths of the time. Those who favor the endorsement process claim it provides an ideal means of unifying a party and selecting the strongest candidate.

> Perhaps the best argument for the more active and powerful political parties is the need to restrain the influence of specialized interests on government and to restore the party's role as an aggregator and mediator of those interests. In doing so the party can provide a buffer between the more aggressive interests and public officials such as governors and legislators. The case for a stronger party role in the nominating process rests on the need to select candidates who are capable and experienced and who are in the mainstream of the political party rather than being the creatures of narrower interests.[25]

Those who would like to strengthen state parties further occasionally suggest encouraging the use of closed primary laws; enacting campaign finance laws that permit parties to contribute party funds in a primary, or even to use state party funds on behalf of endorsees; and guaranteeing the top space of the primary ballot to those endorsed at the party's state convention. But party renewers still find considerable opposition to many of these ideas.

Elections: A Case Study

Perhaps the most distinctive features of American politics are the number and variety of elections. Western Europeans, who are used to voting for one or two candidates at the national and local levels, and voting only once every two or three years, are flabbergasted on learning that Americans engage almost continuously in elections. Selection of town and local officials in the late winter may be followed by primaries to choose delegates to conventions, then primaries to choose party candidates, then general elections, all interspersed with special elections, special town or state referenda, and even, in some states, recall elections to throw an official out of office. Even more bewildering is the number of offices voted on at a particular election, from president to probate judge, from senator to sheriff, from governor to member of the library board. This is the long ballot in operation. Europeans are more accustomed to electing a handful of key officials, who in turn appoint career officials.

Generalizing about all these elections is dangerous, yet experienced politicians might suggest the following rules of thumb:

1. By and large, the more local the election, the less the excitement and interest aroused among the electorate, and the less the participation.
2. Except in areas with strong party organizations, candidates usually run on their own; they win through their personal organizations rather than through efforts by the party (partly because there are so many candidates running for so many offices, the party cannot give much help to any one of them).
3. Voter familiarity with names rather than issues is of relatively greater importance in local elections.
4. The candidates get most of their money from friends and interest groups, not from their parties.
5. Although there is no substitute for personal contact between the candidate and the voters, especially in local campaigns, more and more state and city elections are determined by the extent and quality of direct mail and radio and television ad campaigns. Hi-tech campaign strategies, once the major factor only in presidential and large, populous statewide elections, are now a factor everywhere except in *very* local races.

CAMPAIGNING FOR CITY HALL—CHICAGO

For observers of roughhouse local politics, there is no place like Chicago. In recent years the city has had a black mayor, a fiesty woman mayor, machine politics, notable black-white divisions, and two famous mayors named Daley—

Richard J. Daley, the legendary mayor from 1955 until his death while still in office in 1976, and his firstborn son, Richard M. Daley, elected to office in 1989.[26]

Chicago politics has often defied the rules that characterize local politics in America. In some ways, however, it illustrates many of the patterns of party and organizational politics found elsewhere. In the past decade two candidates won City Hall in upset victories. In 1979 Jane Byrne defeated the Chicago machine and its incumbent mayor, Michael Bilandic, who had succeeded Mayor Richard J. Daley when Daley died in office. Byrne's victory astonished people in Chicago who just assumed that the famed Chicago Democratic political organization would continue in office as it had for nearly fifty years. But Jane Byrne beat the machine, and then she tried to put the pieces back together again. For the most part she succeeded. Her four-year tenure was marked by controversy: Her critics said she was often too temperamental and that she too often alienated the city's growing minority population. But she was also a tough and shrewd politician. After all, she knew the Chicago machine; she had worked within it for years, rising up through its ranks and holding high appointive office under Daley.

In late 1982, when Mayor Byrne prepared her reelection bid for City Hall, most observers expected her to win easily. She had taken effective control over patronage, and in a city where at that time a few thousand jobs were still "controlled" by City Hall, this was presumed to be a major advantage. She also proved to be an awesome fundraiser, eventually raising $10 million in her bid to win a second term.

A major rival emerged as her chief threat when Richard M. Daley, state's attorney for Cook County (of which Chicago is the major city), announced his candidacy in November 1982. As the son of the former mayor, and with considerable experience in state and local politics, young Daley was considered a serious candidate and challenger.

Soon a third candidate emerged—Congressman Harold Washington, a former state legislator who was then representing Chicago's First District in the United States House of Representatives. Washington, a Chicago-born attorney, was black. Some observers say Washington was a very reluctant candidate. Few thought he could beat the Byrne machine. Some Daley campaign advisers believed Mayor Byrne actually encouraged Harold Washington's candidacy and even provided some of his early financial assistance because she believed this would ensure her victory. She reasoned, they charged, that young Daley would get most of the black and Hispanic vote, and that this would make Daley an extremely tough opponent. But with Washington in the race, Byrne's opposition would be divided and Washington would attract much of the city's growing black vote.

As the campaign progressed into the winter of 1983, Byrne was everybody's "front-runner." She had the money. She had the name recognition. She controlled the patronage and the influence that City Hall could exercise in the Chicago business community. But it was also clear that the old Daley Democratic machine was being tested and strained.

All three candidates waged vigorous campaigns. The incumbent's record was regularly attacked and scrutinized. The candidates engaged in four debates during the last stretch of the campaign—debates in which Harold Washington emerged as an impressive candidate. Expert observers said he "won" these debates. Blacks rallied to Washington in an unprecedented way. Some liberals swung in as well.

As the March 1983 primary election neared, experts were predicting a close race, but a race in which Byrne still was the likely victor. Harold Washington, however, came from behind in the three-way race and emerged the clear victor.

For a time there was some grumbling as to whether the Democrats would support their black nominee for mayor. Byrne considered running as a write-in candidate. Others suggested that perhaps the Republican nominee should step aside and allow Byrne to be the Republican candidate. The Democratic party became splintered and was unsure of what to do or to whom to turn.

Harold Washington had grown up in the black neighborhoods of Chicago. He had been a top student, worked hard, "paid his dues," and gradually worked his way up the social and political ladder. The son of a Democratic precinct captain, Washington himself had served in the lower ranks of the party and later had graduated from Northwestern Law School and practiced law. He later worked in the Daley machine in a variety of capacities, and he—along with countless other black Chicagoans—had helped to deliver precincts and wards for the Democratic party for some forty years or more. Now "it was their turn," said Washington, and he asked for the kind of support he and members of his race had given the white Democrats over the years.

Yet that white Democratic support was slow in coming. Old-line Democrats criticized Washington for tax evasion (of which he had been convicted in the past and for which he had even served a short jail sentence) and for running a campaign that mainly emphasized racial divisions. Whites in large numbers joined the Bernard Epton campaign. Epton, the Republican nominee, was a former state legislator and a successful Chicago insurance businessman. Prior to the surprise outcome of the Democratic primary, he had virtually no name recognition and no chance to win. Suddenly his campaign was the only alternative to that of a black candidate for mayor. Epton's media advisers promoted Epton's candidacy with the slogan: "Elect Epton—Before It's Too Late"—a slogan that angered blacks and liberals alike because of its implication that if not Epton, the blacks would take over City Hall, Chicago, and Democratic party patronage.

The ensuing campaign was one of the most divisive the country witnessed in at least a generation. Racism was rife, and emotions ran high. National television and magazines featured the race prominently. Finally, in April 1983, in an election with high voter turnout, Harold Washington emerged the victor with about 51 percent of the vote. He won enormous backing from blacks and Hispanics as well as scattered white support, mainly from liberals and highly educated professional people. Republican Epton won 82 percent of the white vote.

Somehow Chicago endured it—thinly disguised racism and all. Still, the famed Democratic political machine was fractured. Mayor Washington tried in vain to revitalize the Democrats' organization, but it would never be the same. Some questioned whether Chicago would ever be as governable as it had been in the 1950s and 1960s. Everyone anticipated difficulties between the mayor and the regular Democrats on the council, who represented the predominantly white populated wards. Few observers, however, realized just how bitter the situation would be. A majority bloc of the fifty-person city council opposed Washington on many issues and refused to act on the more than fifty nominations to boards and commissions he made during his first three years in office.

Harold Washington, however, was easily reelected in 1987 and was credited with opening city government to many of Chicago's citizens who felt excluded and ignored. Although elected in a highly polarized contest that had deeply divided the city in 1983, Washington's subsequent performance had begun a healing process. When Washington died, shortly into his second term, City Councilman Eugene Sawyer, also a black, was chosen acting mayor by the white dominated Board of Aldermen.

In early 1989 a new election took place to select a mayor to serve out the last two years of Harold Washington's four-year term. In February 1989 Cook County Prosecutor Richard M. Daley defeated Sawyer in a relatively low-key primary campaign in which both candidates repeatedly called for racial harmony. "But in this city, often regarded as the most residentially segregated in the country, racial tensions were never far below the surface, and charges of racism on both sides flared repeatedly in the final weeks of the campaign."[27] Daley won 91 percent of the white vote and only 5 percent of the black vote; Sawyer took 94 percent of the black and only 8 percent of the white vote.

In the April general election, Daley won a decisive victory over his Republican and independent opponents. His main opponent, Timothy Evans, won strong backing from Jesse Jackson but failed to gain more than 5 percent of the white vote and overwhelmingly lost the Hispanic vote to Daley. The population of Chicago, the nation's third largest city, is about evenly divided between blacks and whites, but there are roughly 150,000 more white than black voters.

Daley raised over $6 million in his race to win this coveted mayor's post. He ran a clever "law and order" media campaign and campaigned at countless ethnic and neighborhood events, including many in black neighborhoods. He tried hard to avoid running "as the white candidate" yet his chief opponent in the general election warned that Daley sought "to reopen his father's plantation" and would lead with an autocratic style that would ignore the needs of the poor, especially blacks. Daley won only about 7 percent of the black vote.

Upon winning Daley promised he would have an open City Hall and he extended the hand of the city to all its citizens. He pledged, too, to improve the city's troubled school system, reduce crime, and work fairly with all segments of the city. Unlike his father, the new mayor controls only about a thousand of the more than 40,000 city jobs; the courts have outlawed most of the patronage that served as the muscle behind his father's style of machine politics. Mayor Richard

M. Daley is expected to be less ruthless than his father in running City Hall. He has already appointed many more blacks, Hispanics, and women to key administrative positions than his father did.

These Chicago campaigns suggest several patterns. The key to success in Chicago politics is still winning the Democratic primary. Money is still a crucial factor. A black candidate can win in a racially divided city only by putting together a coalition of committed blacks and Hispanics along with at least some of the liberal white community. Mayor Harold Washington did that. Eugene Sawyer and Timothy Evans failed. Chicago's election of a white mayor after a black had run City Hall suggests that cities with large black populations will not necessarily win and retain a permanent hold on City Hall (this has also happened in Cleveland and Charlotte, North Carolina). Although election campaigns in Chicago typify American party organizational politics in many ways, events in the city during the past decade illustrate how nothing can be taken for granted in politics—especially in Chicago.

Summary

1. American states and localities are characterized more by dispersion of political influence than by concentration. The diversity of elective offices gives influence to many different officials and tends to fragment political parties. In a positive vein this gives us more openings or "cracks" in the system for access purposes. In a negative vein it makes it hard to bring about changes and govern creatively.

2. The primary system of nominating candidates further diffuses power within the parties. A local newspaper publisher may, in effect, have a press monopoly, but he or she often faces competition from other media sources, such as television and radio. The nominating system generally offers considerable access to the centers of influence.

3. Most states and localities have reasonably open and porous systems that are a long way from rule by an establishment or by a boss. This does not mean every voter has roughly the same influence on political decisions. Power tends to center in separate clusters of decision makers, and large numbers of people have little influence. Under the American system these people could have a more active role, but lack of education, information, and money, as well as other factors keep many voters from wielding much influence.

4. Students should look at their own states and communities and ask hard questions. Who has influence and who does not? Who is excluded from the system? What are the rules of the game? Under what conditions is influence exercised? *How* is it exercised—through authority, friendship, propaganda, deals, manipulation, coercion? And in whose behalf? What are the terms under which influence is pyramided and expended? What kind of influence do political leaders sacrifice in order to get the decisions they want? In short, if most of these political systems are marked by deals, bargains, and exchanges, then who gains and loses what? Does fragmented power prevent leaders from making joint efforts on behalf of the great mass of people? Finally, what are the available means of keeping public servants, elected and appointed, accountable and responsive between elections?

Further Reading

DIANE D. BLAIR. *Arkansas Politics and Government* (University of Nebraska Press, 1988).

JOHN GAVENTA. *Power and Powerlessness: Quiescence and Rebellion in an Appalachian Valley* (University of Illinois Press, 1980).

VIRGINIA GRAY, HERBERT JACOBS, and KENNETH VINES, eds. *Politics in the American States*, 5th ed. (Scott, Foresman, 1990).

MALCOLM E. JEWELL. *Parties and Primaries: Nominating State Governors* (Praeger, 1984).

MALCOLM E. JEWELL and DAVID N. OLSON. *American State Political Parties and Elections*, rev. ed. (Dorsey Press, 1982).

DENNIS R. JUDD. *The Politics of American Cities: Private Power and Public Policy*, 3d ed. (Scott, Foresman, 1988).

V. O. KEY, JR. *American State Politics* (Knopf, 1956).

NEAL R. PEIRCE and JERRY HAGSTROM. *The Book of America: Inside Fifty States Today* (Norton, 1983).

ALAN ROSENTHAL and MAUREEN MOAKLEY, eds. *The Political Life of the American States* (Praeger, 1984).

ROBERT A. SLAYTON. *Back of the Yards: The Making of Local Democracy* (University of Chicago Press, 1986).

CLARENCE N. STONE. *Regime Politics: Governing Atlanta, 1946–1948* (University Press of Kansas, 1989).

JAMES D. THOMAS and WILLIAM H. STEWART. *Alabama Government and Politics* (University of Nebraska Press, 1988).

JACK M. TREADWAY. *Public Policymaking in the American States* (Praeger, 1985).

Notes

1. Robert S. Lynd and Helen M. Lynd, *Middletown* (Harcourt, 1929). See also their treatment of Muncie ten years later, *Middletown in Transition* (Harcourt, 1937).

2. Thomas R. Dye, *Politics in States and Communities*, 5th ed. (Prentice Hall, 1985); and Richard I. Hofferbert, *The Study of Public Policy* (Bobbs-Merrill, 1974).

3. See Paul E. Peterson, *City Limits* (University of Chicago Press, 1981).

4. Floyd Hunter, *Community Power Structure* (University of North Carolina Press, 1953). For a reassessment and rebuttal of Hunter's findings, see M. Kent Jennings, *Community Influentials: The Elites of Atlanta* (Free Press, 1964).

5. Robert A. Dahl, *Who Governs? Democracy and Power in an American City* (Yale University Press, 1961). For an example of the power elite or social stratification approach as applied to New Haven, see G. William Domhoff, *Who Really Rules? New Haven and Community Power Reexamined* (Goodyear, 1978).

6. See Nelson W. Polsby, *Community Power and Political Theory*, 2d ed. (Yale University Press,

1980), for the perspective of a critic of social stratification theorists. See Steven Lukes, *Power: A Radical View* (Macmillan, 1974), for the perspective of class conflict theorist, which differs sharply from the Polsby and Dahl analyses.

7. See the interesting study of San Jose, California, along these lines: Phillip J. Troustine and Terry Christensen, *Movers and Shakers: The Study of Community Power* (St. Martin's, 1982).

8. See, for example, Peter Bachrach and Morton S. Baratz, *Power and Poverty: Theory and Practice* (Oxford University Press, 1970); Matthew A. Crenson, *The Unpolitics of Air Pollution: A Study of Non-Decisionmaking in Two Cities* (John Hopkins University Press, 1971); and John Gaventa, *Power and Powerlessness: Quiescence and Rebellion in an Appalachian Valley* (University of Illinois, 1980).

9. Geoffrey Debnam, "Nondecisions and Power: The Two Faces of Bachrach and Baratz," *American Political Science Review* (September 1975), pp. 889–99.

10. Veto message, Governor Adlai Stevenson, to members of the Senate Assembly, Springfield, Illinois, 1949.

11. Michael R. Levy and Michael S. Kramer, *The Ethnic Factor: How American Minorities Decide Elections* (Touchstone, 1973).

12. See, for example, Candace Romig, "Placing Limits on Political Action Committees," *State Legislatures* (January 1984), pp. 19–22; and "States Strengthen Campaign Finance Laws," *State Government News* (November 1984), pp. 7, 31.

13. Jimmy Carter, *Why Not the Best?* (Bantam Books, 1976), p. 101.

14. See L. Harmon Zeigler, "Interest Groups in the States," in Virginia Gray, Herbert Jacob, and Kenneth Vines, eds., *Politics in the American States: A Comparative Analysis*, 4th ed. (Little, Brown, 1983), pp. 97–131.

15. Jesse Unruh, "A Reformed Legislature," *Journal of Public Law*, 16 (1967), p. 13. See also Kerry Drager, "The New Breed of Sacramento Lobbyists," *California Journal* (October 1980), pp. 393–97.

16. Diane D. Blair, *Arkansas Politics and Government* (University of Nebraska Press, 1988), p. 118.

17. Paul E. Peterson, *City Limits* (University of Chicago Press, 1981). The discussion in this section draws from insights developed in this book.

18. Ibid., p. 124.

19. Dahl, *Who Governs?* p. 264. See also Raymond Wolfinger, *The Politics of Progress* (Prentice Hall, 1974), especially chap. 11.

20. On the changing political forces in the South, see Alexander P. Lamis, *The Two-Party South* (Oxford University Press, 1984).

21. The classic picture of this situation at its most extreme was drawn by V. O. Key, Jr., in *Southern Politics in State and Nation* (Knopf, 1949).

22. V. O. Key, Jr., *American State Politics* (Knopf, 1956), pp. 266–67.

23. See Gerald Pomper, ed., *Party Renewal in America: Theory and Practice* (Praeger, 1980); Cornelius P. Cotter, James Gibson, John Bibby, and Robert Huckshorn, *Party Organization in American Politics* (Praeger, 1984); and William J. Crotty, *American Parties in Decline* (Little, Brown, 1985).

24. Leon Epstein, "Will American Political Parties Be Privatized?" *The Journal of Law and Politics* (Winter, 1989), pp. 239–74.

25. Some of these drawbacks are discussed in Malcolm E. Jewell, *Parties and Primaries: Nominating State Governors* (Praeger, 1984).

26. For different insights into Mayor Richard J. Daley and his machine, see Mike Royko, *Boss: Richard J. Daley of Chicago* (Dutton, 1971); Milton L. Rakove, *Don't Make No Waves, Don't Back No Losers: An Insider's Analysis of the Daley Machine* (Indiana University Press, 1975); and Thomas M. Guterbock, *Machine Politics in Transition: Party and Community in Chicago* (University of Chicago Press, 1980).

27. Dirk Johnson, "Daley Wins Primary in Chicago," *The New York Times* (March 1, 1989).

2

American Federalism: Problems and Prospects

"There are two ways to empty a room in Washington: Hold a fund raiser for a defeated candidate or a debate on federalism."[1] Outside of Washington as well, when you talk about federalism you are likely to make people's eyes glaze over.

Federalism, however, closely affects our lives, as the framers clearly recognized. For early American citizens who feared governmental threats to their liberties—and most thinking Americans in the 1780s put this at the top of their worry list—both the *division* of powers between national and state governments (federalism) and the *separation* of powers at each level of government, along with the checks and balances, promised to serve as potent barriers against tyrannical action in the national or state capitals. In effect these devices "divided the enemy"—the government. If the national government threatened people's liberties, the states would protect them—and vice versa. If the executive, the legislature, or the judiciary at any level threatened people's liberties, one of the other branches would protect them. In general the more "vetoes" built into government, the more the government would keep "hands off the people's liberties," and our rights as outlined in the Bill of Rights and other provisions of the Constitution would be protected.

At the same time, for those persons who hoped that governments could be used to protect their rights and liberties—blacks or many women for example— divided government could have the reverse impact. Indeed, efforts to ban child labor in the United States had to overcome so many obstacles created in large part by our federal system, that action was delayed for over a half century. And it took decades to bring national civil rights laws into play to protect blacks against abridgment of their rights by state governments—again in large measure because of having to work through a federal system.

Thus whether federalism makes it easier to protect rights or more difficult to secure them depends upon which rights *and on* whether contending groups are seeking to protect rights *from* government or to broaden them *through* government. The framers of our Constitution, by and large, had no doubts. They believed that federalism—along with other structures of governments such as separation of powers, and checks and balances that divide governmental powers into various pockets to constrain government officials—are more important to preserving liberty and protecting our rights than is the Bill of Rights.

Imagine how the events of 1787 seemed to Americans of two centuries ago. Or to put it in modern terms, suppose you heard Congress had sent a delegation to Ottawa to meet with representatives from Canada and Mexico to draft a constitution for the United Governments of North America. Such a situation would only roughly parallel what happened in the summer of 1787, yet it gives you some idea of the worries that citizens of Massachusetts, Virginia, and the other states felt when they heard rumors about the drafting of a constitution in Philadelphia. The new government, it was rumored, was to have powers to tax and regulate the lives of the people. Citizens' apprehensions were heightened when the proposed constitution was published; most of the rumors were true.

The issues of federalism did not end with the founding period. In 1861 men and women fought and died for Virginia or Texas or for the Union (although it would be a mistake to think of the Civil War as merely a particularly heated debate over the principles of federalism).

What is a federal system? The mere existence of both national and state governments does not make our system federal. What is important is that a *constitution* divides governmental powers between the general, or national, government and the constituent governments (called states in the United States), giving substantial functions to each. Neither the central nor the constituent government receives its powers from the other; both derive them from a common source—a constitution. This constitutional distribution of powers cannot be changed by the ordinary process of legislation—for example, by an act of either a national or state legislature. Finally, both levels of government operate through their own agents and exercise power directly over individuals. Among the countries that have federal systems of government are the United States, Canada, Switzerland, Mexico, and Australia. "Nearly 40 percent of the world's population now lives within polities that are formally federal; another third live in polities that apply federal arrangements in some way."[2]

Constitutionally, our federal system consists only of the national government and the fifty states. "Cities are not," as the Supreme Court has reminded us, "sovereign entities." But in a practical sense, we are a nation of over 83,000 governmental units—from the national government to the school board district. This does not make for a tidy, efficient, easy-to-understand system, but, as we shall see, it does have its virtues.

That ours is a federal system makes a lot of difference, even if we are not always aware that this is so. Almost every aspect of our lives is affected by several

Number of Governments			
States	50	School Districts	14,741
Counties	3,042	Special Districts	29,481
Municipalities	19,205	**Total**	**83,180**
Towns	16,691		

Source: *1987 Census of Governments*, U.S. Department of Commerce, Bureau of the Census.

layers of government. Consider your college or university, public or independent. About half of the students are likely to be receiving some form of national or state financial assistance to help pay their tuition and fees. The college itself is chartered by the state. Most of the funds that pay for the teachers, staff, and buildings come from state appropriations, state bonds, private gifts encouraged by national tax laws, or a combination of national, state, and private sources. The research your faculty is doing, especially in the sciences, and the public-service programs in which they are involved, are likely to be supported by some combination of national, state, and private (yet tax-deductible) dollars. The conditions under which students are admitted, how their grades are posted and reported, and how faculty and staff are appointed and evaluated are subject to national and state regulations. The use of experimental animals is subject to supervision by national and state governments, and national and state inspectors check to ensure that laboratories properly dispose of used chemicals.

What are the alternatives to federalism? There are **unitary systems** of government in which a constitution vests all governmental power in the central government. The central government, if it so chooses, may delegate authority to constituent units, but what it delegates it may also take away. Britain, France, Israel, and the Philippines have this form of government. In the United States the relationship between states and their local governments, such as counties and cities, is usually of this sort.

Then there are **confederations** in which the constituent governments create a central government by constitutional compact, but do not give it power to regulate the conduct of individuals. The central government makes regulations for the constituent governments, but it exists and operates only at their direction. The thirteen states under the Articles of Confederation operated in this manner, as did the Southern Confederacy during the Civil War.

It complicates our understanding of federalism that the founders of our Constitution used the term *federal* to describe what we would now call a *confederate* form of government. Moreover, today "federal" is frequently used as a synonym for national. People often refer to the government in Washington as "the federal government." But, in fact, it is the states and the national government *together* that make up our federal system.

Why Federalism?

In 1787 federalism was an obvious choice. Confederation had been tried and found wanting, but a unitary system was out of the question. Most of the people were too deeply attached to their state governments to permit them to be subordinated to central rule. Even if a unitary state had been politically possible in 1787, it would not have been chosen. Federalism was, and still is, thought to be ideally suited to the needs of a heterogeneous people spread over a large continent, suspicious of concentrated power, and desiring unity but not uniformity. Federalism offered many advantages for such a people.

FEDERALISM ALLOWS UNITY WITHOUT UNIFORMITY

National politicians and parties do not have to iron out every difference on every issue in every state. Such issues as divorce, gun-control, comparable worth, capital punishment, and the creation, operation, and financing of community colleges are debated in state legislatures and city halls; there is no need to enforce a single national standard. As a result, it is easier to develop consensus on truly national problems.

FEDERALISM CHECKS THE GROWTH OF TYRANNY

Although in the rest of the world federal forms have not been notably successful in preventing tyranny, and many unitary governments are democratic, Americans tend to equate freedom with federalism.[3] As Madison pointed out in *The Federalist*, No. 10: "[If] factious leaders . . . kindle a flame within their particular states," national leaders can check the spread of the "conflagration into other states." Shays's Rebellion was a dramatic example. Moreover, when one political party loses control of the national government, it is still likely to hold office in a number of states. It can then regroup, develop new policies and new leaders, and continue to challenge the party in power at the national level.

Such diffusion of power creates its own problems. It makes it difficult for a national majority to carry out a program of action, and it permits those who control a state government to frustrate the consensus expressed through Congress and national agencies. To some of our country's founders this was an advantage. They were more fearful that a single-interest national majority might capture the national government and attempt to suppress the interests of others than they were that minority interests might frustrate the national will. Of course—and this point is often overlooked today (but emphasized by Madison in *Federalist*, No. 10)—the size of the nation and the many interests within it are the greatest obstacles to the formation of a single-interest majority. However, even if such a majority should form, having to work through a federal system would act as a check on it.

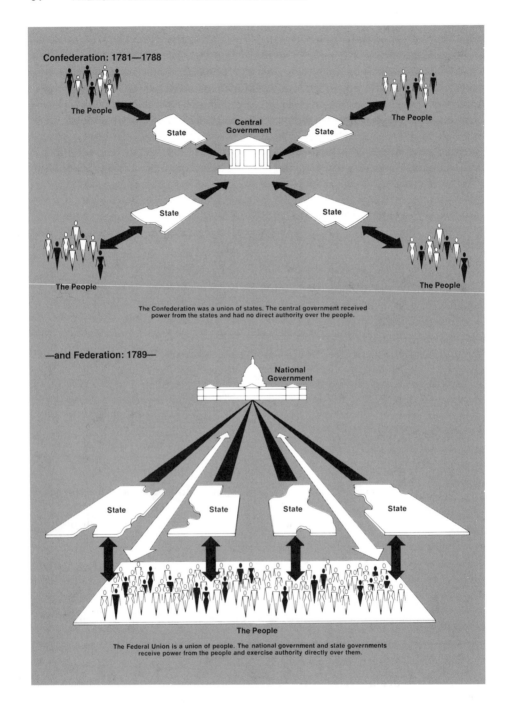

Confederation: 1781—1788

The People

State

Central Government

State

The People

The People

State

State

The People

The Confederation was a union of states. The central government received power from the states and had no direct authority over the people.

—and Federation: 1789—

National Government

State   State   State   State

The People

The Federal Union is a union of people. The national government and state governments receive power from the people and exercise authority directly over them.

Statehood (1787–1959)

This list gives dates when states either ratified the U.S. Constitution or gained formal admittance to the Union.

Delaware	12/1787	Michigan	1/1837
Pennsylvania	12/1787	Florida	3/1845
New Jersey	12/1787	Texas	12/1845
Georgia	1/1788	Iowa	12/1846
Connecticut	1/1788	Wisconsin	5/1848
Massachusetts	2/1788	California	9/1850
Maryland	4/1788	Minnesota	5/1858
South Carolina	5/1788	Oregon	2/1859
New Hampshire	6/1788	Kansas	1/1861
Virginia	6/1788	West Virginia	6/1863
New York	7/1788	Nevada	10/1864
North Carolina	11/1789	Nebraska	3/1867
Rhode Island	5/1790	Colorado	8/1876
Vermont	3/1791	North Dakota	11/1889
Kentucky	6/1792	South Dakota	11/1889
Tennessee	6/1796	Montana	11/1889
Ohio	3/1803	Washington	11/1889
Louisiana	4/1812	Idaho	7/1890
Indiana	12/1816	Wyoming	7/1890
Mississippi	12/1817	Utah	1/1896
Illinois	12/1818	Oklahoma	1/1907
Alabama	12/1819	New Mexico	1/1912
Maine	3/1820	Arizona	2/1912
Missouri	8/1821	Alaska	1/1959
Arkansas	6/1836	Hawaii	8/1959

Note: This information is not provided to be memorized (!), but to suggest the evolution and expansion of the nation.

FEDERALISM ENCOURAGES EXPERIMENTATION

Justice Louis Brandeis, the celebrated Supreme Court justice (on the Court from 1916 to 1939), pointed out that state governments provide great laboratories for experimentation with public policy. This role "in policy experimentation may become" more important as the federal government confronts fiscal and political limits. . . . and as the nation confronts such matters as . . . the revolution in family life, including, for example, surrogate motherhood, test-tube babies, adoption, and care of the elderly."[4] States serve as proving grounds. If they adopt programs that fail, the negative effects are limited; if programs succeed, they can be adopted by other states and by the national government. Georgia, for example, was the first state to permit 18-year-olds to vote; New York has been vigorous in its assault on water pollution; California has pioneered air pollution control programs. After federal leadership waned in the 1970s, New Jersey assumed leadership in programs to handle toxic wastes; it initiated radon gas testing, and was the first state to adopt a state-wide mandatory recycling law.[5] Many states legalized

TABLE 2–1
The Most Popular Level of Government

From which level of government do you feel you get the most for your money—federal, state, or local? (Percent of U.S. public)

LEVEL	1974	1976	1978	1980	1982	1984	1986	1988
National	29	36	35	33	35	24	32	28
Local	28	25	26	26	28	35	33	29
State	24	20	20	22	20	27	22	27
Don't know	19	19	19	19	17	14	13	16

Source: Debra L. Dean, Advisory Commission on Intergovernmental Relations, "Closing the Opinion Gap: State and Local Governments Fare Well in ACIR Poll," Intergovernmental Perspective (Fall 1988), p. 24.

abortion under certain conditions before the Supreme Court acted (whether this is progress or regression depends on one's values, as do so many questions of politics). Sunset laws, equal housing, no-fault insurance, and "lemon" laws providing consumer protection for faulty automobiles are a few other examples of programs that originated in the states.

FEDERALISM KEEPS GOVERNMENT CLOSE TO THE PEOPLE

Federalism, by providing numerous areas for decision making, involves many people and helps keep government closer to the people. Just think of the thousands of people who every night attend school board meetings, water district hearings, city council sessions, county planning board sessions, or are going to their state capitol to make presentations to their legislators. Literally thousands of Americans run our governments day by day.

We should be cautious, however, about generalizing that state and local governments are necessarily "closer to the people" than the national government is. True, more people are involved in local and state politics than in national affairs, and in recent years confidence in the ability of state governments has gone up. Yet national affairs are more on the minds of most people than are state or even local politics. Fewer voters participate in state elections than in congressional and presidential elections. Still, states and their local units remain very much a part of the political life of those concerned with public affairs.

Constitutional Structure of American Federalism

Dividing powers and responsibilities among the national and state governments requires thousands of court decisions, hundreds of books, and a million speeches to explain—and even then the division lacks precise definition. The formal constitutional framework of our federal system, however, may be stated relatively simply:

1. The national government has only those powers (with the one important exception of foreign affairs) *delegated* to it by the Constitution.
2. The state governments have the powers not delegated to the central government, except those *denied* to them by the Constitution and their state constitutions.
3. Within the scope of its operations, the national government is *supreme*.
4. Some powers are specifically denied to *both* the national and state governments; others are specifically denied *only* to the states; still others are denied *only* to the national government.

POWERS OF THE NATIONAL GOVERNMENT

The Constitution, chiefly in the first three articles, delegates legislative, executive, and judicial powers to the national government. In addition to these **express powers,** the Constitution delegates to Congress those **implied powers** that may be reasonably inferred from the express powers. The constitutional basis for the implied powers of Congress is the **necessary and proper clause** (Article I, Section 8), which gives Congress the right "to make all Laws which shall be necessary and proper for carrying into Execution the foregoing Powers, and all other Powers vested . . . in the Government of the United States."

In the field of foreign affairs, the national government has **inherent powers** that do not depend on specific constitutional grants. The national government has the same authority in dealing with other nations as if it were a unitary government. For example, the government of the United States may acquire territory by discovery and occupation, even though no specific clause in the Constitution allows such acquisition. Even if the Constitution were silent about foreign affairs—which it is not—the national government would have the right to declare war, make treaties, and appoint and receive ambassadors.

National Supremacy Clause Article VI states: "This Constitution, and the Laws of the United States which shall be made in Pursuance thereof; and all Treaties made . . . under the Authority of the United States, shall be the supreme Law of the Land; and the Judges in every State shall be bound thereby; any Thing in the Constitution or Laws of any State to the Contrary notwithstanding." All officials, state as well as national, are bound by constitutional oath to support the Constitution of the United States. States may not use their reserved powers to override national policies. (Local units of government are agents of the states. What states cannot constitutionally do, local units cannot do. In our discussion of the constitutional structure of federalism, local units are included in all references to states.) National laws and regulations of federal agencies *preempt* the field so that conflicting state and local rules and regulations are unenforceable.

POWERS OF THE STATES

The Constitution reserves for the states all powers not granted to the national government, subject only to the limitations of the Constitution. Powers that are not given exclusively to the national government, by provision of the Constitution or by judicial interpretation, may be concurrently exercised by the states, as long as there is no conflict with national law. For example, each state has **concurrent powers** with the national government to levy taxes and to regulate commerce internal to each state. How federalism limits the states' taxing powers is neither simple to explain nor simple to understand. In general, a state may levy a tax on the same item as the national government, but a state cannot, by a tax, "unduly burden" commerce among the states, or interfere with a function of the national government, or complicate the operation of a national law, or abridge the terms of a treaty of the United States. Who decides whether a state tax is an "undue burden" on a national function or commerce among the states? Ultimately, the Supreme Court decides.

Federalism issues are even more complicated when states attempt to protect the public health and well-being. When Congress has not acted, states may regulate even interstate businesses, provided these regulations do not cover matters requiring uniform national treatment or are not unduly burdening interstate commerce. Who decides what requires uniform national treatment or might be an undue burden on interstate commerce? Congress does, subject to final review by the Supreme Court. When Congress is silent or does not clearly state its intentions, courts, ultimately the Supreme Court, decide if there is a conflict with the national Constitution or a national law or national regulation, or if there has been federal preemption.

CONSTITUTIONAL LIMITS AND OBLIGATIONS

To make federalism work, the Constitution imposes certain restraints on the national and state governments. States are prohibited from

1. Making treaties with foreign governments
2. Authorizing private persons to prey on the shipping and commerce of other nations—what the Constitution refers to as "granting letters of Marque and Reprisal"
3. Coining money, issuing bills of credit, or making anything but gold and silver coin a tender in payment of debts.

Nor may states, without the consent of Congress,

1. Tax imports or exports
2. Tax foreign ships

3. Keep troops or ships in time of peace (except for the state militia, now called the National Guard)

4. Enter into compacts with other states or foreign nations that "tend to increase the political power in the States, which may encroach upon or interfere" with the supremacy of the national government

5. Engage in war, unless invaded or in such imminent danger as will not admit of delay (of course, an invasion of one state would be an invasion of the United States itself).

The national government, in turn, is required by the Constitution to refrain from exercising its powers, especially its powers to tax and to regulate interstate commerce, in such a way as to interfere substantially with the ability of the states

CONSTITUTIONAL DISTRIBUTION OF POWERS

Powers Denied to State Governments

e.g., Impairing obligations of contracts, or depriving any person of life, liberty, or property without due process, or denying to any person equal protection of the laws.

Powers Denied All Governments

e.g., passing bills of attainder, depriving persons of life, liberty, or property without due process

Powers Denied to National Government

e.g., all of the Bill of Rights

Reserved Powers of State Governments

Ordinary powers of internal government, e.g., controlling elections, local government, public health, safety, morals

TOWN HALL

Concurrent Powers

e.g., taxation and spending for general welfare

PAY STATE TAXES HERE

PAY NATIONAL TAXES HERE

ROADS

Granted, Implied, and Inherent Powers of National Government

Control over external affairs and matters of national concern, e.g., raising and supporting armies and navies, regulating interstate commerce, establishing uniform rules of naturalization

STATE

STATE AND NATIONAL

NATIONAL

to perform their responsibilities. Making this generalization about how the principles of federalism limit national powers is easier than citing specific modern-day examples of how in fact the Supreme Court has struck down any actions of the national government because of interference with state sovereignty. Today whatever protection states have comes from the political process—the built-in restraints that our system provides because individuals elected from the states participate in the decisions of Congress—rather than from judicially enforced limitations.[6]

The Constitution also requires the national government to guarantee to each state a **republican form of government.** The framers used this term to distinguish a republic from a monarchy, on the one side, and from a pure, direct democracy, on the other. Congress, not the courts, enforces this guarantee and determines what is or is not a republican form of government. By permitting the congressional delegation of a state to take its seat in Congress, Congress is in effect deciding that the state has the republican form of government guaranteed by the Constitution.

In addition, the national government is obliged by the Constitution to protect states against *domestic insurrection.* Congress has delegated to the president the authority to dispatch troops to put down such insurrections when so requested by the proper state authorities. (If there are contesting state authorities, the president decides which ones are the proper ones.)[7] The president does not have to wait, however, for a request from state authorities to send federal troops into a state to enforce federal laws. Today it is hard to imagine a situation of domestic insurrection against a state that would not also involve federal matters.

HORIZONTAL FEDERALISM: INTERSTATE CONSTITUTIONAL RELATIONS

Three clauses in the Constitution that were taken from the Articles of Confederation require the states to give full faith and credit to one another's public acts, records, and judicial proceedings; to extend to one another's citizens the privileges and immunities of their own citizens; and to return persons who are fleeing from justice.

Full Faith and Credit The **full faith and credit clause** is one of the more technical provisions of the Constitution. In general, it requires each state court to enforce civil judgments of other state courts and to accept their public records and acts as valid documents. (It does not require states to enforce the criminal laws of other states; in most cases, for one state to enforce the criminal laws of another would be unconstitutional.) The clause applies especially to noncriminal judicial proceedings.

Interstate Privileges and Immunities States must extend to citizens of other states the privileges and immunities granted to their own citizens, including the protection of the laws, the right to engage in peaceful occupations, access to the courts, and freedom from discriminatory taxes. Further, because of this clause, states may not impose unreasonable "durational residency" requirements to withhold political rights such as voting or to withhold such benefits as medical help from United States citizens who move into their boundaries and thereby become state citizens. How long a residency requirement may a state impose? A day seems to be about as long as the Court will tolerate for welfare payments or medical care, fifty days or so for voting privileges, and one year for payment of in-state tuition for state-supported colleges and universities. (Persons who are financially independent who move into a state just prior to enrolling in a state-supported university or college may be required to prove that they intend to remain after finishing their schooling, and to supply proof of becoming a citizen of the state by such evidence as tax payments, driver's licenses, car registrations, voter registrations, and continuous, year-round off-campus residence.)

Extradition The Constitution asserts that when criminals have fled from one state to another, the state to which they have fled is to deliver them to the proper officials upon the demand of the executive authority of the state from which they fled. "The obvious objective of the Extradition Clause is that no State should become a safe haven for the fugitives from a sister State's criminal justice system."[8] Congress has supplemented this constitutional provision by making the governor of the state to which fugitives have fled the agent responsible for returning them. Despite the use of the word "shall" in the Constitution, an 1861 Supreme Court decision, based on an antiquated view of federalism, controlled extradition until 1987, and federal courts would not order governors to surrender (extradite) persons wanted in other states. This is no longer so, since the 1861 decision has been reversed.[9] Usually federal courts do not become involved, and extradition is a routine matter. Recently, however, disputes over the custody of children that sometimes lead to criminal charges of parental kidnapping have complicated extradition procedures.

Interstate Compacts In addition to these three obligations, the Constitution also requires states to settle disputes with one another without the use of force. States may carry their legal disputes to the Supreme Court, or they may negotiate **interstate compacts.** More often, interstate compacts are used to establish interstate agencies to handle interstate problems. Before most interstate compacts become effective, congressional approval is required. After a compact has been signed and approved by Congress, it becomes binding on all signatory states, and its terms are enforceable by the Supreme Court. A typical state belongs to twenty compacts dealing with such subjects as environmental protection, crime control, water rights, and higher education exchanges.[10]

THE REALITIES TODAY

This outline of the constitutional structure of federalism is oversimplified and— especially in terms of the division of powers between the national government and the states—even misleading. The formal structures of our federal system have not changed much since 1787, but the political realities, especially during the last half century, have greatly altered how they are used. During the Great Depression of the 1930s, the nation debated whether Congress had the constitutional authority to enact legislation dealing with agriculture, labor, education, housing, and welfare. Only twenty-five years ago some questioned the constitutional authority of Congress to legislate against racial discrimination. Even today it remains technically correct that Congress lacks any general grant of authority to do whatever it thinks necessary and proper in order to promote the general welfare or preserve domestic tranquility. But as a result of the rise of a national economy, the growth of national demands on Washington, and the emergence of a world in which a nuclear attack could destroy us in a matter of minutes, our constitutional system has so evolved that the national government has authority to deal with almost every issue. Today, restraints on national power stem from constitutional provisions protecting the liberties of the people rather than from those relating to the powers of state governments.

Triumph of the Nationalist Interpretation

The preceding summary of the constitutional construction of our federal system jumps over two hundred years of conflict and proclaims victory, at least for the moment, for the nationalist interpretation. The debate between those who favor national action (**centralists**) and those who favor state and local levels (**decentralists**) continues, yet generally it does so outside the framework of constitutional principles. This victory for the nationalists is recent. Throughout most of our history, powerful groups have favored states' rights.

The constitutional arguments revolving around federalism grew out of specific issues: Did the national government have the authority to outlaw slavery in the territories? Did states have the authority to operate racially segregated schools? Could Congress regulate labor relations? The debates were frequently phrased in constitutional language, and appeals were made to the great principles of federalism. But they were also arguments over who was to get what, where, and how, and who was to do what to whom.

Among those favoring the states' rights interpretation, with varying emphasis, were Thomas Jefferson, John C. Calhoun, the Supreme Court from the 1920s to 1937, and, more recently, Ronald Reagan, George Bush, Chief Justice Rehnquist, and Justice O'Connor. They contend that the Constitution is a treaty among sovereign states that created the central government and gave it carefully limited authority. As a result, the national government is nothing more than an agent of the states, and every one of its powers should be narrowly defined. Any question of whether the states have given a particular function to the central government or have reserved it for themselves should be resolved in favor of the states.

States' righters hold that the national government should not be permitted to exercise its delegated powers in a way that interferes with activities reserved for the states. The Tenth Amendment, they claim, makes this clear: "The powers not delegated to the United States by the Constitution, nor prohibited by it to the States, are reserved to the States respectively, or to the people." Decentralists insist state governments are closer to the people and reflect the people's wishes more accurately than does the national government. The national government, they add, is inherently heavy-handed and bureaucratic; to preserve our federal system and our liberties, central authority must be kept under control.

The nationalist position, supported by Chief Justice John Marshall, Abraham Lincoln, Theodore Roosevelt, Franklin Roosevelt, and throughout most of our history by the Supreme Court, rejects the whole concept of the Constitution as an interstate compact. Rather, it views the Constitution as a supreme law established by the people. The national government is an agent of the people, not of the states, because it was the people who drew up the Constitution and created the national government. The sovereign people gave the national government sufficient power to accomplish the great objectives listed in the Preamble. They intended that the central government's powers should be liberally defined and that the central government should be denied authority only when the Constitution clearly prohibits it from acting.

Nationalists argue the national government is a government of all the people, and that each state speaks only for some of the people. Although the Tenth Amendment clearly reserves powers for the states, as Chief Justice Harlan Stone said: "The Tenth Amendment states but a truism that all is retained which has not been surrendered" (*United States* v. *Darby*, 1941).[11] The Amendment does not deny the national government the right to exercise to the fullest extent all the powers given to it by the Constitution. On the other hand, the supremacy of the national government, it is argued, restricts the states, because governments representing part of the people cannot be allowed to interfere with a government representing all of them.

McCULLOCH VERSUS MARYLAND

In **McCulloch v. Maryland** (1819) the Supreme Court had the first of many chances to choose between these two interpretations of our federal system.[12] Maryland had levied a tax against the Baltimore branch of the Bank of the United States, a semipublic agency established by Congress. James William McCulloch, the cashier of the bank, refused to pay on the grounds that a state could not tax an instrument of the national government. Maryland's attorneys responded that, in the first place, the national government did not have the power to incorporate a bank, but even if it did, the state had the power to tax it.

Maryland was represented before the Court by some of the country's most distinguished lawyers, including Luther Martin, a delegate to the Constitutional Convention who had left early when it became apparent that a strong national government was in the making. Martin, basing his argument on the states' rights view of federalism, said the power to incorporate a bank is not expressly delegated to the national government. He contended that Article I, Section 8, Clause 18,

Centralists versus Decentralists

CENTRALISTS' ARGUMENTS

1. State and local governments lack expertise.
2. State and local officials tend to be parochial.
3. State and local governments are unable or unwilling to raise enough money to meet demands.
4. State and local governments are more apt to reflect race and ethnic biases.
5. State and local governments are more likely to be dominated by conservative elites.
6. State and local governments are structurally incapable of dealing with problems of redistribution from the rich to the poor.
7. Given . . . the mobility of corporate and residential taxpayers, states and localities are not able to regulate business effectively.

DECENTRALISTS' RESPONSES

1. Changes in population have made the states more competent and sensitive to urban needs.
2. Changes in tax structure have made states and local governments more flexible and progressive raisers of revenue.
3. Legal and political changes have made states and localities as sensitive to the needs of the poor and minorities as the national government.
4. Political reform movements have made state and local governments more effective governments.

Look closely at the operation of your state and city governments. Do the facts as you know them support the contentions of the centralists?

Source: Jeffrey R. Henig, *Public Policy and Federalism: Issues in State and Local Politics*, pp. 34–41. Copyright © 1985 by St. Martin's Press, Inc. Reprinted by permission of St. Martin's Press, Incorporated.

which gives Congress the right to choose whatever means are necessary and proper to carry out its delegated powers, gives Congress only the power to choose those means and to pass those laws absolutely essential to the execution of its expressly granted powers. Because a bank is not absolutely necessary to the exercise of any of its delegated powers, Congress has no authority to establish it. As for Maryland's right to tax the bank, Martin's position was clear: The power to tax is one of the powers reserved to the states; they may use it as they see fit.

The national government was represented by equally distinguished counsel, chief among whom was Daniel Webster. Webster conceded that the power to create a bank is not one of the express powers of the national government. However, the power to pass laws *necessary* and *proper* to carry out enumerated powers is expressly delegated to Congress, and this should be interpreted to mean Congress has authority to enact any legislation convenient and useful in carrying out delegated national powers. Therefore, Congress may incorporate a bank as an appropriate, convenient, and useful means of exercising the granted powers of collecting taxes, borrowing money, and caring for the property of the United States.

Webster contended that although the power to tax is reserved to the states, states cannot use their reserved powers to interfere with the operations of the national government. The Constitution leaves no room for doubt; in cases of conflict between the national and state governments, the national is supreme.

Speaking for a unanimous Court, Marshall rejected every one of Maryland's contentions. He wrote: "We must never forget that it is a constitution we are expounding . . . a constitution intended to endure for ages to come, and consequently, to be adapted to the various crises of human affairs. . . . The government of the Union, then, . . . is, emphatically, and truly, a government of the people. In form and substance it emanates from them. Its powers are granted by them, and are to be exercised directly on them, and for their benefit. . . . It can never be to their interest and cannot be presumed to have been their intention, to clog and embarrass its execution, by withholding the most appropriate means." Marshall summarized his views on the powers of the national government in these now-famous words: "Let the end be legitimate, let it be within the scope of the Constitution, and all means which are appropriate, which are plainly adapted to that end, which are not prohibited, but consist with the letter and spirit of the constitution, are constitutional."

Having thus established the doctrine of implied national powers, Marshall set forth the doctrine of **national supremacy.** No state, he said, can use its reserved taxing powers to tax a national instrument. "The power to tax involves the power to destroy. . . . If the right of the states to tax the means employed by the general government be conceded, the declaration that the Constitution, and the laws made in pursuance thereof, shall be the supreme law of the land, is empty and unmeaning declamation."

The long-range significance of *McCulloch* v. *Maryland* in providing support for the developing forces of nationalism cannot be overstated. The arguments of the states' righters, if accepted, would have strapped the national government in a constitutional straitjacket and denied it powers needed to handle the problems of an expanding nation.

THE CONSTITUTIONAL BASIS OF THE GROWTH OF THE NATIONAL GOVERNMENT

The formal constitutional powers of the national government are essentially the same today as they were in 1789. But the Supreme Court (building on Marshall's work in *McCulloch* v. *Maryland*), Congress, the president, and the people have taken advantage of the Constitution's flexibility to permit the national government to use whatever powers it needs to fight wars and depressions and to serve the needs of a modern industrial nation operating in a global economy. The expansion of central government functions has rested on three major constitutional pillars.

The War Power The national government is responsible for protecting the nation from external aggression and, when necessary, for waging war. In today's world military strength depends not only on troops in the field, but also on our ability to mobilize the nation's industrial might and to apply our scientific knowledge to the tasks of defense. The national government has the power to wage war and to do what is necessary and proper to do so successfully. This means that the national government has the power to do almost anything that is not in direct conflict with constitutional guarantees.

The Power to Regulate Interstate and Foreign Commerce Congressional authority extends to all commerce that affects more than one state and to all those activities, wherever they exist or whatever their nature, whose control Congress decides is necessary and proper to regulate interstate and foreign commerce. The term *commerce* includes the production, buying, selling, renting, and transporting of goods, services, and properties.[13] The commerce clause—Article 1, Section 8, Clause 3—packs a tremendous constitutional punch. In these few words the national government has been able to find constitutional justification for regulating a wide range of human activity and property. Few, if any, aspects of our economy today affect commerce in only one state and are thus outside the scope of the national government's constitutional authority.

The commerce clause can also be used to sustain legislation that goes beyond commercial matters. When the Supreme Court upheld the 1964 Civil Rights Act forbidding discrimination because of race, religion, or national origin in places of public accommodation, it said: "Congress' action in removing the disruptive effect which it found racial discrimination has on interstate travel is not invalidated because Congress was also legislating against what it considers to be moral wrongs." Discrimination restricts the flow of interstate commerce; interstate commerce was being used to support discrimination; therefore, Congress could legislate against the discrimination. Moreover, the law could be applied even to local places of public accommodation because local incidents of discrimination have a substantial and harmful impact on interstate commerce. "If it is interstate commerce that feels the pinch, it does not matter how local the operation that applies the squeeze."[14]

Territorial Expansion

Part of the genius and flexibility of our constitutional system has been the way in which we have acquired territory and later extended rights and guarantees by means of statehood, commonwealth, or territorial status.

Louisiana Purchase	1803	The Philippines	1898–1946
Florida	1819	Puerto Rico	1899
Texas	1845	Guam	1899
Oregon	1846	American Samoa	1900
Mexican Cession	1848	Canal Zone	1904
Gadsden Purchase	1853	U.S. Virgin Islands	1917
Alaska	1867	Pacific Islands	
Hawaii	1898	Trust Territory	1947

The Power to Tax and Spend Congress lacks constitutional authority to pass laws solely on the ground that they will promote the general welfare, but it may raise taxes and spend money for this purpose. This distinction between legislating and appropriating makes little difference most of the time. Congress, for example, lacks constitutional power to regulate education or agriculture directly, but it does have the power to appropriate money to support education or to pay farmers subsidies. By attaching conditions to its grants of money, Congress may regulate what it cannot directly control by law.

Because Congress puts up the money, it determines how the money will be spent. By withholding or threatening to withhold funds, the national government can influence—or control—state operations and regulate individual conduct. For example, Congress has stipulated that federal funds should be withdrawn from any program in which any person is denied benefits because of race, color, or national origin; subsequently the categories of sex and physical handicap were added. Congress has also used its power of the purse to force states to raise the drinking age to 21 by tying such a condition to federal dollars for highways.

These three constitutional powers—the war power, the power over interstate commerce, and, most especially, the power to tax and spend for the general welfare—have made possible a tremendous expansion of federal functions.

Umpires of the Federal System

Today there are few doubts about the national government's constitutional authority to deal with issues affecting the nation, whether they concern civil rights, speed limits on highways, or the sale of holiday lights. Nonetheless, we still argue about (1) whether Congress intended to regulate a subject completely or to leave some regulation to state discretion, and (2) whether, in the absence of congressional action, states may deal with subjects that affect commerce or people in other states.

Although couched in terms of federalism, such arguments reflect differences between various interests. The national and state governments are the arenas in which, and through which, clashes take place between consumers and producers, workers and employers, airlines and railroads, pro-choice and right to life, pro-growth and anti-growth, and all the other contending groups that make up our political system. Although Congress and the political process ultimately decide how power shall be divided between the national and state governments, federal courthouses remain major forums where hundreds of disputes about which government should do what for and to whom are increasingly being decided daily.

THE ROLE OF THE FEDERAL COURTS

Federal judges' authority to review the activities of state and local governments expanded dramatically in recent decades as a result of modern judicial interpretations of the Thirteenth, Fourteenth, and Fifteenth Amendments (especially the

Fourteenth) and the congressional legislation enacted to implement these amendments. Along with an earlier congressional and judicial expansion of the habeas corpus jurisdiction of the federal district courts (see Chapter 6), these developments ensure that almost every action by state and local officials can be challenged before a federal judge as a violation of the Constitution or of federal law. In carrying out their judgments, federal judges sometimes have, in effect, taken over the supervision of state prison systems, public hospitals, public schools, and other public facilities.

One of the major instruments for opening these matters for review by federal courts is the Supreme Court's revitalization—some would say the rewriting—during recent decades of an 1871 rights act originally written to combat the Ku Klux Klan. This Act, now called Section 1983 after its designation in Title 42 of the United States Code, permits individuals to go into federal court to sue for damages or seek injunctions against any person acting under the color of law whom they believe has deprived them of any right secured by the Constitution or by any one of the several thousands of federal laws.[15] As a result of these Section 1983 actions, cities are now facing millions of dollars worth of damage claims (states can be ordered to stop doing something, but there are Eleventh Amendment constraints upon damage suits against the states). Among other Section 1983 claims against state and local officials have been thousands of suits by state prison inmates; by Jerry Tarkanian, the Nevada (UNLV) basketball coach against the N.C.A.A. which he unsuccessfully charged was acting as an agent of Nevada; by a father who sued a school district because he was not permitted to see his children's records; and by real-estate developers who allege that county and city land-use regulations are depriving them of their rights.[16]

Over the years the decisions of federal judges, under the leadership of the Supreme Court, have favored national powers (including their own); nonetheless, few would deny the Supreme Court the power to review and set aside state actions. As Justice Oliver Wendell Holmes once remarked: "I do not think the United States would come to an end if we lost our power to declare an Act of Congress void. I do think the Union would be imperiled if we could not make that declaration as to the laws of the several States."[17]

A MESSAGE FROM GARCIA—
FEDERALISM AS A POLITICAL AND NOT A LEGAL CONSTRAINT

Until 1937 the Supreme Court generally espoused the **doctrine of dual federalism,** which views national and state governments as equal sovereigns, each operating within its own restricted sphere, with the Supreme Court enforcing the boundary between the two. In 1976, echoes of this doctrine could be heard in *National League of Cities* v. *Usery*, in which the Court, by five to four, held unconstitutional a 1974 amendment of the Fair Labor Standards Act extending federal minimum wage and maximum hours provisions to employees of state and local governments.[18] Then, in 1985, again by a five to four vote, *National League of Cities* was overturned by *Garcia* v. *San Antonio Metro.* In *Garcia* the Court said, in essence, that Congress, not the courts, decides which actions of the states should be regulated by the national government. "Although *Garcia* left open the possibility that some extraordinary defects in the national political process might render congressional regulation of state activities invalid," nothing in the Tenth Amendment "authorizes courts to second-guess the substantive basis for congressional legislation 'affecting state action.' "[19] "The States," said the Supreme Court in reaffirming the *Garcia* doctrine, "must find their protection from congressional regulation through the national political process" rather than look to judges to shield them from it.[20]

All the Reagan appointees, except Justice Anthony Kennedy, who has not spoken on this issue as yet, dissented from the *Garcia* view that the political process is the states' only constitutional protection. One of them, Justice Sandra Day O'Connor, predicted "this Court will in time again assume its constitutional responsibility" of defining the scope of state autonomy protected by federalism. She is probably right, since President Bush is likely to nominate judges and justices sympathetic to her version of federalism. It seems likely that the message from Garcia is not the final word on this matter.[21] Yet the dissenting and more conservative justices have acknowledged that even if the courts were to resume the task of protecting the states, the set of activities protected by state sovereignty from the reach of the national government "may well be negligible."[22]

OTHER UMPIRES (AND CONTESTANTS) OF THE FEDERAL SYSTEM

Congress always has the most to say about whether federal or state standards or some combination of them will prevail. It authorizes programs, appropriates the funds, and establishes general rules for how the programs will operate. The president and federal administrators also get into the act. They issue the specific guidelines, decide which projects to approve, and largely determine how federal standards will be applied.

It should not be thought, however, that states and local governments are merely passive partners waiting to learn from federal officials what to do and how to do it. It is one thing to get a law through Congress; it is quite another to impose national standards on state and local officials and the people they represent. If local and state political groups fail to persuade Congress to build safeguards into a law to protect their interests, they may still use the ambiguities of the law to do what they want done, rather than what the federal agencies intend. In the implementation battles that routinely follow the enactment of legislation, the greater political power may be with state and local officials.[23]

Federal Grants

Even after the rather successful "Reagan Revolution" resulted in the "devolution" of some functions back to the states, the national government continues to do much more than it did even two decades ago, although the number of federal employees is about the same today as it was then. State and local governments have gotten larger; the federal government has not. Rather than expanding the size of the federal government, Congress has chosen to use the states, the cities, the counties, the universities—and at times even private agencies—to administer many new programs, deliver services, and carry out federal mandates.

Congress has done this by using four general types of federal grants: categorical-formula grants, project grants, block grants, and revenue sharing.

1. **Categorical-formula grants.** Congress appropriates funds for specific purposes—welfare, school lunches, the building of airports and highways. The funds are allocated by formula and are subject to detailed federal conditions, often on a matching basis; that is, the government receiving the funds must put up some of its own dollars. There are hundreds of such grant programs, but two dozen account for almost 90 percent of total spending for categoricals. These include Medicaid, child nutrition grants, wastewater treatment plant construction, Aid to Families with Dependent Children (AFDC), training and employment programs, low-rent public housing, and community development programs.[24]

2. **Project grants.** Congress appropriates a certain sum, but the dollars are allocated to state and local units—in some instances to nongovernmental agencies—on the basis of applications from those who wish to participate.

3. **Block grants.** These grants, promoted by the Advisory Commission on Intergovernmental Relations and favored by presidents, especially Republicans, are broad grants to states for certain prescribed activities—elementary and secondary education, social services, preventive health, and health services—with only a few specific strings attached.

4. **Revenue sharing.** From 1972 to 1987, substantial federal funds were given to state and local units of government to be used at their discretion, subject only to very general conditions. When in the second Reagan Administration federal budget deficits soared and, "there was no revenue to share," revenue sharing was terminated—to the states in 1986 and to local governments in 1987.

THE POLITICS OF FEDERAL GRANTS

Arguments about the forms of federal aid involve more than considerations of efficiency. They reflect differences about what constitutes desirable public policy, where power should be located, and who will gain or lose by the various types of grants. Republican presidents "have consistently favored fewer strings, less federal supervision, and the delegation of spending discretion to the state and local governments, whereas Democratic presidents have advocated the opposite. Congress has divided similarly, with Democrats generally voting for centralization, and Republicans decentralization."[25]

Although chief executives—governors and presidents—generally tend to urge the consolidation of categorical-formula grants into larger blocks, legislators and groups who benefit from existing programs are likely to resist, and most of the time they do so successfully. Consider the battle over libraries. "[The] Administration proposed the consolidation of several narrow library grants. The Congress resisted, and the reason is simple. It can be expressed quantitatively: 99.99% of the public is not interested in library grant reform. Of the .01 percent who are interested, all are librarians and oppose it."[26]

IRON TRIANGLES OR ISSUE NETWORKS

The debate about the form of grants is not just a dispute over whether state and local governments can be trusted to spend federal dollars wisely, but is a debate about which state and local officials should be given control over the spending. Specialists who work for state and local governments often have more in common with specialists working for the national government than they do with their own governors, mayors, or state legislators. These specialists (highway engineers, welfare administrators, educators) confer at meetings, read common journals, and jointly defend the independence of their programs from attempts by "politicians" (elected national or state officials) to regulate them.[27] When these executive branch specialists join forces with their counterparts among the interest groups and specialists working for congressional committees they create powerful "guilds."[28] The result is "iron triangles"—of interest groups, congressional committee staffers, and federal bureaucrats (who in turn are connected to state and local bureaucrats)—of great effectiveness.

FEDERAL GRANTS UNDER REAGAN AND BUSH

Ronald Reagan, during the first year of his presidency, was able to convince Congress to consolidate fifty-seven categorical grant programs consisting of 10 percent of all federal aid to state and local governments into nine block grants. But that was as far as Congress has been willing to go.

What have been the results of these consolidations? Not as much money has been saved as proponents of block grants claimed would be, but there has not been as much diversion away from the poor as the opponents of such grants feared. Most states picked up some of the slack. Nonetheless, there has been some diversion of funds away from some groups targeted by the categorical grants that the block grants replaced. And after block grants were established, there was considerable pressure to reduce their funding. For "once a block grant becomes nothing more than a small fraction of a state's general program budget . . . it may seem to lose its rationale for existence."[29] Yet on balance, according to one set of experts, "The administrative rationale of block-grant consolidation, and even the political rationale for returning decision-making authority to the states, has been largely vindicated. . . ."[30]

The battle over "which piper calls the tune when one government raises the money and another spends it" tends to be cyclical. "Complaints about excessive federal control tend to be followed by proposals to shift more power to state and local governments. Then, when problems arise in state and local administration—and problems inevitably arise when any organization tries to administer anything—demands for closer federal supervision and tighter federal controls follow."[31] The trend at the moment is toward fewer federal dollars, more block grants, and fewer program-specific national controls, but despite the decentralist rhetoric, new ways have been found to impose national controls.

Federal Regulations

State and local governments have received fewer federal dollars via federal grants recently, relatively speaking, but federal controls are as strong as ever. In fact, the federal government has new ways to regulate the way states and local governments spend federal dollars, and in some instances even their own state and local dollars. State and local officials complain that these regulations are far more intrusive than the more obvious conditions a state or local government must meet in order to be eligible for a federal grant.

There are four types of federal regulations of state and local governments:

1. *Direct orders.* In a few instances, federal regulation takes the form of direct orders that must be complied with under threat of criminal or civil sanction. Examples are the Equal Opportunity Act of 1982, barring job discrimination by state and local governments on the basis of race, color, religion, sex, and national origin, and the Marine Protection Amendments of 1977, prohibiting cities from dumping sewage into the ocean. Because such direct orders raise mild constitutional concerns and more serious political ones, Congress favors other techniques to impose the federal will on the states.

2. *Cross-cutting requirements.* The first and most famous of these requirements (so-called because a condition on one federal grant is extended to all activities supported by federal funds regardless of their source) is Title VI of the 1964 Civil Rights Act, which holds that no person may be discriminated against in the use of federal funds because of race, color, national origin, sex, or handicapped status. Over sixty cross-cutting requirements concern the environment, historical preservation, contract wage rates, access to governmental information, the care of experimental animals, the treatment of human subjects in research projects, and so on.

3. *Cross-over sanctions.* These sanctions permit the "feds" to use federal dollars in one program to influence state and local policy in another. One example is the Emergency Highway Energy Conservation Act of 1974, which prohibits the Secretary of Transportation from approving federal funding for highway construction in states having a speed limit in excess of 55 miles per hour (since amended to allow the limit to be raised to 65 in certain rural areas). Another example is a 1984 act that threatened to reduce federal highway

aid by up to 15 percent for any state that failed to adopt a minimum drinking age of 21 by 1987.

4. *Partial preemption.* This kind of control rests not upon the national government's power to spend, but on its powers under the supremacy and commerce clauses to preempt conflicting state and local activities. Building on this constitutional authority, federal law in certain areas establishes basic policies but requires states to administer them. Some programs give states the option and funds to administer them, if they meet the nationally determined conditions or standards. However, if a state chooses not to participate, the national government then steps in and directly runs the programs. The Clean Air Act Amendments of 1970 calls for mandatory partial preemption; the federal government sets national air-quality standards but requires states to devise plans for their implementation and enforcement.[32]

These new forms of federal regulation accelerated during the 1970s; they abated only slightly during the 1980s. Despite the Reagan-Bush emphasis on retrenchment of federal regulations, the Reagan administration pressured for national controls to force states to adopt drunk-driving legislation, to cut off federal funds to cities enacting rent controls, and to force on states and localities certain busing, abortion, and school-prayer policies. Apparently liberals and conservatives alike favor fewer federal controls over state and local officials in the abstract, yet are willing to make exceptions in policy areas when they feel strongly that something must be done to correct or prevent an injustice. Because there are plenty of injustices, federal regulation of state and local governments remains a continuing feature of our political system.

Two Levels or Three? Crazy-Quilt Federalism[33]

During the 1960s' urban crisis, the national government started in earnest to provide large-scale, direct federal aid to cities, counties, school districts, flood-control districts, and other kinds of local units. In some ways Congress "became the city council of the nation," and the "president—acting very much like a Mayor"—started "taking on the meanest housekeeping concerns of daily existence."[34] As a result, there was "virtually no function of local government from police to community arts promotion, for which there [wasn't] a counterpart federal aid program."[35] The combination of a strengthened national-city link and the corresponding state bypass resulted—at least in part—from the belief that Congress and federal authorities are more likely than state officials to ensure that the "poor and the black, especially the latter" will get their fair share from tax dollars.

Plainly, governors and state legislators do not like to see federal funds go directly to city officials; city officials of course favor such direct federal aid, or any other means by which the federal government might provide money. (Some federal programs, attempting to bypass City Hall, provided federal dollars directly to community agencies created especially to represent the poor. Because neither state nor city officials liked this approach, such programs did not last long.)

In the 1980s the number and size of federal programs providing direct federal aid to cities was dramatically reduced—by more than $30 billion a year. Abandoned by the national government, cities and counties turned once again to their own state capitols. Tensions between state and city officials started to ease. It became clear that the national government was not necessarily a more reliable source of funds for a city than its own state. Moreover, changing demographic factors and an altering political climate have made state officials more responsive to city issues. Pollution, crime, poverty, unemployment, and other problems, once thought to belong exclusively to cities, have become suburban problems as well.

The states have responded to the reduction in federal funding for urban governments with mixed results. Wealthier states such as Massachusetts and New Jersey have done more to replace the withdrawn federal funds for their cities and schools than have such economically troubled states such as Louisiana. And although state help to localities is growing, many city officials and county authorities continue to complain they have been left in the lurch.

In short, the national/city link has not been broken, but it is no longer expanding—for the moment. States are reemerging as the primary channel between Washington and local governments.

The Politics of Federalism

Americans have long argued about the "proper" division of powers between central and local governments, and from time to time various governmental commissions and "experts" have tried to set definitive criteria. But the experts discovered, as did our country's founders, that few objective standards exist. Rather, the problems are largely political. At one time or another Northerners, Southerners, business people, farmers, workers, Federalists, Democrats, Whigs, and Republicans have championed states' rights, but underlying their arguments have been such issues as slavery, labor-management relations, government regulation of business, civil rights, welfare politics, environmental regulations, and so on. Until the Civil Rights Revolution of the 1960s, for example, segregationists feared that national officials— responding to different political majorities—would work for racial integration. Thus they praised local governments, emphasized the dangers of overcentralization, and argued that the protection of civil rights was not a proper function of the national government.

Today the politics of federalism is more complicated than it was in the past. Even in the area of civil rights,[36] as a result of changing political power distributions, it is no longer safe to predict that the national government will be more favorable to the claims of minorities than most state or city governments. State and local governments, for example, "have become the principal agents for advancing the cause of comparable worth. This role challenges the conventional wisdom that only centrist alternatives can advance equal opportunity and civil rights for all citizens."[37]

Moreover, as states more actively regulate the economy, some business interests have been running back to Washington asking for preemptive federal regulation to save them not only from stringent state regulations, but from having to adjust to fifty different state laws.[38] On the whole, however, conservative ideology continues to favor state and local action, while liberal ideology continues to favor national action. Conservative theorists still tend to champion local autonomy as the "means of protecting individual freedom." Local autonomy continues to be suspect by representatives of minorities, feminists, and the disadvantaged in general as "an exclusive haven for white privilege."[39] Yet these "solid" positions about the appropriate functions of the national government versus state and local governments have begun to crumble.

THE POLITICS OF NATIONAL GROWTH

Over the past two hundred years there has been a steady drift of power from other institutions—families, churches and synagogues, the marketplace—to governments, and especially to the national government. "No one planned the growth . . . but everyone played a part in it."[40] How did this come about? For a variety of reasons. One is that many of our problems became national in scope. Much that was local in 1789, in 1860, or in 1930 is now national—even global. State governments could supervise the relations between small merchants and their few employees, but only the national government can supervise relations between an international industry and its thousands of employees, all organized in national unions. Big business, big agriculture, and big labor all add up to big government.

As industrialization progressed, powerful interests made demands on the national government. Business groups called on the government for aid in the form of tariffs, a national banking system, and subsidies to railroads and the merchant marine. Farmers learned that the national government could give more aid than the states, and they too began to demand help. By the beginning of this century, urban groups in general, and organized labor in particular, pressed their claims.

The growth of the national economy and the creation of a national transportation and communications network altered people's attitudes toward the national government. Prior to the Civil War the national government was viewed as a distant, even foreign, government. Today, in part because of television, most people identify as closely with Washington as with their state capitals.

The Great Depression of the 1930s stimulated extensive national action on such issues as relief, unemployment, and agricultural surpluses. World War II brought federal regulation of wages, prices, and employment, as well as national efforts to allocate resources, train personnel, and support engineering and inventions. After the war the national government helped veterans and inaugurated a vast system of support for university research. Moreover, the United States became the most powerful member of the free world and had to maintain substantial military forces, even during times of peace.

The **Great Society** programs of the 1960s poured out grants-in-aid to states and localities. City dwellers, including blacks who had migrated from the rural South to northern cities, began to seek federal funds for—at the very least—housing, education, and mass transportation.

Although economic and social conditions generated many of the pressures for expansion of the national government, so did political ones. Members of Congress, presidents, federal judges, and federal administrators have actively promoted federal initiatives. Congress in particular has encouraged this trend. True, when there is widespread conflict about what to do—how to reduce the federal deficit, regulate energy policy, reform social security, provide health care for the indigent—Congress waits for a national consensus and looks to presidents for leadership. But when an organized constituency wants something and there is no counterpressure, Congress, "responds often to everyone, and with great vigour."[41]

Once established, federal programs generate groups with vested interests in promoting, defending, and expanding them. Associations are formed; alliances are made. "In a word, the growth of government has created a constituency of, by, and for government."[42]

THE REAGAN LEGACY AND THE BUSH PROMISES

The trend toward federal expansion, like most trends, generated a reaction. In fact, the high point of federal aid in terms of real dollars occurred in 1978.[43] By the beginning of the 1980s, as national budget deficits mounted, liberals and conservatives, Republicans and Democrats, all agreed that the expansion of the national government had gone too far. First the Carter administration curtailed some federal programs. Then the Reagan and Bush administrations made the reduction of the role of the national government one of their domestic priorities. They made considerable progress. Many programs have been eliminated and even more have been sharply reduced. General revenue sharing was eliminated. Between 1980 and 1990 categorical-formula grants for states and local governments were reduced by one-third. Federal aid has dropped from almost 32 percent of all state-local own-source revenues in 1980 to an estimated 20 percent in 1990. More than half of the eighty federal regulations the National Governors' Association targeted as being especially burdensome to the states have been cut.[44] Faced with an overwhelming federal deficit, neither Congress nor President Bush found it easy to inaugurate any substantial new federal programs.

When the national government slowed down the rate of growth of its domestic spending, states took over some of its responsibilities.[45] And "to a greater extent than almost anyone thought possible, [Reagan] . . . achieved his long-cherished goal of shifting the initiative and responsibility for domestic programs out of Washington and back to the states and cities."[46]

The national government, however, is not likely to retreat to a pre-1930 posture or even a pre-1960 one. The underlying economic and social conditions

"Remember, son, we are a government of loopholes, not of men."

Drawing by Dana Fradon; © 1976 The New Yorker Magazine, Inc.

that generated the demand for federal action have not substantially altered. On the contrary, in addition to such traditional issues as jobs and preventing inflation and depressions that still require national action, countless new issues have been added to the national agenda by the transformation of our industrial economy to a global economy based on high technology, service, and information. Although it is worth remembering that in terms of gross national product, many American states are larger than many nations—California has an economy larger than that of Great Britain—and that during the last two decades the states have strengthened their governmental machinery and are more politically responsive than at any time in our history, nonetheless, the states—at least most of them—still lack the jurisdiction by themselves to clean up the air, modernize the air traffic control system, regulate the economy, prevent pollution of our rivers, and deal with drug abuse. There are also all the problems of public health—such as preventing the spread of AIDS and finding a cure for it, as well as issues relating to the lack of decent housing for inner-city blacks and Hispanics that are beyond the capacity of the states to solve alone.

THE FUTURE OF THE STATES AND OUR FEDERAL SYSTEM

In 1933, seeing state governments helpless during the Great Depression, one writer stated: "I do not predict that the states will go, but affirm that they have gone."[47] Thirty years later Senator Everett McKinley Dirksen from Illinois intoned that before too long, "the only people interested in state boundaries will be Rand-McNally."[48]

These prophets of doom were wrong. States are stronger than ever. "A revolution—albeit a quiet one—has transformed the states over the past quarter of a century."[49] "Almost unnoticed in Washington, there has been a revolution in state capitals from Albany to Santa Fe, from Olympia to Tallahassee, and from Richmond to St. Paul. No longer the province primarily of hangers-on and political hacks, most state governments today are remarkably sophisticated and professional, competent to address problems that only a decade ago seemed beyond their

TABLE 2–2
Which of These Statements Comes Closest to Your View about Government
Power Today?

	1983 WHITES	1983 NON-WHITES	1984 WHITES	1984 NON-WHITES	1986 WHITES	1986 NON-WHITES
The federal government:						
1. Has too much power.	41%	21%	36%	29%	29%	22%
2. Has about the right amount of power.	18	15	25	20	25	18
3. Should use its power more vigorously.	28	45	33	41	40	52
4. Don't know/No answer.	13	19	6	10	6	8

Source: Advisory Commission on Intergovernmental Relations.
Figures represent percentage of U.S. public.

grasp."[50] Most have improved their governmental structures, taken on greater roles in funding education, launched programs to help distressed cities, and—despite new constitutional limitations—expanded their taxing bases. Outstanding men and women have been attracted to many governorships.[51] "Today, states, in formal representational, policymaking, and implementation terms at least, are more representative, more responsive, more activist, and more professional in their operations than they ever have been. They face their expanded roles better equipped to assume and fulfill them."[52]

Clearly the constitutional and political durability of our states is secure. Federalism remains strong. And considering how much federalism has changed in the last 200 years, more changes can be expected as we move into the next century.

Summary

1. Our federal constitutional system has evolved into something only slightly different in form, but significantly different in operation, from the 1789 version. Whether or not we ever had a system in which it was possible to talk about neat divisions between the powers of the national and the state governments, we certainly can no longer do so accurately.

2. To recognize that the national government has the constitutional authority to do whatever Congress thinks may be necessary and proper to do is not the same as saying federalism is dead. Although during the last two centuries constitutional power has moved toward the national center, political power remains dispersed. States remain active and significant political entities.

3. Ideological bias in favor of either national or state action is likely to reflect concrete political objectives. In recent years the conservatives' stand in favor of states' rights

and the liberals' stand in favor of national action are no longer as predictable. Shifting political issues continue to lead to shifting allegiances among the various levels of government.

4. The drift toward increasing federal action has been fueled more by underlying economic and social changes than by concerns about federalism, but we detect a vigorous trend toward the view that federalism as a political principle is worthy of being preserved.

5. The major instrument of federal intervention in recent decades has been various kinds of grants-in-aid, of which the most prominent are categorical-formula grants, project grants, block grants, and revenue sharing.

6. Additional forms of federal intervention to control the activities of state and local governments have become more important in recent decades; these include direct orders, cross-cutting requirements on federal funds, cross-over sanctions in the use of federal funds, and partial preemption.

7. In the 1980s there was a substantial return of policy responsibilities back to the states and a pause in the expanding role of the national government.

8. Today we no longer spend so much time debating the *law* of federalism; we have moved to the *politics* of federalism. As now interpreted, the Constitution gives us the option to decide through the political process what we want to do, who is going to pay, and how we are going to get it done.

Further Reading

Advisory Commission on Intergovernmental Relations. *An Agenda for American Federalism: Restoring Confidence and Competence* (1981). Final volume of an 11-volume study under the general title, *The Federal Role in the Federal System: The Dynamics of Growth.*

Advisory Commission on Intergovernmental Relations. *Intergovernmental Perspective.* Published four times a year (U.S. Government Printing Office).

THOMAS J. ANTON, *American Federalism and Public Policy* (Temple University Press, 1989).

RAOUL BERGER. *Federalism: The Founders' Design* (University of Oklahoma Press, 1987).

ANN O'M. BOWMAN and RICHARD C. KEARNEY. *The Resurgence of the States* (Prentice Hall, 1986).

The Center for the Study of Federalism. *Publius: The Journal of Federalism.* Published quarterly (Temple University), one of the issues is an *Annual Review of the State of American Federalism.*

TIMOTHY J. CONLAN. *New Federalism: Intergovernmental Reform from Nixon to Reagan* (The Brookings Institution, 1988).

DANIEL J. ELAZAR. *American Federalism: A View from the States,* 3d ed. (Harper & Row, 1984).

DANIEL J. ELAZAR. *Exploring Federalism* (University of Alabama Press, 1987).

PARRIS N. GLENDENING and MAVIS MANN REEVES. *Pragmatic Federalism: An Intergovernmental View of American Government,* 2d ed. (Palisades Publishers, 1984).

JEFFREY HENIG. *Public Policy and Federalism* (St. Martin's, 1985).

GOVERNOR SCOTT M. MATHESON with JAMES E. KEE. *Out of Balance* (Peregrine Smith Books, 1986).

LAURENCE J. O'TOOLE, JR., ed. *American Intergovernmental Relations* (Congressional Quarterly Press, 1985).

MICHAEL D. REAGAN and JOHN G. SANZONE. *The New Federalism,* 2d ed. (Oxford University Press, 1981).

WILLIAM H. RIKER. *The Development of American Federalism* (Kluwer Academic Publishers, 1987).

HARRY N. SCHEIBER. *Federalism: Studies in History, Law, and Policy* (Institute of Governmental Studies, University of California at Berkeley, 1985).

WILLIAM H. STEWART. *Concepts of Federalism* (University Press of America, 1984).

DAVID B. WALKER. *Toward a Functioning Federalism* (Winthrop, 1981).

N otes

1. Governor (now Senator) Charles Robb, quoted in *The New York Times* (December 15, 1985), p. A80.

2. Daniel J. Elazar, *Exploring Federalism* (University of Alabama Press, 1987), p. 6.

3. William H. Riker, *The Development of American Federalism* (Academic Publishers, 1987), pp. 14–15. Riker contends that not only does federalism not guarantee freedom, but that the framers of our federal system, as well as those of other nations, were not animated by considerations of safeguarding freedom but by practical considerations of preservation of their unity.

4. John Kincaid, "State Constitutions in the Federal System," *The Annals of the American Academy of Political and Social Sciences, State Constitutions in a Federal System* (March 1988), p. 17. See also David Osborne, *Laboratories of Democracy: A New Breed of Governor Creates Models for National Growth* (Harvard Business School Press, 1988), p. 1.

5. Paul M. Barrett, "New Jersey, After Federal Leadership Waned, Has Become Environmental Protection Pioneer," *The Wall Street Journal* (July 5, 1988), p. 40.

6. *Garcia* v. *San Antonio Metro*, 469 U.S. 528 (1985); James R. Alexander, "State Sovereignty in the Federal System" *Publius* (Spring 1986), pp. 1–15.

7. *Luther* v. *Borden*, 7 How. 1 (1849).

8. *California* v. *Superior Court of California*, 482 U.S. 400 (1987).

9. *Puerto Rico* v. *Brandstadt*, 423 U.S. 219.

10. David C. Nice, "State Participation in Interstate Compacts," *Publius*, vol. 17, no 2 (Spring 1987), p. 70.

11. 312 U.S. 100 (1941).

12. 4 Wheaton 316 (1819).

13. *Gibbons* v. *Ogden*, 9 Wheaton 1 (1824).

14. *Heart of Atlanta Motel* v. *United States*, 379 U.S. 241 (1964).

15. *Oklahoma City* v. *Tuttle*, 471 U.S. 808 (1985); *Maine* v. *Thiboutot*, 448 U.S. 1 (1980); *Monell* v. *New York City Dept. of Social Welfare*, 436 U.S. 658 (1978). See Cynthia Cates Colella, "The United States Supreme Court and Intergovernmental Relations," in Robert J. Dilger, ed., *American Intergovernmental Relations Today: Perspectives and Controversies* (Prentice Hall, 1985), p. 66.

16. Linda Greenhouse, "1871 Rights Law Now Used for Many Causes," *The New York Times* (August 26, 1988), p. Y17.

17. Oliver Wendell Holmes, Jr., *Collected Legal Papers* (Harcourt, 1920), pp. 295–96.

18. 426 U.S. 833 (1976).

19. *South Carolina* v. *Baker*, 99 L Ed 2d 592 (1988).

20. Ibid. Whether Congress is a reliable protector of federalism is a subject of research debate among political scientists; see Rodney E. Hero, "The U.S. Congress and American Federalism: Are 'Subnational' Governments Protected?" *Western Political Quarterly*, 42 (March 1989), pp. 93–106.

21. Justice Sandra O'Connor dissenting in *Garcia* v. *San Antonio Metro*.

22. Ibid.

23. Michael J. Rich, "Distributive Politics and the Allocation of Federal Grants," *The American Political Science Review*, vol. 83, no. 1 (March 1989), p. 209.

24. George J. Gordon, *Public Administration in America*, 3d ed. (St. Martin's, 1986), p. 149.

25. John E. Chubb, "The Political Economy of Federalism," *The American Political Science Review*, vol. 79 (December 1985), p. 1005.

26. Richard P. Nathan, "Special Revenue Sharing: Simple, Neat, and Correct." Unpublished manuscript.

27. Deil S. Wright, *Understanding Intergovernmental Relations*, 3d ed. (Brooks-Cole, 1982).
28. Harold Seidman and Robert Gilmour, *Politics, Position and Power*, rev. ed. (Oxford University Press, 1985).
29. George E. Peterson et al., *The Reagan Block Grants: What Have We Learned?* (The Urban Institute Press, 1985), p. 29.
30. Ibid.
31. Donald F. Kettl, *The Regulation of American Federalism* (Johns Hopkins University Press, 1987), pp. 154–55.
32. Mel Dubnick and Alan Gitelson, "Nationalizing State Policies," in Jerome J. Hanus, ed., *The Nationalization of State Government* (D.C. Heath, 1981), pp. 56–57.
33. W. John Moore, "Crazy-Quilt Federalism," *National Journal* (November 26, 1988), p. 3004.
34. H. F. Graff, "Presidents Are Now Mayors," *The New York Times* (July 18, 1979), p. A23.
35. Neal R. Peirce, "The State of American Federalism," *Civic Review* (January 1980), p. 32.
36. Daniel J. Elazar, *American Federalism: A View from the States*, 3d ed. (Harper & Row, 1984), p. 241.
37. Debra A. Stewart, "State Initiatives in the Federal System: The Politics and Policy of Comparable Worth in 1984," *Publius* (Summer 1985), p. 93.
38. Martha M. Hamilton, "If You Want Something Done Right, Do It Yourself," *The Washington Post National Weekly Edition* (September 5–11, 1988), p. 31.
39. Gordon L. Clark, *Judges and the Cities: Interpreting Local Autonomy* (The University of Chicago Press, 1985), p. 8.
40. Advisory Commission on Intergovernmental Relations, *Restoring Confidence and Competence* (ACIR, 1981), p. 30.
41. Cynthia Cates Colella, "The Creation, Care and Feeding of the Leviathan: Who and What Makes Government Grow," *Intergovernmental Perspective* (Fall 1979), p. 9.
42. Aaron Wildavsky, "Bare Bones: Putting Flesh on the Skeleton of American Federalism," in Advisory Commission on Intergovernmental Relations, *The Future of Federalism in the 1980s* (ACIR Publication M–126, 1981), p. 79.
43. Richard P. Nathan and Fred C. Doolittle, "Federal Grants: Giving and Taking Away," *Political Science Quarterly* (Spring 1985), p. 55.
44. John Kincaid, "The State of American Federalism—1987," *Publius*, vol. 18 (Summer 1988), p. 1.
45. John Herbers, "The New Federalism: Unplanned, Innovative, and Here to Stay," *Governing* (October 1987).
46. David S. Broder, "What Reagan Did—and Didn't Do," *The Washington Post National Weekly Edition* (January 23, 1989), p. 4.
47. Luther Gulick, "Reorganization of the States," *Civil Engineering* (August 1933), pp. 420–21.
48. Quoted by Terry Sanford in *Storm over the States* (McGraw-Hill, 1967), p. 37.
49. Carl Stenberg, in Mavis Mann Reeves, *The Question of State Government Capability: A Commission Report* (Advisory Commission on Intergovernmental Relations, 1985), p. 320. See also, Ann O'M. Bowman and Richard C. Kearney, *The Resurgence of the States* (Prentice Hall, 1986).
50. Denis P. Doyle and Terry W. Hartle, "A Funny Thing Happened on the Way to New Federalism . . . ," *Washington Post National Weekly Edition* (December 2, 1985), p. 23.
51. Osborne, *Laboratories of Democracy*.
52. Ibid., p. 363.

3

State Constitutions: Charters or Straitjackets?

While you're celebrating the bicentennial era of our nation's Bill of Rights, you might also give some thought to your state constitution. There will be no "state" birthdays in the years immediately ahead. Although anniversaries of state constitutions are not usually observed with much fanfare, they deserve to be, because some state documents are actually older than our federal Constitution. Virginia added its Bill of Rights to its constitution in 1776, thirteen years before the national one was proposed by Congress. Massachusetts and New Hampshire can boast of charters older than the federal document. Other states—Georgia and Montana, for example—have adopted constitutions during your own lifetime.

State constitutions, like the federal one, are both *instruments of* and *limitations on* government. However, state constitutions, unlike the federal one, are not symbols of state unity. On trips to your state capital you are unlikely to find the state constitution "displayed as is the federal Constitution, in a setting similar to a Shinto shrine."[1]

The first state constitutions were outgrowths of colonial charters. In 1787 the framers of the federal Constitution drew heavily on their experience with these state charters and constitutions. Later state constitutions, in turn, benefited in large measure from their framers' experience with the federal Constitution. As people moved westward and created new states, they copied the constitutions of the older states. The federal and the state constitutions were all adopted in conventions convened for that specific purpose. These conventions then submitted their new charters to the people for ratification.

The people of each state, subject only to the broad limitations of the federal Constitution, are free to create whatever kind of republican government they wish. Yet all state constitutions are similar in general outline. No state has established a parliamentary system, and none has deprived its judges of the power of judicial review. The usual state constitution consists of a preamble, a bill of rights, articles providing for separation of powers, a two-house legislature, an executive department, an independent judiciary with power of judicial review, a description of the form and powers of local units of government, an amendatory article, and miscellaneous provisions dealing with corporations, railroads, finances, and other specific topics.

Studying state constitutions obviously tells us much about how power is distributed within the states, and by studying them we learn of the essential similarity in the structure of state governments. Yet similarity of formal constitutions does not mean similarity in actual governmental processes. Much more has to be considered in determining who governs our states, as the preceding chapter suggests. The constitution is just a place to begin.

Constitutional Rigidity and Change

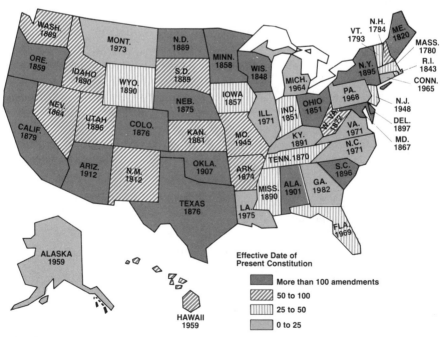

SOURCE: *The Book of the States, 1984–85.*

Constitutional Rigidity and Evasion

State constitutions contain more detail than the national Constitution does. They are longer and less flexible, and they require more frequent formal amendment. Further, states frequently change their constitutions. (Louisiana has had eleven constitutions; Georgia has had ten; South Carolina, seven; and Alabama, Florida, and Virginia, six.) State constitutions vary in length—from the 6600 words of Vermont's, the only state constitution shorter than the Constitution of the United States as amended, to the 174,000 of Alabama's.[2]

The federal Constitution grants powers in broad and sweeping terms, allowing each generation to write in the details and adapt the basic charter of government to new conditions. Most state constitutions, on the other hand, prescribe in detail what can be done and how it can be done. Compare, for example, the difference between how the national and a typical state constitution spell out the way taxes can be levied and public moneys spent. The federal Constitution uses only one clause to authorize Congress to spend money, but state constitutions require dozens of pages to specify the purposes for which the money may be spent, how much may be spent, and in what manner. These details sometimes get in the way of action.

Although most state constitutional provisions deal with matters of significance, some deal with trivial subjects. California's much-amended constitution (it has had over 475 amendments since it was adopted in 1879), for example, goes into great detail about such matters as the taxation of fish and the internal organization of several major departments. Oklahoma's constitution proclaims: "Until changed by the Legislature, the flash test for all kerosene oil for illuminating purposes shall be 115 degrees Fahrenheit; and the specific gravity test for all such oil shall be 40 degrees." And the South Dakota constitution provides for authorizing a twine and cordage plant at the state penitentiary.

CONSTITUTIONS AS ROADBLOCKS

A written constitution sets forth, among other things, the terms upon which public officials are authorized to act in behalf of the people. The more detailed the constitution, the less discretion public officials enjoy. The earliest state constitutions granted authority to the legislatures without much restriction on how their power should be exercised. But after many legislatures gave special privileges to railroads, canal builders, and other interests, constitutional amendments were adopted to prevent such abuses. Reform groups, distrusting the legislatures, began to insist that their programs be incorporated into the constitution. In time, state constitutions became encrusted in layer after layer of procedural detail. Further, unlike the national Constitution that mainly prescribes a set of institutions, processes, and procedures for making public policies without attempting to spell out specific policies, state constitutions often prescribe what the policy should be in many areas.

What does this mean for democratic government? Most simply, it means that state constitutions—intended as charters of self-government—are often like straitjackets imposed on the living present by the dead past. Listing powers in detail soon renders a constitution out of date. Some outdated provisions, of course, do no harm, but more often they are roadblocks to effective government. For example, fixed salaries do not reflect changing economic conditions, and a rigidly organized administrative structure is incapable of adjusting to new needs. Further, detailed and restrictive state constitutions enhance the position of those who wish to preserve the status quo.

Under these conditions the people's representatives—the legislature—cannot act on many problems; instead, the voters are regularly asked to pass constitutional amendments on subjects about which they may know very little. Consider the formerly overworked voters of Louisiana. Between 1921, when their next-to-the-most-recent constitution was adopted, and 1974, when their new one was adopted, they were presented with about 750 proposed amendments, two-thirds of which they approved. In 1988, California voters were given a ballot that, along with a long list of candidates for national and state offices and local issues, asked them to vote on eight bond issues, eight legislatively proposed constitutional amendments, and twelve constitutional proposals submitted by the initiative process, including five highly technical ones having to do with automobile insurance.

GETTING AROUND THE CONSTITUTION

Does all this mean that state constitutions can forever prevent the wishes of the majority from being carried out? Not necessarily. The constitutional system of our states, like that of the national government, includes more than the formal written document. Unwritten rules, practices, political parties, and interest groups also shape events. When large groups of people want their officials to act, they usually find some way to overcome formal barriers. One device they rely on is judicial interpretation, whereby judges can remove a law's restrictive force by a broad interpretation of its meaning. Some sections of state constitutions have been invalidated by national action, especially in the area of civil rights and suffrage. Nevertheless, rigid state constitutions can create a "constitutional autocracy" by making it more difficult for new majorities to achieve their aims.

Detailed state constitutions also increase the authority of judges. The more complex the constitution, the easier it is for judges to veto legislation. One reason for the growing length of some constitutions is that amendments are often required to reverse judicial interpretations.

TAKING STATE CONSTITUTIONS SERIOUSLY [3]

State supreme courts in recent decades have drawn considerable attention as they have used the bill of rights in their own state constitutions to review the actions of state and local officials. Even more recently the entire constitution, as well as the bill of rights of the state constitutions, has become increasingly involved in state court litigation.

State constitutions are being used by some state judges to require their state legislatures to provide better schools for children living in poor neighborhoods, to build more low-income housing, and to protect the environment. Because of this renewed interest in state constitutional law, the National Association of Attorneys General publishes a monthly bulletin on state constitutional law and sponsors an annual seminar, and the Advisory Commission on Intergovernmental Relations (ACIR) has published the first modern casebook on state constitutional law.[4]

Amending State Constitutions

Constitutional amendments must first be *proposed* (initiated) and then *ratified*. There are three ways to propose amendments: (1) by legislative acts; (2) by constitutional conventions; and (3) by initiative petitions.

All states permit their legislatures to propose amendments; in fact, this is the most commonly used method. Although provisions vary, the general practice is to require the approval of two-thirds of the elected members in each chamber of the legislature. Some states, however, permit proposal of an amendment by a simple majority in two successive legislatures.

After an amendment has been proposed, it must be ratified. In all states except Delaware (where the legislature can ratify as well as propose amendments), ratification is by the voters. In most states, an amendment becomes part of the constitution when approved by a majority of those voting on the amendment. In a few states, however, approval of a majority of all those voting in the election is required. This makes ratification difficult, because some people who vote for candidates do not vote at all on amendments. Still, about 60 percent of all amendments submitted by legislatures to the voters are ratified.

CONSTITUTIONAL CONVENTIONS

Because amendments involve piecemeal change, many people in many states advocate writing a new constitution rather than amending the current one. Americans love constitutional conventions; we have had over 230 of them. The most recent one was held by Rhode Island in 1986. We have always insisted on written constitutions, and have always viewed them as expressions of popular will and as fundamental law binding on all public officials. As such they can be changed only by prescribed methods. We have preferred to have our constitutions drawn up by some agency more in touch with the people's wishes than a legislature is. The constitutional convention has been by far the preferred method of writing new constitutions.

Forty-one state constitutions authorize their legislatures to submit to the voters the question of calling a convention; in the other states the legislatures are assumed to have the power to do so. Fourteen state constitutions require the legislatures to submit this question to the voters at fixed intervals. If the voters approve, the next step is to elect delegates. Some constitutions contain elaborate procedures governing the number of delegates, the method of election, and the time and place of the conventions. Others leave the details to the legislatures. The way convention delegates are selected seems to affect the kind of document the convention proposes. Nonpartisan multimember district selection devices are more likely to result in a "reform" convention than those in which parties play a major role.[5]

After the delegates have been chosen for the specific job of drafting a new constitution, they usually assemble at the state capital. When the convention has prepared a draft of the new constitution, the document is submitted to the voters. But first the convention delegates have to make a difficult choice: Should the voters be asked to accept or reject the new constitution as a whole? Or should they be given a chance to vote on each section as though it were an amendment to the old constitution?

The advantage of the first method is that one provision of a constitution ties in with another, and in order to secure all the advantages of revision, the entire constitution should be adopted. The disadvantage is that those who oppose a particular provision may vote against the entire constitution in order to defeat the offending provision. When the convention delegates know that one provision is controversial, they may decide to submit at least that provision separately. Whichever method they choose, the supporters of change must rally their forces to gain voter approval of their work.

Conventions: Political Aspects Constitutions are not a neutral set of rules perched above the world of everyday politics; rather, they significantly affect who gets what from government. How a constitution is changed can help or hinder various groups; constitutional change is, therefore, a difficult process. "If the document is exceptionally innovative, those status quo supporting groups and interests who have lost in the selection and convention process will oppose and defeat the document. If the document is not innovative, those reform groups who initially lobbied for conventions will oppose and defeat the document."[6]

Many people simply do not care. It is difficult to work up much excitement in a campaign for revision of a state constitution except among those with intense feelings, and they are more likely to oppose than to favor adoption. Those who like the status quo thus have a built-in advantage, which, combined with obstacles to the amending process in the constitution itself, helps explain the lack of action.

Revision Commissions Instead of calling a constitutional convention, the legislature may appoint a small commission to make recommendations. A commission is less expensive, does not require initial voter approval, and gives the legislature final control of what is presented to the electorate. Florida, Virginia, and Louisiana have used the commission procedure to bring about significant constitutional change. Mississippi has been using the commission device to develop support to change its 1890 constitution, a constitution that had been designed to keep blacks out of the political process. The governor urged the commission "to recommend changes that will move this state forward into the next century."[7]

In some states the revision commission has not worked well, perhaps because it has not been responsive to political currents or representative of enough interests. Although a commission may provide more objective consideration of amendments than either the legislature or a convention, if it proposes changes that do not reflect political realities, its proposals will be rejected by the legislature or by the voters. Still, revision commissions are becoming more popular.

Rhode Island Amends Its Constitution   Rhode Island's 1986 constitutional convention produced fourteen separate propositions for amending its 1983 constitution. On November 4, 1986, the voters approved eight of the fourteen provisions, rejecting attempts to increase compensation of state legislators, merit selection of judges, and a provision to create a "paramount right to life without regard to age, health, function or condition of dependency" that would have banned abortions or public funding of them. The voters approved provisions strengthening free speech, due process, and equal protection rights and expanding rights to fish and access to the shore, as well as a statement that the rights protected by the Rhode Island constitution "stand independent of the U.S. Constitution."

Texas Tries to Revise Its Constitution   Texas has a lengthy constitution, to which more than 218 amendments have been added. In 1972, when political scandals brought in a new governor, Dolph Briscoe, and a reform-oriented state legislature, the time for constitutional revision appeared ripe. After pushing through a variety of reforms dealing with ethics of officeholders, campaign practices, and registration of lobbyists, the legislature called a convention to revise the 1876 constitution. However, unlike most constitutional conventions, members of the legislature, rather than a specially elected body, served as the constitutional convention.

After working for seventeen months, the legislator-delegates came up with a much revised and shortened document intended to modernize many obsolete governmental practices. Because the convention deadlocked over whether to give constitutional status to the state right-to-work law, which prohibits labor contracts requiring union membership as a condition of employment, this issue was referred to the voters. Nonetheless, neither the AFL-CIO nor Governor Briscoe would support all of the convention's recommendations. The governor was especially opposed to the proposal for annual legislative sessions, which he argued would cause higher taxes. Revisionists tried to salvage their work by offering substantial parts of the new charter to the voters as amendments to the existing constitution. Conservatives praised the old constitution, claiming it had served Texas well for one hundred years. Progressives complained that the old constitution was elitist, permitted only the narrowest governmental objectives, and made real change nearly impossible. In November 1975, Texas voters rejected the new amendments by a two to one vote.[8]

Louisiana Revises Its Constitution   The Louisiana constitutional revision commission set out during 1973 and 1974 to write a streamlined "people's constitution"— one the average person could understand.[9] The AFL-CIO, NAACP, League of Women Voters, Committee for a Better Louisiana, National Municipal League, and many other lobbying groups became involved in shaping the new constitution. It took well over a year to write, and it cost approximately $4 million. In the end, however, a readable 26,000-word document replaced the existing 265,000-word document that contained detailed legislative items and some 536 amendments. In April 1974, Louisiana voters approved the new charter by a large margin. The Louisiana constitution can no longer be cited as the chief example of an unworkable state constitution.

Changing the Hawaiian Constitution (1978), and Leaving It Alone (1986)
Hawaiians take constitution making and constitution changing very seriously: Hawaii's constitution allows the voters to hold a constitutional convention every ten years! Over 800 proposals for constitutional changes were submitted to the Hawaiian convention of 1978. The League of Women Voters and other groups conducted extensive information and discussion meetings, and the convention itself held many public hearings on key issues. The 102 delegates to the state constitutional convention met for nearly three months during the summer of 1978. After extensive debate the convention narrowed the proposals down to thirty-four questions to be placed on the fall ballot. These questions reflected both traditional and new thinking in constitutional revision: convention delegates rejected proposals for the initiative, referendum, and recall; for a unicameral legislature; and for an elected (as against appointed) attorney general.

The delegates were not opposed to all government "reforms," however, for they endorsed a two-term limit for governor and lieutenant governor, moved to make Hawaiian party primaries more "open" by allowing voters to cast ballots without declaring party preference, and authorized the state legislature to provide partial public funding for election campaigns and to establish spending limits. The convention reflected current concern over government spending by setting tougher debt and spending limits for the state. It also strengthened environmental safeguards and gave further constitutional and financial protection to the special status of native Hawaiians.

When these and other recommendations were placed before the voters on November 7, 1978, in the form of proposed amendments to the Hawaii constitution, all thirty-four were adopted. Seventy-four percent of the voters went to the polls; of those who voted, all but approximately 20 percent supported all the proposals as a package or individually by majority vote. The delegates had no sooner celebrated the favorable response to their work, however, when the election results were challenged in the courts. Opponents claimed, among other things, that the ballot contained an inherent bias toward a "yes" vote by making it harder to vote "no" than "yes." The Hawaii Supreme Court rejected the challenge.

Ten years later, in November 1986, Hawaiians rejected the periodic question of whether to call a convention by a vote of 139,236 (for) to 173,977 (against).

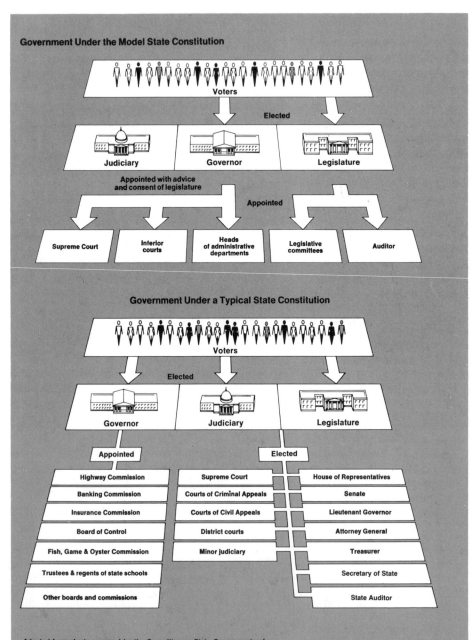

Government Under the Model State Constitution

Voters

Elected

Judiciary · Governor · Legislature

Appointed with advice and consent of legislature

Appointed

Supreme Court · Inferior courts · Heads of administrative departments · Legislative committees · Auditor

Government Under a Typical State Constitution

Voters

Elected

Governor · Judiciary · Legislature

Appointed

Highway Commission
Banking Commission
Insurance Commission
Board of Control
Fish, Game & Oyster Commission
Trustees & regents of state schools
Other boards and commissions

Elected

Supreme Court
Courts of Criminal Appeals
Courts of Civil Appeals
District courts
Minor judiciary

House of Representatives
Senate
Lieutenant Governor
Attorney General
Treasurer
Secretary of State
State Auditor

Adapted from charts prepared for the Committee on State Governments of the National Municipal League for the 1948 edition of the Model State Constitution, modified to reflect provisions of the 1967 revision.

Hawaii's experience with revision in 1978 and 1986 is a potent reminder that constitution making cannot be separated from the political process.

Arkansas's Eighth Constitutional Convention　Arkansas's eighth constitutional convention was a protracted affair. The one hundred delegates who were elected in 1978 held their organizational session in the winter of that year but did not get down to work until the spring of 1979. Then, having reconvened in June 1980 to revise the final draft, they submitted the proposed constitution to the voters in November 1980.

Opposition later developed to a provision in the new constitution allowing the legislature, by a two-thirds vote, to set interest rates rather than limit them, as in the current constitution. Others opposed a new provision enlarging the taxing powers of the local governments. Even though the new constitution was endorsed by the governor, the Democratic Party, and the Arkansas Bar Association, it was opposed by the AFL-CIO and the Arkansas Education Association. The voters rejected it by a two to one margin.

A Constitution for "New Columbia"　Also of interest is the work of a constitutional convention of the District of Columbia. Forty-five delegates proposed a constitution that was adopted by the voters of the District in November 1982, and subsequently submitted to Congress along with a petition for the admission of the District as a new state, to be called New Columbia. After hearings and public discussion, the Council of the District of Columbia in 1987 approved a revised document for transmission to Congress.

The proposed constitution calls for a unicameral legislature elected by a combination of single-member and at-large election districts, a relatively strong governor, a two-tier judicial branch with merit selection of judges for fifteen years, and a bill of rights that is similar to the U.S. Bill of Rights, except that an equality clause replaces the Tenth Amendment.

CONSTITUTIONAL CHANGE BY POPULAR INITIATIVE

At the end of the nineteenth century, the prestige of state governments was at a new low. Out of this disillusionment came a variety of reforms. Among them was the constitutional **initiative petition,** a device that permits voters to force specific constitutional amendments onto the ballot. Seventeen states allow amendments to be proposed by such petitions. A percentage of signatures, ranging from 4 percent to 16 percent of either the total electorate or the number of voters who voted in the last election, is required on the initiative petition. Once approved by the appropriate state official (attorney general or secretary of state), the amendment is placed directly on the ballot at the next election. In recent years, although approving slightly more than 60 percent of the amendments proposed by state legislatures, voters have approved only about 30 percent of the amendments that originated as the result of citizen initiative procedures.

Plainly, a variety of factors account for the low adoption rate of initiative measures. For example, initiatives tend to be used for controversial issues that have already been rejected by the legislature or that proponents believe do not have a chance of passage. Also, initiatives are often proposed by a small number of interest groups or by reform-minded elites who do not have broad enough support for their views. Sometimes measures are proposed more to launch educational campaigns than to win adoption.

Some critics charge that the initiative asks voters to make too many decisions for which they are not especially well prepared. Others argue that the use of the initiative petition can prevent elected representatives from exercising their proper authority. Still others hold that a constitution should be a blueprint that outlines not the rules for the moment but the overriding principles for an unknowable future. It should certainly not, they say, be too specific about how governments are to operate on a day-to-day basis.

Critics also charge that recently the initiative process in some states has become the tool of well-organized single-interest groups who present voters with simplistic "yes" or "no" choices on complex taxation matters. The celebrated Proposition 13, approved by California voters in mid-1978, came about by the initiative process. It resulted in dramatic reductions of property taxes, the chief source of revenue for local government.

Defenders of the constitutional initiative petition contend that it is a valuable safety valve against unresponsive legislatures. When a legislature is tied so closely to special interests that it refuses even to acknowledge the real needs and demands of a majority of citizens, they contend, the initiative process can be used as a corrective. Also, defenders contend voters are much smarter than critics say, and that they have, in fact, acted rather prudently when asked to decide most constitutional questions.[10]

In a sense, then, constitutional conventions—and especially the constitutional initiative process—are yet other examples of the diffusion of power that characterizes our national and state political systems.

Summary

1. State constitutions attempt to spell out the fundamental laws of the states. Although they vary considerably in detail, each outlines the organizational framework of the state, vesting powers in the legislature and other departments. Each provides for a bill of rights, sets procedures for holding elections, provides for local governments, and contains a variety of provisions dealing with finances, education, and other state issues.
2. A constitution typically reveals little about the politics of a state. But to study the constitutional development of a state is to study its political heritage, the battles among interest groups, and the struggles to adapt to changing conditions.
3. Most state constitutions are cumbersome documents, containing more detail than the national Constitution, and writing into "fundamental law" matters that most consti-

tutional scholars believe should be left to statutory law. The distinction between fundamental and ordinary law is blurred.

4. Despite the considerable constitutional change brought about during the last half century through amendments, voters have often been resistant to sweeping constitutional revision.

Further Reading

ELMER E. CORNWELL, JR., JAY S. GOODMAN, and WAYNE R. SWANSON. *State Constitutional Conventions: The Politics of the Revision Process in Seven States* (Praeger, 1975).

JOHN KINCAID. "State Constitutions in the Federal System," *The Annals* (March 1988).

BERNARD REAMS, JR. *The Constitutions of the States* (Oceana Publications, 1988).

ALBERT L. STURM and JANICE C. MAY. "State Constitutions 1986–1987," *The Book of the States, 1988–89* (The Council of State Governments, 1988), and equivalent articles in each edition of *The Book of the States.*

ALAN G. TARR. *State Constitutions of the United States* (Greenwood Press). Fifty-two volumes are in publication, to be completed by 1995. Each volume will provide a comprehensive commentary on state constitutions.

Notes

1. Gerald Benjamin, "The Functions of State Constitutions in a Federal System," American Political Science Association Round Table, Washington, D.C., 1984.

2. Albert L. Sturm and Janice C. May, "State Constitutions and Constitutional Revision: 1986–87," *The Book of the States, 1986–87* (Council of State Governments, 1988); John Kincaid, "State Constitutions in the Federal System," *The Annals,* (March 1988), p. 14.

3. Title taken from article of the same name by Robert Welsh and Ronald K. L. Collins, *The Center Magazine* (September–October 1981), p. 6.

4. Elder Witt, "State Supreme Courts: Tilting the Balance Toward Change," *Governing* (August 1988), p. 33.

5. Ibid, p. 129.

6. Elmer E. Cornwell, Jr., Jay S. Goodman, and Wayne R. Swanson, "State Constitutional Conventions: Delegates, Roll Calls, and Issues,"

Midwest Journal of Political Science (February 1970), pp. 105–30.

7. "Mississippi Begins Analyzing Its Racist Constitution of 1890," *The New York Times* (December 12, 1985), p. B2.

8. See Beryl E. Pettus and Randall W. Bland, *Texas Government Today* (Dorsey Press, 1979), pp. 34–36. See also Janice May, "Texas Constitutional Revision: Lessons and Laments," *National Civic Review* (February 1977), pp. 64–69.

9. Cecil Morgan, "A New Constitution for Louisiana," *National Civic Review* (July 1974), pp. 343–56.

10. See Thomas E. Cronin, *Direct Democracy: The Politics of Initiative, Referendum and Recall* (Harvard University Press, 1989) for a comprehensive discussion of these matters. See also David B. Magleby, "Taking the Initiative: Direct Legislation and Direct Democracy in the 1980s," *PS* (Summer 1988), pp. 600–11.

4

State Legislatures

State legislatures are the oldest part of our government; the Massachusetts legislature, for example, is in its fourth century. State legislatures existed before we had the U.S. Constitution. Moreover, they were the most powerful governing institution in America during the revolutionary period. Indeed, the coming of the Constitution was in part a reaction to the excessive power of the state legislatures.

The Constitution worked. It did diminish the influence of state legislatures. Two hundred years after its adoption state legislatures are not as powerful as they were in 1787—at least when compared to other governmental institutions.

But state legislatures are important, very important. State legislatures used to be among the public's favorite punching bags. Comedians, journalists, and governors won easy laughs poking fun at certain frivolous or inept legislative antics. Such joking is no longer warranted. Nowadays, state legislatures play a vital role in state politics and state policy making. Heeding their constituents, state legislators strive to solve more problems and provide more and better services—but with fewer taxes and less bureaucracy. Legislators these days seek to make the legislature a counterbalance to governors and especially to state bureaucracies.

Legislatures are sometimes overshadowed by strong and vigorous governors. This is understandable; their many members often concern themselves with dozens of different issues at once. Under such circumstances it is difficult for such a diverse and divergent body to provide unified, swift policy leadership. Some state legislatures lack influence over policy making because they lack the staff and the time to compete with governors, bureaucrats, and interest group leaders—many of whom are better informed. Many state legislators, especially in the smaller states, are still part-timers; they have not been there long and will not stay there long (about three or four terms is the average). Even the best-paid and best-staffed legislatures are often not the dominant branch in state policy making.

The legislatures' *political* functions, however, may be as important now as their law-making or policy-making functions. Legislatures are constantly reconciling pressures among competing interest groups. Representing local views at the state level, they dramatize issues and bring them into the open. In effect, a legislature serves as a lightning rod to which most of the conflicting pressures of American society are drawn, "and its primary job is to defuse these pressures so that the political system can function intact without blowing wide apart."[1]

You or your family probably know someone who is or has tried to become a state legislator, for about 12,000 to 15,000 people seek this job every two years. Sometimes there is no real contest; able incumbents are often unopposed. Nearly 80 percent of incumbents run for reelection, and they have a nearly 90 percent chance of winning renomination and reelection. An incumbent seeking reelection has many advantages over a challenger. These include name recognition, better access to campaign funds, experience in running campaigns, and many opportunities to provide constituent services. Still, few of them feel politically secure, even when they have not been opposed in the last election. "They are always wary of potentially strong opponents and work hard to build a record at the polls and in office that will discourage such persons from running."[2]

State legislators today are better educated, have more professional staffs, are better paid, and have better committee systems and better leadership than they did just twenty-five years ago. They put in far more time on their work than did their predecessors twenty-five years ago.[3] In general, they are also deciding to stay a term or two longer than their earlier counterparts.

Why do so many people seek this office? For many reasons—"the excitement, power and deference, personal gain, a chance to advertise themselves, a need for self-esteem, the challenge of making good public policy, or a sense of loyalty to their political party."[4] Often the reason is a mixture of these factors, as well as a desire to be where the action is. Once elected, state legislators translate diverse public wants and aspirations into practical laws and regulations.

Most state legislators concentrate on being *lawmakers* when meeting at their state capitols. Yet they also try to be *representatives*—listen, learn, and find out what the people like and don't like—when they are at home in their legislative districts. Invariably, too, state legislators wind up doing a lot of favors—getting a merchant a license to sell lottery tickets, persuading some state agency to look into safety standards at the local hospital, pushing for funds to repair county roads, arranging for a campaign supporter to be appointed to the state labor commission, and so on.

State legislators are very accessible. Citizens and students can nearly always contact their legislators and talk with them on the telephone or in person.

The Legislative Branch

All states except Nebraska have a two-house, or **bicameral legislature.** The larger chamber is generally called the house of representatives. It contains from as few as 40 members in Alaska and Nevada to as many as 400 members in New Hampshire; the typical number is around 100. In all but four states the representatives serve two-year terms. The smaller chamber, known as the senate, is composed of about forty members. State senators have four-year terms in most states.

Most state legislatures meet every year from January through May or June. Legislatures in about a dozen mostly smaller or less populous states meet only every other year. Some state constitutions limit their legislatures to regular sessions of a fixed number of days, usually sixty or ninety. Several means, such as the "special session," have been developed to get around this limitation. Such restrictions reflect the old distrust of government, the feeling that "the faster we get it over with, the better." The governor has the power to call the legislature into special session—and in some states to determine the issues that may be discussed in the special session—a power frequently used because of the just-mentioned constitutional limitations.

The organization and procedures of the state legislatures are similar to those of the United States Congress. A speaker, usually chosen by the majority party presides over the lower house. In many states speakers have more power to control proceedings than their national counterpart has. For example, most speakers have the right to appoint committees and thus possess a key role in determining policy. In less than half of the states lieutenant governors preside over the senate, though usually they are mere figureheads; in other states the presiding officer is chosen by the majority party in the senate. The committee system prevails, as in Congress. In several states, such as Massachusetts, **joint committees** are used to speed up legislative action. However, state legislative committees usually do not have the same power over bills as do their national counterparts; they often lack adequate professional assistance; the seniority system is not as closely followed as in Congress; and turnover is somewhat higher.

Although the formal structures and procedures of the legislatures are similar from state to state, their actual operations are not. Several states, like New York and Ohio, have strong political parties that take an active part in policy making. In these states, the party caucus is an important part of the legislative machinery; in others, the parties assume little or no responsibility for the actions of their legislative members. In some states, governors lead the way; in others they are relatively unimportant.

Striking differences exist among state legislatures. Often these differences stem from historical or ethnic traditions. Sometimes they arise because of urban-rural or east-west factional splits, and sometimes because of notable regional differences—as is the case with the "Hill people" versus the "Delta people" in

Mississippi. Here is how one expert on state politics sees some of the more distinctive characteristics shaping state politics in America.

> In New York professional politics, political wheeling and dealing, and frantic activity are characteristic. In Virginia, one gets a sense of tradition, conservatism, and gentility. . . . Louisiana's politics are wild and flamboyant. By contrast, moderation and caution are features of Iowa. A strong disposition of compromise pervades Oregon, with politicians disposed to act as brokers and deal pragmatically rather than dogmatically. In Kansas hard work, respect for authority, fiscal prudence, and a general conservatism and resistance to rapid social change are pervasive features of the state environment. Indiana is intensely partisan. Wyoming is mainly individualistic and Ohio is fundamentally conservative. In Hawaii the relative recent political dominance of Japanese, and the secondary status of Chinese, native Hawaiians, Hawaiians, and Haoles (whites) makes for tough ethnic politics. Yankee Republicans used to run Massachusetts, but now the Irish dominate. Their personalized style, which blends gregariousness and political loyalty, results in a politics of the clan. Mormonism of course dominates Utah.[5]

Still, legislatures have much in common, and it is important to know (1) what they are supposed to do; (2) what their members' backgrounds are; and (3) what influences their behavior and their vote.

WHAT STATE LEGISLATURES CAN—AND CANNOT—DO

What do the 7461 state legislators do? Among other things, they enact the laws that create state parks, specify the salaries for state officials, draw up the rules governing state elections, fix the state tax rates, determine the quantity and quality of state correctional, mental health, and educational institutions, and much more. State legislators in most of the states are more and more involved in overseeing the administration of public policy. Although they do not administer programs directly, through hearings, investigations, audits, and increased involvement in the budgetary process, legislators can and do determine whether programs are being carried out according to legislative intentions.[6]

State legislatures have various functions within the larger federal system, such as ratifying proposed amendments to the U.S. Constitution, exercising the right to petition Congress to call for a constitutional convention to propose an amendment to the national Constitution, and approving interstate compacts on matters affecting state policies and their implementation.

State legislatures have all the powers that are not given to some other agency. The Tenth Amendment to the federal Constitution makes it clear that power not given to the national government nor denied to the states lies with the states or with the people. The state constitutions, in turn, give some of this reserved power

What Makes a Good Legislator?

There are many ways to be an effective legislator. Many specialize in issues, others in procedures or helping their districts through casework, and still others become chamber or party leaders. Nearly everyone learns that there is more to the job than making a lot of speeches or trying to get more bills passed than your colleagues do.

Legislators themselves say they admire colleagues who are confident but not arrogant, cooperative but not spineless, principled but flexible, and humorous but not silly.

Retired lawmakers suggest these rules:

Learn to count.
Keep your word.
Be patient.
Be honest.
Don't promise too soon.
Make friends with the staff.
Never surprise a politician.
Learn how to build alliances.
Learn the procedures.
Think beyond party labels.
Know that timing is often the key.
Don't hog the credit.

exclusively to *non*legislative agencies and specifically deny some to the legislature. What is left is inherited by the state legislatures.

Despite all these restrictions, the legislatures still have a powerful voice in deciding crucial political questions in their states. Thus, for example, they levy state taxes, appropriate money, create agencies to carry out the tasks of government, and investigate these agencies to make sure they are doing what the lawmakers intended them to do. State legislators, like their national counterparts, also participate in amending constitutions, have authority to impeach and try state officials, and exercise some appointive powers.

Each state's constitution usually prescribes the procedures its legislators must follow in order to make laws. In addition, limits on the rate of taxation, the kinds of taxes, the subjects that may be taxed, and the purposes of taxation are often spelled out in the constitution.

With the growth of state functions, legislators are spending increasing amounts of time on casework or constituency services. Constituent relations are often the most time-consuming aspect of a legislator's job. Concerns of constituents usually arise during campaign time. Local city and school officials always need the help of legislators, and dozens of interest groups from back home are always pressing their views on legislators. Legislators usually work hard to attract constituency casework and recognize its political value. The more help they give to their home district citizens and businesses, they reason, the more they will probably be respected and reelected.

WHO ARE THE STATE LEGISLATORS?

The typical American state legislator is a 43-year-old white, male, Protestant businessman or lawyer of Anglo-Saxon origin who has had previous political experience—usually elective—at the city or county level. About 40 percent are Republi-

cans. Lawyers continue to be the largest occupational group in most state legislatures. Many young attorneys, in fact, enter the legislature to perform a public
service, secure a reputation, and build up a practice. But there has been a decline
in the number of lawyers in state legislatures in recent years and an increase in
the number of teachers.

Real estate and insurance dealers, salespeople, and farmers are also found
in legislatures in significant numbers. The number of farmers is decreasing, however, as a result of reapportionment, the decline in the overall number of farmers,
and the longer sessions of the legislatures. When legislatures used to meet for
just a few winter months, farmers were able to fit their schedules to the legislative
cycle.

More and more women and blacks are winning election to state legislatures,
but both groups are still notably in the minority. Out of 7461 state legislators,
about 17 percent, or 1250, are women, over 400 are blacks, and about 125 are
Hispanics. Women's political groups point out that it took 144 years for women
to get the vote. They note also the increasing number of highly qualified women
running for statewide political offices. Women are determined to have an equal
voice in government.[7]

**The Statehouse
as a Second Job**
Percentage of state legislators
holding other jobs.

Lawyers
16%

Business
owners
14%

All others
23%

Farmers
10%

Full-time
legislators
11%

Educators
8%

Employees
11%

Retired
7%

SOURCE: National Conference of State Legislatures,
from a survey in 1986. *New York Times*, June 4,
1989, p.Y13.

Because legislators must have flexible schedules, the job often attracts young people right out of college, retired people, and those whose businesses or law practices have been so successful that they can afford to take the time off. In the more populous and wealthy states, the trend is toward annual legislative sessions with reasonable salaries. New York legislators earn $57,500 a year plus $75 per day for expenses. Pennsylvania pays their legislators $47,000 annually plus $85 per day for expenses. California and a few other states pay at least $40,000. A few other states, such as Maryland, Ohio, and Wisconsin, also provide living wages. But in most states legislators receive modest salaries. Thus, Texas pays $7,200, and Georgia almost $10,000. In some, legislators go to the capitol for only a few months a year and are paid so little that many are able to serve only if they are independently wealthy, if they can live off their parents or spouses, or if they have other jobs that can be readily combined with legislative service. The 400 members of the New Hampshire House earn only $100 a year.

State legislators are generally better educated and have better jobs than the average person. Also, they tend to come more from middle- and upper-income groups. They are usually hard-working, public-spirited citizens who believe serving in the legislature is a good opportunity for service.

State legislators enjoy less prestige than members of Congress, especially in states that have large legislatures. Discouraged by modest salaries and long hours, many serve a few terms and then either retire voluntarily or run for higher office. About 20 percent of all legislators are newcomers, but there has been a gradual increase in the number of legislators seeking reelection. Some state legislators probably leave after just a couple of terms because they get bored listening to matters that frankly do not interest them. As one one-termer advised: "In short, a great deal in the political process does not—repeat does not—involve the glamorous policy issues. Most of the work is sheer routine and hardly awe-inspiring."[8] State legislatures also serve as a significant transit point to higher office.

LOBBYISTS AND THE STATE LEGISLATURE

Those who dislike the laws that are passed, or who like the laws that are defeated, often claim that the fault lies in the integrity of the legislators. Although state legislatures do have their share of dishonest people, their number is probably no greater than in business, sports, or the entertainment field. Many people who may be affected by decisions seek to bend those decisions to their advantage. Anyone who reads major state newspapers knows that certain bankers, insurance companies, road builders, developers, and large landholders have sought contracts or special rulings by illegal means.

A larger problem has long challenged the integrity of representative government in America. "If there is any safe axiom in American politics," writes David Broder, "it is that our legislators get the funds with which they run from the very people who have the greatest direct stake in the legislation they will pass." Broder describes the problem well:

The arrangements are not subtle. Fund-raising dinners are held during the legislative sessions, and the distribution of campaign contributions is often done personally by the same lobbyists who are negotiating with those legislators on provisions of specific bills. The cynical remark of a Florida lobbyist, who had been "invited" to one of those mid-session "appreciation dinners" given by and for a key legislator, was that "you've got to appreciate someone for their past service—or their future service." At that point, the difference between a contribution and a bribe becomes so blurred as to be almost invisible.[9]

To **lobby** is to conduct activities aimed at influencing public officials, especially members of legislative bodies, and the policies they enact. The right to lobby is, of course, based on the First Amendment to the Constitution, which expresses the right of people to petition the government for a redress of grievances. This provision is applicable to the states through judicial interpretation of the Fourteenth Amendment, and similar language is now found in state constitutions.

Illegal use of lobbying techniques, primarily bribery, can still be found in a few states. But direct, illegal bribery is not a major problem. Writing about his own experiences in the Vermont state senate. Frank Smallwood observes that as a general rule, most of the lobbyists "were articulate, hard-working, and extremely well informed in their particular areas of expertise. This last attribute—information—represented their chief weapon and gave them real clout. As far as I could find out, the lobbyists didn't offer legislators any money or other direct inducements, at least, they never offered me anything, not even a sociable drink. Instead they relied on information."[10]

Effective lobbyists are specialists in both subject matter and legislative procedure. Lobbyists for organized interests know the schedule of general hearings, committee meetings, floor debates, and social events. They also know as much as possible about the legislators, their electoral support, their values, their hobbies, and who has their "ear." Some of the most powerful and effective lobbyists are former legislators. They are present and prepared when their interests are affected. In short, veteran lobbyists know how to win friends and influence. One of their rules of thumb is "It's a hell of a lot easier to kill a bill than to pass it." "If a bill hits the floor [of the Senate or the House] you don't have the foggiest idea how the vote will go unless you do an awful lot of homework. . . . To kill a bill all you need is a majority of a committee, but to pass it you need a majority of the House."[11]

How important are interest groups and state political-action committees as a source of influence on state legislatures? Teacher organizations, trade associations, labor groups, and insurance, mining, real estate, and banking interests are often the most visible special-interest groups—varying, of course, from state to state. In states with an obvious major economic interest, legislators pay close attention to the needs of that interest regardless of whether the group employs lobbyists. "Agricultural interests in Iowa, the oil companies in Oklahoma, the automobile

How A Bill Becomes Law: The Massachusetts Model

Petitions are filed in the office of the House or Senate Clerk.

Clerk assigns a number to the petition and refers it to a committee.

Joint Committee holds public hearing before making report.

An unfavorable report, if accepted by the House or Senate, kills the bill. A favorable report is considered the first reading.

If the bill relates to state finances, it is referred to the Ways and Means Committee. When the Ways and Means Committee makes its recommendations, the bill is put on the next day's calendar for a second reading.

Before voting on "ordering the bill a third reading," a bill is subject to debate and amendment. If favorable action is taken and the bill is ordered a third reading, it is then referred to the Committee on Bills in the Third Reading.

Following a third reading, a vote is taken on "passing the bill to be engrossed." A favorable vote sends the bill to the other branch where it follows the same procedure.

If a bill passes the second branch in an amended version, it is sent back to the originating branch for concurrence. If concurrence is rejected, the bill may go to a conference committee.

When agreement is reached by both branches, the bill is prepared for final passage.

Vote on enactment is taken in the House and then the Senate.

The bill is sent to the Governor.

The Governor, during the ten day period allotted him by the constitution, may:

—sign the bill into law

—let it become law by taking no action

—send it back with recommended amendments

—veto it. A two-thirds vote of both branches is required to override a veto.

—let it die by taking no action within ten days after the session has ended and the legislature has prorogued. This is called a pocket veto.

Source: Prepared and published as part of the pamphlet *Inside the State House* by the Massachusetts Legislature and the League of Women Voters of Massachusetts.

industry in Michigan, or the lumbering industry in Oregon do not need to engage much in lobbying the state legislature."[12] The legislatures in these states are not likely to pass legislation hostile to their own state's principal economic interests.

Hundreds of lobbyists openly ply their trade in the committee rooms and corridors of the state capitols. The bigger states register thousands of lobbyists. As of 1990, even little Vermont had nearly 650 lobbyists registered with the secretary of state's office. Much of the most effective lobbying requires generating grass-roots mail and arranging for face-to-face constituent persuasion. "The secret is to be able to find and move the persons back home who are in turn willing and able to move the legislator in the desired direction. These may be the local banker, the local union leadership, the chairman of the county Democratic executive committee, the president of the local chamber of commerce, a minister; the person or persons back home with influence upon the legislator will vary from one issue to another as well as from one member to another."[13]

On balance, probably too much is made of the negative aspects of lobbying. Even the occasional corrupt practices, however, have done much to damage Americans' faith in their state governments. Most state legislators would like to improve the image of the state legislature. In recent years most states have sought to solve the problems of conflict of interest, regulation of lobbyists, and financing of political campaigns. Common Cause, the League of Women Voters, and other groups helped to encourage better financial disclosure, open meetings, and campaign finance reforms.

Not all of these reforms have been easy to enforce, nor have they all worked according to the original intentions. In many states attempts have been made to control lobbying and to regulate how much persons may spend to influence either elections or the legislative process. These laws are difficult to enforce. Further, it is sometimes unclear whether they infringe on the constitutional right of persons to petition their government or to spend their funds for political purposes. These problems will not be easily solved. "The fight for good campaign finance laws is complicated and potentially frustrating," says John D. Feerick, chairman of the New York State Commission on Government and Integrity. "But it is a good and important fight, vital to the health of our democracy."[14]

PARTIES IN THE STATE LEGISLATURE

Except in Nebraska, where legislators are elected on a nonpartisan ballot (one without party labels), all candidates for state legislatures are nominated by political parties in primaries and are elected as party members. A study in Connecticut found that although the official party organization is not a domineering force in recruiting state legislative candidates, a candidate nonetheless has to go through the party to gain the nomination. Candidates sense that parties are weaker than they used to be. And while candidates welcome what help they can get from the parties, they in fact get little money from the parties and clearly have to form their own personal organization, separate from the local party apparatus, to wage a winning campaign.[15]

The role of the political parties in the management of legislatures and in policy making varies widely from state to state. In nearly half the states—especially in the urban, industrialized states and the Northeast—the political party is the most important factor in decision making. In other states—in the Southwest, for example—parties appear to be somewhat less significant. Instead, rural-urban splits, conservative-liberal coalitions or regional blocs serve as the major sources of conflict.

In nearly every state where there are two substantial parties, the political party is the device for the selection of legislative leaders and the assignment of members to committees. Party leaders in many states distribute sought-after perks, ranging from committee assignments to parking spaces. Legislative party caucuses sometimes also distribute campaign funds to their members and to specifically targeted districts.

Party discipline on policy matters is more likely to be found in states with a highly competitive two-party system. Here party caucuses are likely to be the place where party positions are developed, and members of a party are expected to support its policies within their legislative chambers. In fact, in a few states binding votes in party caucuses virtually force party members to vote as a unified bloc on the floor of their chamber. Such binding caucus votes, however, are taken on relatively few issues.

The party caucus is a principal instrument for legislative decision making in about half the states, including Colorado, Delaware, Idaho, Montana, and Utah. In several states, such as Illinois, New York, New Jersey, Pennsylvania, and Minnesota, parties play an even more prominent role than they do in Congress.

In states where one political party is so large that it dominates the legislature, the party caucus is usually not likely to play a central role in policy making. Of course it is hard to generalize about the precise role parties play in legislatures, especially in states where there is neither a highly competitive two-party system nor a one-party system, but something in between. In such states you may find

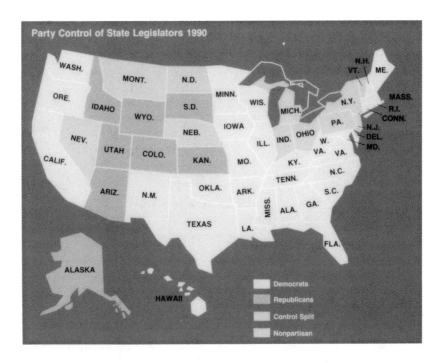

that both parties are highly organized and influence both the procedures and the substantive outcomes inside the state legislatures. Yet in some states only the major political party plays this role. In still other such states, the parties may not be important in deciding what gets done in the legislatures.

In legislatures in which a single party has had a longstanding dominance or even overwhelming control, as in some southern states, parties are generally less important in conducting and shaping legislative business. Because of the rise of the Republican party in the South and Southwest, however, parties and partisanship are gradually increasing in strength in such states as Florida, Texas, and North Carolina. A rebirth of partisanship and growing attention to elections of legislators are apparently making the parties more important than they have been in over half of the states. Voting regularly with his or her party and being a member of the majority party can help legislators win discretionary grants for their districts.[16]

LEGISLATIVE COMMITTEES

Committee recommendations also influence legislative decision making. Committees vary in power and influence depending on the state; as a general rule, however, the influence of committees has increased in the past decade or two. They used to be pale shadows of their counterparts in Congress. They often still are in the less populous states, because of short sessions, limited staffing, and turnover of both staff and legislators.

Still, legislative committees process and shape hundreds or even thousands of bills and resolutions. The typical state legislature must deal with between several hundred and a few thousand bills a session. Here are some of the functions expected of a standing committee and, to a lesser extent, of interim committees created for assignments between sessions.

Studying pending legislation carefully
Conducting public hearings on proposed bills and resolutions
Debating and modifying initial proposals
Screening, eliminating, or burying undesirable legislation
Grading legislation in terms of desirability
Confirming key administrative personnel
Monitoring or overseeing administrative practices and regulations

Above all, a committee system allows members to concentrate their energies on particular areas of governmental operations. Over time, legislative committees and their members develop extensive knowledge about these activities and provide useful information to their colleagues. It's impossible these days for everybody to be an expert on all aspects of state government. Committees, properly staffed and run, can evaluate the merits and faults of a proposed law more effectively than can any individual legislator.

"If you don't get committee support, your legislative program is in jeopardy," says a Michigan state legislator. "There's kind of an unwritten rule that you follow the recommendation of the committee. You may debate the committee suggestions. You may try to alter some of their suggestions. But you generally accept—unless you're opposed to the idea completely."[17]

In short, legislative committees do the homework of the legislature. Some division of labor is absolutely essential. Committees weed out the weakest bills, provide citizens and interest groups an opportunity to testify before their hearings, and enable the better bills to move from one stage of the legislative process to the next.

A few states appoint citizens to play a special role in legislative policy decision making. Wisconsin, for example, is one of the handful of states whose legislatures appoint public members to interim study committees. Citizen members of these between-session legislative committees in Wisconsin are selected for their special knowledge of or interest in the issues under study. Often, as many as 250 citizens serve on these interim legislative committees; they thus equal or even outnumber the legislators on them in a given period. These members draft reports and prepare legislative proposals for submission at the next session. They receive no salary, but they are reimbursed for their expenses. "Frequently, council study measures have a much higher rate of passage than the other bills. For example, in 1983 and 1984, 70 percent of all legislative council bills [in Wisconsin] were enacted by the legislature, compared with the usual passage rate of one bill in four.[18]

OTHER INFLUENCES ON STATE LEGISLATORS

Plainly, the influences that are significant in determining how state legislators cast their votes vary from issue to issue. *Political party leaders* are likely to be most influential on such matters as legislative redistricting, selecting the legislature's leaders, and other issues relating to institutional interests. On issues concerning matters such as banking interests, *interest groups* such as the state Savings and Loan League are likely to be more significant. *Constituents* are likely to have more influence on tax issues. Again, as always in trying to generalize about the politics of fifty different states, one must be cautious.[19]

Although state legislators are elected to represent the people and their views at the statehouse, few lawmakers think they should merely mirror or re-present the views of constituents. Most legislators consider themselves *trustees* of their constituents, claiming to rely on their own consciences, or on their considered judgments of the facts before them. Legislators who considered themselves *delegates*, on the other hand, adhere more closely to instructions from their district's constituents. Not surprisingly, the trustee role is not only the most popular but also the easiest and most realistic to practice. Given the complexity of government and the difficulty of finding out where citizens stand on a wide variety of issues,

---

Influences On Legislators' Voting

Personal political philosophies	Party leaders and party splits
Legislative colleagues	Constituent mail and opinion
Legislative staff specialists	Urban and rural splits in the state
Committee recommendations	Regional blocs within the state
Interest-group lobbyists	National trends
The governor	Programs that have worked in
Cabinet and agency heads	other states

---

the trustee role is more practical in the day-to-day decision making of a legislator during legislative sessions.

On most issues that arise during the session, the explicit needs of the legislative district are not usually a major factor. On those that are important to the district, a legislator generally behaves according to implicit instructions. Thus, state lawmakers in effect act as trustees on some issues and delegates on others, yet "conscience" is seldom the only or even the most important guide. Colleagues, committee recommendations, party leadership advice, staff counsel, lobbying by the affected interests, and a variety of similar factors are ordinarily the guides.

New legislators soon learn that it makes sense to depend on colleagues to inform them about issues assigned to their committees. "Very early in the session you try to find other representatives who sit on other committees and who are similar to you in their outlook politically." According to a Pennsylvania legislator "When a bill comes to the floor for a vote, you have to look to that person, you have to trust him."[20] In a sense you must follow such advice unless you know the subject well enough to have your own informed opinion.

Another aspect of state politics that often fuels legislation is the action taken by other states. Legislators frequently ask their staffs, "What is Florida or Arizona or Oregon doing on this problem?" Sometimes another state's policy affects the legislator's state, such as in the area of diesel fuel rates or college tuitions. Legislators are always on the lookout, too, for innovative tax, educational, or prison policies implemented in another state. Legislators are keenly interested in how their state ranks in a certain area, for example, on sales taxes, high school dropouts, or clean air. The press often uses such rankings in their headlines or in their assesments of the legislature. Of course, actions taken by the federal government influence state laws and regulations. Reagan's cutbacks and Bush's anti-drug programs are examples.

In sum, most state legislators are influenced by their colleagues and legislative leaders and by a variety of forces outside the legislature itself. These may include leaders and opinion makers in their legislative districts, governors, state and local party leaders, interest-group spokespeople, experts in the bureaucracy, and new ideas that have been implemented elsewhere.

Legislative Folkways

The terms *legislative folkways* or *legislative norms* refer to the shared standards of members' individual conduct, especially to what is regarded as appropriate behavior or what is expected of a member in that particular legislature. Most of these norms are commonly also found in business and other professional groups and are by no means unique to a legislature. Political scientists are not exactly sure why these are held more important in some states than in others; we do know, however, that most of the norms listed here are honored as part of the professionalism in nearly every state legislature.[21] Occasional mavericks violate the "rules of the game," but most newcomers to a legislature soon discover these and similar norms and abide by them.

> Treat your colleagues with respect; don't make personal attacks on them or harass them.
>
> Serve an apprenticeship; take some time to do your homework and go through a learning process before charging around acting like a "know-it-all."
>
> Don't be a publicity hound; stay away from the microphone unless you really have something to say.
>
> Don't conceal the real purpose of a bill or purposely overlook some portion of it in order to assure its passage.
>
> Don't make a commitment on a vote until you are ready to be bound by it; keep your word, be reliable when you have made a commitment.
>
> Committee work is your punishment for getting elected; effective legislators specialize enough in their subject areas to be able to advise their colleagues—especially those not on their committees.
>
> Reciprocate when you can; support your friends and colleagues whenever possible so that they will support you whenever they can.
>
> Defend the legislature when it comes under attack from the press, the governor, or other critics—institutional patriotism is much admired by your colleagues.
>
> Don't burn your bridges; learn to get along with others. Remember, today's foe may be tomorrow's ally in a crucially close vote on some new matter. A policy of "No Permanent Enemies" usually works best.

Legislative Modernization

Criticisms of some state legislatures, although less justified than they were a generation ago, are much like those of Congress: Legislative business is not conducted efficiently, committee work is not well planned, careful records are not kept, and expert information is not systematically sought. Other criticisms are: Introduc-

---

State Legislators: Their Many Roles

Studying the problems of their districts and states.

Preparing for and helping enact legislative programs.

Developing support for priority programs.

Keeping informed on all bills and amendments.

Attending sessions, taking part in debate, and voting on business before the legislative chambers.

Attending committee meetings and hearings.

Responding to calls and letters from constituents.

Exercising legislative oversight over the administrations and the state budgets

through hearings, personal visits, inspections, and so on.

Participating in the confirmation and impeachment processes involving various state officials.

Serving as connecting links between local officials and state officials, and between state officials and national officials.

Maintaining their own campaign organizations and perhaps playing active roles in their county and state political-party organizations.

Taking part in ceremonial functions.

Ratifying proposed amendments to U.S. Constitution and approving various interstate compacts with other states.

Source: Adapted in part from *A Guidebook for Ohio Legislators* (Ohio Legislative Service Commission)

---

ing special and private legislation is too easy, and parliamentary rules prevent action and play into the hands of those who would cling to the status quo. Other reported weaknesses are peculiar to certain states: The length of sessions is unnecessarily restricted; salaries in many states are low; the speaker is too powerful; and many legislatures lack the staff resources needed for policy making in today's complex society.

Such structural or procedural inadequacies may, in fact, make state legislatures less efficient. For example, low pay and short sessions are thought to guarantee too little deliberation on major issues, and lack of professional staff leads to an amateur committee system or an overreliance on lobbyists. State legislatures cannot perform efficiently if (1) they are shackled by outmoded constitutions; (2) their structures are inflexible, weak, and rickety; (3) they are unable to induce outstanding citizens to run for office; (4) they are not given powers commensurate with their responsibilities; (5) they are run by factions that cannot be held accountable for their actions; (6) they have as many leaders as followers; (7) they cannot act unless prodded by the governor; and (8)—in sum—they cannot harness their powers in such a way as to transform majority preferences in the electorate, when they exist, into the public policy of the legislature.

IMPROVING STATE LEGISLATURES

Following are some specific recommendations made by one group of experts a generation ago to improve legislative procedures in the states:

1. Constitutions should leave legislatures as unhampered as possible to encourage the development of their own self-reliance. Limitations on a legislature's power to appropriate public funds and to address itself to public questions should be eliminated.

2. Enactment of private bills, bills affecting few persons, and local and special bills should be minimized.

3. Legislatures should be small enough to make the position of legislator more important and visible.

4. To develop more responsibility in legislative performance and more independence, legislatures should be continuing bodies meeting in annual sessions, without limitation of time or subject. Legislatures should be able to call themselves into session.

5. Competent professional staff should be provided, including staff for the leadership, both majority and minority.

6. State legislatures should utilize a strong system of standing committees, few in number, with broad, well-defined jurisdictions.

7. Codes of ethics should be adopted that apply to career, appointed, and elected officials in all branches of state government.[22]

In the early 1970s a group then known as the Citizens' Conference on State Legislatures used some of the standards contained in these recommendations to rank the fifty state legislatures. They sought, for example, to measure how accountable, informed, independent, and representative each legislature was in relation to those of the other forty-nine states. Based on these measures, the California legislature ranked first, followed by New York and Illinois. Critics suggest that the group used the California legislature as its model, thus biasing the whole project. Experts agree that these rankings became badly out of date within just a few years. Further, their evaluation dealt only with *structure* and *procedures*.

Other groups have tried to evaluate state legislatures. It is relatively easy to measure them against certain proclaimed standards in terms of procedures and processes, yet to do so in terms of what they enact and fund is impossible except in political terms. Most evaluations of legislatures, like evaluations of legislators, tell us more about the values of the evaluator than the performance of what is being measured. Of course, the fact that there are no objective standards to determine which policies are "best" is why we have democratically elected legislatures in the first place.

Many of these improvements recommended a generation ago were adopted in most states. Many legislatures now have longer sessions, professional staffs, streamlined rules and procedures, fewer and more responsible committees, and increased salaries. About half the states now employ joint legislative committees. Interstate cooperation and better research and training have been brought about through the National Conference of State Legislatures. Legislative attempts to control federal funds, legislative review of administrative regulations, and legislative efforts in the area of program evaluation and **sunset processes** (consideration of agency termination) are all intended to improve legislative effectiveness[23] In short, the largely amateur, part-time state legislatures of thirty years ago are now being professionalized. This reflects a growing determination on the part of legislators—especially state legislative leaders—to be the bosses in their own branch.

TWO HOUSES OR ONE?

Although two-chamber legislatures became the established pattern in the United States early in our history, Georgia, Pennsylvania, and Vermont experimented with one-house legislatures. During colonial days the two chambers represented distinct interests; the senates stood for royal authority, the assemblies for the colonial cause. The desire to balance the aristocratic against the popular interest, and the belief in a government of checks and balances, led to the retention of bicameral legislatures after independence. During the first decades of our republic, the requirements to vote for senator and the qualifications to serve in the state senate were stricter than those for the house. By the middle of the nineteenth century, however, the same electorate was choosing the members of both houses. Today the two houses represent the same people (but in districts of different sizes). Why do we retain the two-house system?

Defenders of bicameralism insist that two chambers check hasty or ill-considered legislation. Yet even in some states with two chambers, legislation is rushed through, especially in the closing days of a session. Sometimes the second chamber discovers errors in bills enacted by the other house and makes the necessary corrective amendments. Some bills proposed by one chamber are defeated by the other, but it is impossible to develop objective standards to determine whether the defeated legislation was poor to begin with. Critics of bicameralism are persuaded that the governor's veto, the courts, and the electorate are better checks. The case for a **unicameral legislature** has been made by those who believe

1. A one-house legislature would be more efficient, avoid needless delays and duplication, and permit higher salaries.
2. A one-house legislature would permit the voters more knowledge about whom to blame and whom to credit and would thereby increase accountability.
3. One strong, well-staffed house would be a more efficient counterbalance to the governor.
4. The one-chamber arrangement has worked well in Nebraska, in all our cities, and in the Canadian provinces. Further, it works well in our state constitutional conventions, just as it did in our 1787 national constitutional convention.

The case for the two-house legislature rests on the following claims as well as on tradition:

1. A two-house legislature permits greater scrutiny of all new laws, making it more difficult for rash, arbitrary, or emotional legislation to be enacted.
2. A two-house legislature provides for more access, more debate, and more representation of diverse points of view.
3. A two-house legislature makes it more difficult for any one person or interest to dominate state decision making; the chances are good that one of the houses will offer effective resistance.

Although there are merits on both sides, the adoption of unicameralism is still viewed as a radical step. Moreover, it is a pretty safe bet that few state legislators will be attracted to a proposal that would put the majority of them out of office. In Nebraska, for example, before the unicameral plan won at the polls, there were thirty-three senators and 100 house members. Afterward there were just forty-nine senators.

The Politics of Reapportionment

State legislatures have the key responsibilites of **reapportionment,** drawing legislative district boundaries for both their own and their state's U.S. House of Representative districts. A few legislatures delegate these responsibilites to reapportionment commissions or panels; most legislatures, however, consider these once-a-decade (after each census) responsibilities to be extremely important and often highly political events. A former speaker of the California state assembly calls legislative reapportionment "quite simply . . . the most political, most crass, most selfish act that any legislator ever engages in."[24]

Reapportionment and redistricting battles were waged in many states after the 1980 census and can be anticipated again after the 1990 census. One of the most bitter took place in California. The legislature was accused of unfairly aiding incumbents, especially Democrats, and the legislative efforts resulted in a referendum campaign, several initiative campaigns, and at least two California Supreme Court decisions. And the bitterness lingers on into the 1990s.

One of the big issues of the past thirty years was the battle over representation in the state legislatures, most of which gave rural and small town voters more votes in the legislature than they would have been entitled to on the basis of their population. City officials complained bitterly that the small-town and farm-dominated legislators were unsympathetic to their problems and were forcing rural notions of right and wrong upon them.

The battle over reapportionment, however, was more complex than just a rural versus city struggle. First, as the century proceeded, the suburbs—not the central cities—came to be most underrepresented in many states. Even more to the point, many who live and do business within the city or live in its suburbs feel closer politically to those who live on farms and small towns than they do to other city dwellers. Thus, many business interests located in cities favored

Legislative Humor

Everyone has committed verbal gaffes at one time or another, but what separates legislators from others is that their job requires so much debating and speechmaking and other public presentations. These are real quotes; legislators really said these things. And of course, the ever-diligent media were on hand to record such misstatements for posterity.

HUMILITY AND INSIGHT

Legislative life attracts individuals with strong egos, but even the most stout-hearted can disarm themselves with a choice phrase:

These are not my figures I'm quoting. They're the figures of someone who knows what he's talking about.

I think I know more about this bill than I understand.

It takes real courage to vote against your convictions.

There comes a time to put principles aside and do what's right.

Anyone can carry a good bill; it is really hard to get a bad bill passed.

We could be guilty of inaction if we don't do something.

I realize my face is not a household word in Maryland.

MANGLED METAPHORS

More than one legislator has mixed apples and oranges in creative ways:

The sword of Damocles is hanging over Pandora's Box.

They're hanging by the thread of their bootstraps.

It's time to swallow the bullet.

I favor this irrigation bill in order that we may turn the barren hills of my state into fruitful valleys.

My colleague is listening with a forked ear.

From now on I'm watching everything you do with a fine-tooth comb.

WHAT I MEANT . . .

Sometimes things turn out much differently than a lawmaker intends:

When I started I was for the bill, but the longer I talk, the more I know I'm against it.

Before I give you the benefit of my remarks, I'd like to know what we're talking about.

I wish some of these ideas were left to stand on their own bottoms.

I'm in favor of letting the status quo stay as it is.

This body is becoming entirely too laxative about some matters.

I misquoted myself.

Source: Veteran state lobbyist Charles Henning, quoted in Malcolm Kushner, "The Serious Use of Humor," *State Legislatures* (May 1985), p. 27.

rural domination of the state legislatures because they thought "cow-country legislators" would be more responsive to their demands and less responsive to the social welfare schemes championed by many urban legislators.

FEDERAL COURTS TO THE RESCUE

But no matter how much they protested, those underrepresented in the state legislatures made little progress. Legislators from small towns and farm areas naturally did not wish to reapportion themselves out of jobs, and their constituents did not wish to lose their influence. Even though the failure of state legislatures to reapportion often violated express provisions of state constitutions and raised serious questions under the federal Constitution, state and federal judges took the position that issues having to do with legislative districting were "political" and outside the scope of judicial authority.

Finally, the United States Supreme Court stepped in. In 1962, in the famous case of **Baker v. Carr,** the Court held that voters do have standing to challenge legislative apportionment and that such questions should be considered by the federal courts. Arbitrary and capriciously drawn districts do deprive people of their constitutional rights, and federal judges may take jurisdiction over such cases.[25] *Baker* v. *Carr* started a small tidal wave.

ONE PERSON, ONE VOTE

In 1964 (*Wesberry* v. *Sanders*) the Supreme Court announced that as far as *congressional* representation is concerned, "as nearly as practicable one man's vote in a congressional election is to be worth as much as another's."[26] And in the same term the Court extended this principle to representation in the *state legislatures*, although subsequently it has slightly modified this decision.

In *Reynolds* v. *Sims* (1964) the Court held that "the fundamental principle of representative government in this country is one of equal representation for equal numbers of people, without regard to race, sex, economic status, or place of residence within a state." In the Court's view, this principle applied not only to the more numerous house of the state legislature, which was usually based on population, but also to the state senate, where representation was often based on area, such as the county or some other governmental unit. Defenders of this pattern had argued that as long as the house or more numerous chamber represented population, the senate could represent geographical units. Look at the federal system embodied in the United States Constitution, they said. Isn't representation in the United States Senate based on area? Although many thought this to be a compelling argument, a majority of the Court did not. Chief Justice Earl Warren explained: "Legislators represent people, not trees or acres. Legislators are elected by voters, not farms or cities or economic interests. . . . The right to elect legislators in a free unimpaired fashion is a bedrock of our political system."[27] The federal analogy, in short, does not hold; political subdivisions are not and never have been sovereign entities.

The Supreme Court has been especially rigid about the states' drawing of congressional districts. A state legislature must justify any variance from strict mathematical equality among such districts by showing that it made a good-faith effort to come as close as possible to this standard. The Supreme Court is, however, less insistent upon absolute equality for state legislative districts. Thus the Court, in 1983, upheld a Wyoming plan that allocated at least one state legislative seat per county, saying that Wyoming's policy was rational and appropriate to the special needs of that sparsely populated state. "This holding, however, represents the exception to the general rule of a 10 percent maximum permissible deviation between state legislative districts."[28] But the requirement that the districts be established in accordance with the one-person, one-vote principle still remains.

UNANSWERED QUESTIONS FOR THE 1990s

Even though the one-person, one-vote principle is firmly established, many issues affecting the nature of legislative representation remain open. In northern metropolitan areas, for instance, the general pattern is for the core city to be Democratic and the surrounding suburbs Republican. If legislative district lines are drawn like spokes from the central city to the suburbs, fewer Republicans will thus be elected than if the district lines are drawn in concentric circles. Although partisan gerrymandering is permissible, because of *Davis* v. *Bandemer*[29] there are constitutional constraints on it.

There has been an increasing attack on the part of representatives of minorities on the multimember district systems, more on the grounds that they result in voting dilution and violating the Voting Rights Act of 1965 than constitutional violations.

Can racial or religious considerations be used in drawing up legislative districts? Racial considerations are not automatically unconstitutional. If district lines are drawn in order to protect the voting strength of blacks, and if they do not force white voters out of the process or unfairly minimize their voting strength, there is no constitutional violation. However, the Constitution does forbid the deliberate attempt to draw district lines in order to "impose a racial slur or stigma, or minimize the voting strength of particular races or religions."[30]

CONSEQUENCES OF BAKER VERSUS CARR

In the more populous northern states, such as New Jersey, Michigan, Illinois, and New York, surburban communities have gained legislative representation due to court-enforced reapportionment. Rural districts have borne the brunt of this change, but there has been some cost to big cities. However, the traditional alliance between suburbs and rural districts against the big city appears not to have changed.

In the South, in states such as Georgia, Florida, and Tennessee (where Atlanta, Miami, and Memphis were so underrepresented), reapportionment has had a dramatic impact. In Georgia it increased the voice of Atlanta's citizens in the state legislature, and it provided opportunities for the election of blacks to that body. In Alabama, Birmingham and Mobile gained new political influence, and an alliance between these two cities could have a long-range impact on the politics of that state. In Florida urban centers have become the dominant voice in the legislature. In the West reapportionment seems to have had less impact, although it may be a factor in creating a more competitive two-party system in the more populous states, such as California. "In Washington, reapportionment created the opportunity for change and the political actors have used that opportunity."[31] Overall, the Democrats appear to be slight gainers from reapportionment. It has tended to benefit surburban Republicans and city Democrats at the expense of rural Republicans in the North and rural Democrats in the South, and to have the effect of moving the states toward more competitive party systems in their legislatures.[32]

What have been the *policy* consequences of reapportionment? Many of its p.roponents hoped that it would lead to legislatures more sympathetic to big-city people and more generous in support of the welfare, transportation, educational, and financial problems of the cities. It was also hoped that state aid and shared-tax formulas would be revised toward a more favorable distribution of state funds to the cities. Opponents of reapportionment feared that it would lead to a decline in the quality of legislators, an increase in taxation and spending, and a reduction of state support to rural areas. So far neither the hopes of proponents nor the fears of opponents have been realized.

REAPPORTIONMENT AND PARTISAN GERRYMANDERING TODAY

The politics of legislative redistricting is only a bit less heated in the 1990s than it was in the 1960s. For officeholders it remains a factor that can make or break political careers. As already noted, in most states the legislature itself redraws the legislative districts every ten years.

Critics of the current system of districts being drawn by the incumbent legislators say one-person, one-vote and fairness principles are often violated when the party in power juggles district lines to its own advantage. A spokesperson for Common Cause says: "The present system stinks. . . . Legislators who set the boundaries for their own districts have a basic conflict of interests. . . . (It's) a crummy system of backscratching."[33] Hence Common Cause, the League of Women Voters, and a few other groups call for the establishment of an independent nonpartisan commission to draw district lines. Such a commission would be prohibited from using information about incumbent legislators, the political affiliations of registered voters, or previous election results to draw boundary lines that favor any group or person or that dilute the influence of racial or minority interests. A handful of states, including Ohio, Montana, and Hawaii, currently use such a system. Legislators, not surprisingly, generally oppose this idea, claiming that it is like trying to take politics out of politics. They say the legislature, because it represents all interests in a state and is regularly accountable to the public, is the single best institution to resolve reapportionment issues.[34]

A fundamental question in any democracy, of course, is how the people are to be represented in the legislative branch of government. This is unavoidably—in the highest sense of the word—a political issue. Repeated attempts have been made to find a body of "experts" who know how to do these things better than the people through the political process. One might argue, for example, that the dominant party will draw up tax legislation or spending programs to reward its supporters and punish its opponents, whereas a body of experts could doubtless design a more "rational" and "fair" system of taxation. But people who believe in democracy might be skeptical. Independent nonpartisan commissions are likely to reflect middle-class and upper-class values and might, in fact, emphasize only these values under the guise of nonpartisanship.

In the early 1990s, some states are looking seriously at their redistricting methods. The more extravagant promises made by independent commissions will probably prove difficult to realize. Still, no one doubts that political controversy will continue to surround reapportionment arrangements no matter what form they take. And no one doubts the ability of incumbents in the majority to "rig" elections through reapportionment. In the words of the old-time politicians: "You tell me the results you want, and I'll draw the district map to do it."

Direct Legislation: Policy Making by the People

Does "We the People" mean the people themselves should govern directly? Around the turn of the century, the Populist and Progressive movements fought to "return the government to the people" through the initiative, referendum, and recall. Give the voters the power to make or veto laws and to recall officials, they said, and the political machines will be destroyed and the special interests beaten. In fact, some of our states have given the people the power to make their own laws.

Populists and **Progressives** had good reason between 1890 and 1912 to want to bypass their legislatures, for in several states the legislatures were indeed either incompetent or under the domination of the political machines. (The Southern Pacific Railroad's political machine in California had dominated the selection of state legislators, governors, and United States senators for years.) The Progressives placed enormous trust in the wisdom of the individual and in the notion that voters would inform themselves about issues and make responsible decisions on a variety of policy questions put before them.

"Before I stand up to be counted on this issue, I want to see who's counting."

Dunagin's People by Ralph Dunagin. Reprinted with special permission of North America Syndicate, Inc.

Americans have recently had the chance to vote on all kinds of state and local ballot issues. About 250 citizen-initiated issues were placed on state ballots in the 1980s. Another one thousand issues were referred to voters by state legislators. Citizens have turned to the initiative process to try to regulate handguns in California, to protect the moose in Maine, to encourage the death penalty in Massachusetts, to approve the sale of wine in local grocery stores in Colorado, to abolish daylight saving time in North Dakota, to pressure the national government for some type of nuclear freeze, to enact English as the official language, and to ban nuclear power.

Critics lament the rise in what they call "public policy making by bumper-sticker." But legislators themselves are in various ways responsible for many of the issues that get placed on the ballot.

> Legislators have developed something of a "multiple personality" relationship with ballot measures. On the one hand, many legislators and staffers recognize that an initiated measure is a form of rejection of representative democracy and a subtle kind of no confidence vote toward the legislatures. On the other hand, many legislatures have "referred" tough policy issues to the public vote. In many instances, the same person who condemns the power of big spending on ballot questions will initiate a petition drive when his or her key issue dies in the legislature.[35]

INITIATIVE

The **initiative petition** procedure permits a designated minimum number of voters to propose a law that will be enacted if approved by a majority of the voters at a subsequent election. Twenty-three states, mostly in the West, authorize the making of laws by means of the initiative petition (see map). In states such as California, Oregon, Washington, North Dakota, Arizona, and Colorado, the initiative has become almost a routine part of the legislative process.

In some states the *direct* initiative applies to constitutional amendments and to legislation; in others it can be used only for one or the other. In a state that permits the direct initiative, any individual or interest group may draft a proposed law and file it with a designated state official—usually the secretary of state. Supporters have only to secure a certain number of signatures (between 5 to 15 percent of those who voted in the last election) to ensure that the measure is placed on the ballot at the next election for approval or disapproval.

The *indirect* initiative is used in a few states. After a certain number of petition signatures have been collected, the state legislature is given an opportunity to act on the measure without alteration; if they approve it, the law simply goes into effect. If they do not approve it, the proposed legislation is then placed on the ballot, although in some states additional signatures are required before the proposal can be placed before the voters.

Citizen-Initiated Initiative, Referendum, and Recall at the State Level

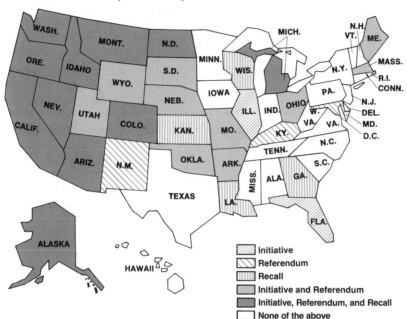

NOTE: The initiative can be used for constitutional amendments only in Florida and in Illinois.
Initiative petitions can only be used for statutory changes in Alaska, Idaho, Maine, Utah, Washington, Wyoming, and the District of Columbia.
The initiative can be used for both constitutional and statutory changes in all the other states noted here as having the initiative.
About 36 states permit recall of various local and elected officials.

REFERENDUM

The **referendum** permits a majority of the voters to veto legislation or reject constitutional amendments. In 1988, for example, Massachusetts voters voted to repeal their legislature's recently adopted pay raise by the referendum process. The referendum is simply a way of letting the people vote on recently passed laws or proposed amendments to a state's constitution. It is required in every state except Delaware for the ratification of constitutional amendments. Legislation may be subject to mandatory or optional referendums. The *mandatory referendum* calls for a waiting period, usually sixty to ninety days, before legislation goes into effect. If during this period a prescribed number of voters sign a referendum petition requesting that the act be referred to the voters, the law does not go into effect unless a majority of the voters give their approval at the next election. The *optional referendum* permits the legislature, at its discretion, to provide that a measure shall not become law until it has been approved by the voters at an election. This second kind is the most common.

Although in several states referendums are often held statewide, referendum democracy flourishes at the local level. The annual volume of referendums presented to voters in school districts, cities, and counties runs to several thousand,

and many of these are on topics of considerable importance and controversy—bonds for school buildings, fluoridation of water, banning of bottles, restrictions on nuclear power facilities, and approval or rejection of convention facilities or dome stadiums.

RECALL

Recall is the means by which voters may remove elected public officials before the end of a term. Fifteen states, mostly in the West, provide for recall of state officers, but many others permit the recall of local officials. Recall also requires a petition, but it needs more signatures (typically 25 percent of voters in the last election for the position of the official to be recalled) than the initiative and referendum. There are various kinds of recall election. In some the official must stand on his or her record; in others candidates are permitted to file and run against the incumbent.

In effect, recall is like impeachment by the public. But unlike impeachment, formal charges of wrongdoing against the incumbent are not required. Rather, recall permits throwing people out of office merely because of policy differences. For recall, voters need only circulate petitions and obtain the required number of signatures. Recall is seldom used at the state level, although one governor and several state legislators have been recalled, including two Michigan state senators and one Oregon lawmaker in the 1980s. In Arizona, a recall campaign against Governor Evan Mecham in 1987 obtained far more than the needed signatures and forced the close scrutiny of Mecham that led to his impeachment and ouster by the Arizona state legislature.

Perhaps as many as 2000 county and municipal officeholders have been discharged around the country since Los Angeles became the first local government to adopt the recall in 1903. Mayors in more than a score of cities have been recalled from Seattle to Atlantic City. Mayor Mike Boyle of Omaha, for example, was turned out of office in a 1987 recall election that brought 56 percent of the eligible voters to the polls—a city election record. Three city councilmembers were ousted by recall in Honolulu in 1985. Six Grand Junction, Colorado city officials were recalled in 1986.

While critics of the recall device say it is an unruly process that deters good people from running and discourages leaders from taking decisive actions, the recall helps to lessen incumbent arrogance. The recall is a helpful, if crude, safety valve, permitting "citizens to eject those officials who violate the public trust. It has not, in any essential way, lessened the independence of well-intentioned public officials."[36]

THE DEBATE OVER DIRECT DEMOCRACY

Political scientists differ over the desirability of direct legislation. Early opponents argued that such measures would undermine the legitimacy of representative government and open the way for radical or special-interest legislation. Critics of the initiative and referendum believe the Progressives who advocated direct legislation were overly idealistic and that these mechanisms are likely to be used less as a citizen's weapon than as a vehicle for special interests. According to these critics, only well-organized interests could gather the appropriate number of signatures and mount the required media campaigns to gain victory.

What have been the results of these populist democracy devices? Historically, direct legislation via the initiative has typically resulted in progressive victories on consumer and many economic issues and conservative verdicts on social issues. Direct democracy has not weakened our legislatures. Seats in state legislatures are still valued, sought after, and competed for by able citizens. Nor has unwise legislation been enacted, as a general rule. The overall record suggests that the voters reject most of the truly unsound ideas that get on the ballot. Surveys indicate that many voters wish they had more information on some of the matters on their ballots; still, studies indicate those who vote decide prudently. Viewed from another perspective, most of the perceived flaws of the populist democracy processes are in many ways also the flaws of democracy. We often wish we had more information about the candidates—especially those running for state and county offices. Delegates at constitutional conventions or national party conventions frequently have similar misgivings when they are forced to render "yes" and "no" votes on complicated issues. So, too, do members of state legislatures, especially in those frantic days near the end of their sessions, yearn for more information, more clarity about consequences, and more discussion and compromise than time will permit.

Still, the critics of direct legislation fear the very fabric of legislative processes and representative government is at stake. To be sure, lack of faith in legislative bodies prompts the use of direct legislation devices. But it is an illusion, they say, to believe that the voter has the proper information to decide on complex,

---

An Initiative and Referendum for New Jersey?

In early 1986 Governor Thomas Kean of N.J. urged passage of a measure that would allow New Jersey voters to vote on policy issues. His reasoning: "We have good government in New Jersey, but we can make it better—more responsive—more efficient. The people of most states have the right to directly change their laws. People in New Jersey deserve the same right. We should not be afraid of the people who elected us. I ask you to pass . . . legislation to give the people the right of initiative and referendum." The I & R won the support of the United Taxpayers of New Jersey, Common Cause, the League of Women Voters, and the state's Public Interest Research Group.

Opposed to the adoption of the I & R were the state's leading business and industry associations, labor unions, and some former governors. A former governor called the proposed I & R costly and cumbersome and said it would detract from the ability of the legislature to weigh state problems and address them after careful study. Dr. Alan Rosenthal of the Eagleton Institute of Politics at Rutgers University said the direct legislation system "shifts power from the people, through their elected representatives, to zealots, power groups and fringe groups."

As of 1990, New Jersey still has no initiative referendum process.

technical matters.[37] The critics also suggest that the best way to restore faith in the legislature is not to bypass it but to elect better people to it.

A new problem is the number of issues on the ballot. In 1988, for example, California voters had to decide at least twenty-nine ballot issues; about a dozen were initiated by interest groups and the rest were placed on the ballot by the legislature. Most citizens told a *Los Angeles Times* survey that there were too many and that "the process had gotten out of hand."

At the same time, however, voters in California and throughout the country insist that citizens ought to occasionally have the right to vote directly on issues. They especially say this when their representatives seem afraid of offending certain interest groups. Further, every survey on direct democracy finds that both voters and nonvoters say they would be more likely to vote and more likely to become interested in politics if some issues appeared along with candidates on their ballots.

Another serious problem has arisen in California. Political consulting firms, for a price, will gather signatures and put nearly anything you want on the ballot. Deceptive pitches are made trying to get enough people to sign petitions. It takes a small fortune to do this, and only the well-organized, well-financed single interest groups can afford it. However, supporters of populist democracy say they have not given up on the legislative process. Rather, they wish to use direct legislation only when legislatures prove unresponsive. If our legislature won't act, they say, give us the opportunity to debate our proposals in the open arena of election politics. Supporters further contend the people *can* make decisions on complex and controversial matters.

Critics of ballot democracy frequently have a view of state legislators that borders on the mythical: highly intelligent; extremely well-informed; as rational as a virtuous, wise, and deliberative statesman; as mangerially competent as a corporate executive; and as substantively informed as an expert professor. These same critics, however, tend to view the people as a "mob" unworthy of being trusted. Yet the people are the voters who elect legislators. Experience suggests that on most issues, especially the well publicized ones, voters do grasp the meaning of the issue on which they are asked to vote, and they cast an informed vote. Most studies indicate that voters who do vote on ballot measures do so more responsibly and intelligently than we have any right to expect.

The legislative process is never perfect. Even with larger staffs, hearings, bicameralism, and other distinctive features of representative democracy, mistakes are made and defective bills are enacted into law by our legislatures. The Supreme Court has overturned hundreds of state measures as unconstitutional, and state legislatures often spend much of their time in their next session amending or otherwise improving measures passed the previous year that didn't quite work out. As a practical matter, the competence and rationality of both the legislative and the direct ballot processes can stand improvement. The charge, however, that voters are not competent enough to decide on occasional issues put before them is usually exaggerated.[38]

Experience suggests that neither the best hopes of the Progressives nor the worst worries of their critics have been realized. Yet, whatever the merits of the initiative, referendum, and recall, it is clear that these mechanisms have severe limits; in no way could they even begin to replace a legislature.

Summary

1. Although Americans greatly value the state legislature as a vital institution in our constitutional form of government, we are quick to criticize its imperfections. Perhaps we overestimate the possibilities for responsive and representative legislatures. Or perhaps we make legislatures the target of our complaints, when the imperfections and the imperfectibility of people are really at the heart of the matter.
2. The nation's 7461 state legislators are called upon to represent our diverse views, help formulate state public policy, oversee the administration of state laws, and help mediate political conflicts that arise in the state.
3. What are the main influences on a state legislator's voting decisions? Colleagues, committee recommendations, district considerations, party leaders, staff reports, the governor's urgings, lobbyists, constituent mail, visits, and phone calls can all be influential depending on the type of issue.
4. State legislators are asked to represent all the people in chambers that are constantly subjected to intense lobbying by organized interests. Lobbyists and interest-group representatives are important sources of information, but often the elected state legislator is the only effective representative and voice for the unorganized citizen.
5. Legislative modernization is taking place in most states, making state legislatures somewhat more accountable and more prepared to do the public's business. Most states now have ethics commissions, open-meeting laws, and staff available to assist with committee work. Many have reasonably good conflict-of-interest and financial disclosure laws.
6. Direct legislative procedures, especially the initiative petition, are a prominent part of the legislative process, particularly in the West. Other direct mechanisms, such as the referendum and the recall, are also available to voters in many states.

Further Reading

DIANE D. BLAIR. *Arkansas Politics and Government: Do the People Rule?* (University of Nebraska Press, 1988).

BRUCE E. CAIN. *The Reapportionment Puzzle* (University of California Press, 1984).

THOMAS E. CRONIN. *Direct Democracy—The Politics of the Initiative, Referendum, and Recall* (Harvard University Press, 1989).

VIRGINIA GRAY, HERBERT JACOB, and KENNETH N. VINES. *Politics in the American States*, 5th ed (Scott, Foresman, 1990).

MALCOLM JEWELL. *Representation in State Legislatures* (University of Kentucky Press, 1982).

MALCOLM JEWELL and SAMUEL C. PATTERSON. *The Legislative Process in the United States* (Random House, 1986).

WILLIAM J. KEEFE and MORRIS S. OGUL. *The American Legislative Process*, 6th ed. (Prentice Hall, 1985).

DAVID MAGLEBY. *Direct Legislation* (Johns Hopkins University Press, 1984).
WILLIAM K. MUIR, JR. *Legislature* (University of Chicago Press, 1983).
ALAN ROSENTHAL. *Legislative Life* (Harper & Row, 1981).
FRANK SMALLWOOD. *Free and Independent: The Initiation of a College Professor into State Politics* (The Stephen Greene Press, 1976).
See the journal *State Legislatures*, published ten times a year by the National Conference of State Legislatures. *Legislative Studies Quarterly* often has articles on state legislatures; this is published by the Legislative Studies Section of the American Political Science Association. Also, *Governing*, published monthly by Congressional Quarterly, Inc., regularly covers state politics and state legislative issues.

N otes

1. Frank Smallwood, *Free and Independent: The Initiation of a College Professor into State Politics* (The Stephen Greene Press, 1976), p. 218.

2. Malcolm Jewell, *Representation in State Legislatures* (University of Kentucky Press, 1982), p. 47. See also Keith E. Hamm and David M. Olson, "The Value of Incumbency in State Legislative Elections," paper delivered at the American Political Science Association annual meeting, September, 1987. See also Malcolm Jewell and David Breaux, "The Effect of Incumbency on State Legislative Elections," *Legislative Studies Quarterly* (Nov. 1988), pp. 495–514.

3. Alan Rosenthal, "The Changing Character of State Legislators," *Public Affairs Review* (1985), pp. 80–93.

4. Samuel C. Patterson, "Legislators and Legislatures in American States," in Virginia Gray et al., eds., *Politics in the American States*, 4th ed. (Little, Brown, 1983), p. 174. See also Alan Rosenthal, *Legislative Life: People, Process and Performance in the States* (Harper & Row, 1981), chap. 2.

5. Alan Rosenthal, *Legislative Life*, pp. 112–13.

6. See Alan Rosenthal, "Legislative Oversight and the Balance of Power in State Government," *State Government*, no. 3 (1983), pp. 90–98. See also John Wanat, Karen Burke, and Marilyn Snodell, "Legislators as Budget Initiators and Lobbyists," *American Politics Quarterly* (April 1984), pp. 389–408; and James J. Gosling, "Patterns of Influence and Choice in the Wisconsin Budgetary Process," *Legislative Studies Quarterly* (November 1985), pp. 457.

7. On women in elections, see Susan J. Carroll, *Women as Candidates in American Politics* (Indiana University Press, 1985) and Ronna Romney and Beppie Harrison, *Momentum: Women in American Politics Now* (Crown, 1988).

8. Smallwood, *Free and Independent*, p. 223. See also Alan Rosenthal, "Turnover in State Legislatures," *American Journal of Political Science* (August 1978), pp. 609–16.

9. David Broder, in Herbert E. Alexander, ed., *Campaign Money: Reform and Reality in the States* (Free Press, 1976), p. 313. See also Michael Johnston, *Political Corruption and Public Policy in America* (Brooks/Cole, 1982), and Ruth Jones, "Financing State Elections," in Michael Malbin, ed., *Money and Politics in The United States* (American Enterprise Institute, 1984).

10. Smallwood, *Free and Independent*, p. 165.

11. Lobbyist, quoted in Smallwood, p. 164.

12. Patterson, "Legislators and Legislatures in the American States," p. 170.

13. Clifton, McCleskey, Allan K. Butcher, Daniel E. Farlow, and J. Pat Stephens, *The Government and Politics of Texas* (Little, Brown, 1982), p. 163. For a useful comparative study of senior citizen lobbies in four states, see William P. Browne, "Variations in the Behavior and Style of State Lobbyists and Interest Groups," *Journal of Politics* (May 1985), pp. 450–68.

14. John D. Ferrick, "Effective Campaign Finance Law: It's a Three-way Street," *Governing* (January 1989), p. 82. See also, Karen Hansen, "Walking the Ethical Tightrope," *State Legislatures* (July 1988), pp. 14–17.

15. Gary L. Rose, "Party Organization Activity during the 1986 Connecticut State Legislative Campaign: A View from the Victorious Candidates," *Party Line: Newsletter of the Committee for Party Renewal* (Summer 1988), pp. 5–13.

16. See Joel A. Thompson and Gary F. Moncrief, "Pursuing the Pork in a State Legislature," *Leg-*

islative Studies Quarterly (August 1988), pp. 393–401.

17. Quoted in Gerald Stollman, *Michigan: State Legislators and Their World* (University Press of America, 1979), p. 56.

18. Lucinda Simon, "Wisconsin Legislature Mobilizes Citizen Input," *State Legislatures* (April 1985), p. 35.

19. Donald R. Songer, Sonja G. Dillon, Darla W. Kite, Patricia E. Jameson, James M. Underwood, and William D. Underwood, "The Influence of Issues on Choices of Voting Cues Utilized in State Legislatures," *Western Political Quarterly* (March 1986), p. 118.

20. Quoted in David Ray, "The Sources of Voting Cues in Three State Legislatures," *Journal of Politics* (November 1982), p. 1081.

21. E. Lee Bernick and Charles W. Wiggins, "Legislative Norms in Eleven States," *Legislative Studies Quarterly* (May 1983), pp. 191–200.

22. Adapted from Alexander Heard, ed., *State Legislatures in American Government* (Prentice Hall, 1966). See also Donald G. Herzberg and Alan Rosenthal, eds., *Strengthening the States: Essays on Legislative Reform* (Doubleday Anchor, 1972).

23. On the promise and limitations of some of these efforts, see Rich Jones, "Legislative Review of Regulations: How Well Is It Working?" *State Legislatures* (September 1982), pp. 7–9, and William Lyons and Patricia Freeman, "Sunset Legislation and the Legislative Process in Tennessee," *Legislative Studies Quarterly*, vol 9 (February 1984), p. 151.

24. Quoted in Bruce E. Cain, *The Reapportionment Puzzle* (University of California Press, 1984), p 1.

25. 369 U.S. 186.

26. 376 U.S. 1.

27. 377 U.S. 533.

28. Jeffrey M. Wice, "Drawing the Lines," *State Legislatures* (July 1988), p. 31.

29. 478 U.S. 109, 1986.

30. *United Jewish Organization of Williamsburg, Inc.* v. *Hugh L. Carey*, 430 U.S. 144 (1977).

31. James J. Best, "The Impact of Reapportionment on the Washington House of Representatives," in James A. Robinson, ed., *State Legislative Innovation* (Praeger, 1973), p. 180.

32. See Timothy G. O'Rourke, *The Impact of Reapportionment* (Transaction Books, 1980). For an analysis that concludes that reapportionment has had little or no policy impact, see Frank M. Bryan. *Politics in the Rural States. People, Parties and Processes* (Westview, 1981), pp. 223, 259.

33. Bruce Adams, quoted in Janet Simons, "Reapportionment Here It Comes Again." *State Legislatures* (November–December 1979), p. 15.

34. This position is presented in Bruce E. Cain, *The Reapportionment Puzzle* (University of California Press, 1984). For related studies, see Bernard Grofman et al., eds. *Representation and Redistricting Issues in the 1980s* (D.C. Heath, 1982).

35. M. Glenn Newkirk, "Initiatives and Referenda: What Did the Voters Say?" *State Legislatures* (January 1983), p. 16.

36. Thomas E. Cronin, *Direct Democracy: The Politics of the Initiative, Referendum, and Recall* (Harvard University Press, 1989), p. 156.

37. See David Magleby, *Direct Legislation* (Johns Hopkins University Press, 1984).

38. Cronin, *Direct Democracy*, Chapters 4 and 8.

5

State Governors

Before the American Revolution the royal governors, appointed by the British crown and responsible to it, had broad powers, including extensive veto powers over the actions of the voter-elected colonial legislatures. As anti-British sentiment increased, royal governors became more and more unpopular.

The post–Declaration of Independence office of governor was thus born in an atmosphere of distrust. Initially, most state legislatures elected their governors, which ensured the governors would remain under the control of the people's representatives. The early state constitutions also gave the governors few powers and terms of just a year or two.

Gradually, however, the office of governor grew in importance; in New York, the position of chief executive was sufficiently formidable by 1787 that it became one of the main models for the proposed American presidency. Thus, despite the distrustful environment in which the governorship was established in our republic, the demands for executive leadership have gradually led to a strengthening of the role and authority of the position. We have also looked to governors for presidential candidates, although they have been eclipsed in the post–World War II period by U.S. senators and vice presidents.

In recent years the office of governor has grown so much in stature and responsibilities that it has attracted many excellent men and women. The office has grown in stature in part because it has been occupied by such able people. In most states the governor has gained authority and formal powers in recent years, and this has improved policy and managerial leadership performances.

The job of governor nowadays is plainly one of the most important and exacting challenges in American politics. The Reagan and Bush administrations succeeded in decentralizing to the states many of the responsibilities once considered national priorities. Governors have to be more than effective managers; they also have to be leaders, asking the right questions, considering long-term implications and side effects of their policies, and involving large numbers of quality advisors and specialists to help point them in the right direction.

Today a governor is expected, among other things, to be the state's chief policymaker, architect of the state budget, a savvy political party leader, chief recruiter of the best available advisors and administrators, and an inspiring renewer of confidence in state programs. They must also champion the state's interests against the encroachments of the federal government (or local governments) and be the state's chief booster to attract tourism. Effective governors now also have to have their own foreign policy—making trips to foreign nations to encourage foreign investment in their states and promote their local products abroad. Governors, whether they want to or not, must also propose "investment taxes" to the legislature and the voters for such programs as education and economic development. A governor in the 1990s also plays an increasingly subtle role as a crucial link between states and between the local and the national governments.

Governors have always been a major source of national leadership. In many ways, in fact, the governorship is a training ground for important national political positions. Fifteen governors became presidents—including William McKinley, Woodrow Wilson, Calvin Coolidge, Franklin Roosevelt, Jimmy Carter, and Ronald Reagan—in this century alone. Massachusetts Governor Michael Dukakis was the Democratic Party's nominee in 1988. Since 1900 about 125 governors have become U.S. senators. Former New Hampshire governor John Sununu became President Bush's chief of staff.

How do we evaluate governors? Pretty much as we assess and rate presidents, although the constitutional powers of governors vary from state to state and their existing formal powers are not necessarily constant.[1] Governors have to be leaders who can devise new initiatives, realize increased savings and efficiency, and inspire people to believe in them and their programs. An effective governor also has to perform countless symbolic and ceremonial functions and win the respect of the people and the legislature in order to exercise fully the executive functions of the office.

We expect governors to be excellent judges of people and to be able to make tough decisions and assume responsibility—especially in crisis situations. We want them to have a zest for combat, when this is needed, and an overall ability to inspire confidence. They must also be able to withstand unfair criticism and have a sense of proportion, compassion, and humor. We also ask: Are their appointments good? Do they formulate policy effectively? Do they grasp the important realities of their states' budgetary and economic development requirements? Do they communicate their views forcefully? Are they able to get programs through the state legislature? Do they run honest and efficient administrations? Can they meet crises such as state prison revolts? What of the tone and style of their leadership and their relations with the people? Do they know what needs doing and get it done? In short, are they effective?[2]

In 1950 about half the states had two-year terms for governors; now all but

TABLE 5-1
Twentieth Century Governors Hall of Fame*

TERM	GOVERNOR	STATE
1901–06	Robert LaFollette	Wisconsin
1911–13	Woodrow Wilson	New Jersey
1919–21	Alfred Smith	New York
1923–28	Alfred Smith	New York
1928–32	Huey Long	Louisiana
1943–54	Earl Warren	California
1943–54	Thomas Dewey	New York
1959–73	Nelson Rockefeller	New York
1961–65	Terry Sanford	North Carolina
1965–77	Daniel Evans	Washington
1971–79	Reubin Askew	Florida

Source: George Weeks, "A Statehouse Hall of Fame," *State Government,* vol. 55, no. 2 (1982), pp. 67–73.

* This list was drawn up by a veteran aide to Governor Milliken of Michigan. He sought advice and nominations from many of the experts in the field. Others might nominate Franklin Delano Roosevelt of New York, Adlai Stevenson of Illinois, Edmund G. Brown of California, John Connally of Texas, William Scranton of Pennsylvania, Richard Hughes of New Jersey, Harold Hughes and Robert Ray of Iowa, Tom McCall of Oregon, Lamar Alexander of Tennessee, or Robert Graham of Florida. Doubtless others among the more than 1000 who have served deserve consideration.

New Hampshire, Rhode Island, and Vermont have four-year terms. Until recently many states forbade a governor to seek immediate reelection; today only three states do so. Nearly half of the states have also strengthened the governorship by making the lieutenant governor run with the governor as a team, so that the chief executive is less likely to be faced with a hostile lieutenant governor. Most important, in almost all states the governor presents the state budget to the legislature and controls spending after the budget has been approved. This means that state officials look to the governor as well as the legislature for funds.

With more powers have come more problems. This is especially true in recent years as the states have taken on more responsibilities. At one time all the governor had to do was balance the state budget, make speeches about the virtues of the state, and criticize national officials. It was relatively easy to avoid hard decisions—or at least to postpone them. Not so today. People now expect the governor to be a problem solver, a leader, an effective manager of state

---

Women Governors

Nellie Taylor Ross, Wyoming	1925–27	Dixie Lee Ray, Washington	1977–81
"Ma" Ferguson, Texas	1925–27,	Martha L. Collins, Kentucky	1983–87
	1933–35	Madeleine Kunin, Vermont	1985–
Lurleen Wallace, Alabama	1967–68	Kay Orr, Nebraska	1987–
Ella Grasso, Connecticut	1975–80	Rose Mofford, Arizona	1988–

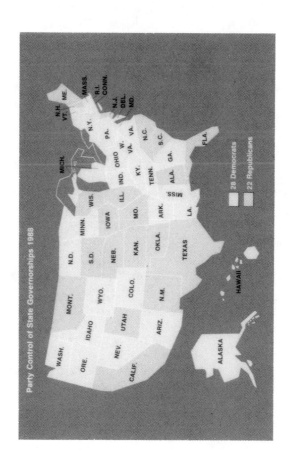

Party Control of State Governorships 1988

28 Democrats

22 Republicans

agencies, a promoter of the state's tourism, and a vigorous champion of economic development programs. Governors can no longer merely preside; they must govern.

Becoming and Remaining Governor

Each state's constitution and laws spell out the rules of eligibility, tenure, and salary for governor. In most states, to run for the office a person must be at least 30 years of age, a citizen of the United States, and a state resident for at least five years immediately preceding the election. The constitution typically reads: "The governor shall be elected, at the regular election every other odd-numbered year, by the direct vote of the people, for a term of four years beginning on the first day of January next following his (or her) election. Any qualified voter of the state who is at least 30 years of age shall be eligible for the office of governor."

In practice, however, there are well-traveled career paths to the governor's office. Most of our governors in the past generation have been white male attorneys who have first won election to city or state legislative positions. A large number were state legislators or held statewide elective office. In one recent year, for example, thirty-one governors were attorneys, two were farmers, one was a dentist, and most of the others were business people. The most common path is election to the state legislature, followed by election to a statewide office such as attorney general, lieutenant governor, or secretary of state. Governor Douglas Wilder of Virginia and Governor Madeleine Kunin of Vermont came to prominence as state legislators. Former Governors White of Texas and Babbitt of Arizona served first as attorneys general in their states. Governor Mario Cuomo of New York served first as an appointed secretary of state and then as an elected lieutenant governor in this state. Several governors won election from their posts as members of the House of Representatives, including the recent governors of Louisiana, Michigan, North and South Carolina, and New Jersey. Oregon's Neil Goldschmidt served as mayor of Portland and as a cabinet member in the Carter Administration before becoming a business executive and then governor.

Sometimes a person who has never held elective office will win a governor-

"Hi there. I'm governor of a large state somewhere out West, and I'm running for President."

Drawing by C. Barsotti; © 1987 The New Yorker Magazine.

ship, but such an individual usually has been actively involved in political life. Although primarily known as an actor or television personality, Ronald Reagan had been a union leader and Republican party activist prior to running successfully for governor of California. William Clements of Texas was an activist oil millionaire as well as a U.S. deputy secretary of defense prior to winning his victory. Sometimes a prominent business leader who has been involved in a state's economic development programs can parlay that leadership into a viable governor's race.

GOVERNORS ON THE SPOT

Once elected, governors generally enjoy high visibility in their states. Salaries range from at least $100,000 in New York, Michigan and North Carolina to $35,000 in states such as Maine and Arkansas; the average is about $75,000. In addition, most governors receive an expense allowance, and all but four are provided an executive mansion.

But just as governors have become increasingly important in recent years, they have also had to work with the twin problems of rising aspirations and scarcity of resources. People want better schools, highways that do not require any land or spoil the environment, adequate welfare programs, aid to local school districts, civil rights, safe streets, and clear air and streams. But they do not want higher taxes. Recent years have been a period of fiscal stress for most states, and governors are often caught in the middle. "We can dream dreams," governors often say, "but if we can't pay the bill, we can't have new programs. The art of the possible makes it difficult to be innovative."

Many governors complain—sometimes bitterly—that federal grant-in-aid programs, guidelines, and formulas shape so much of their activities that there is almost nothing left for them to decide in many areas of public policy. They would prefer to have the federal government give more dollars to the states but without strings. Even more, the governors want federal dollars to be given to agencies they control rather than directly to mayors, city councils, school boards, or welfare agencies. In short, most governors complain that they are faced with a whole range of problems, all of which they are expected to solve, yet few of which are within their authority. A governor is expected to fight on all fronts—and is also expected to emerge victorious—whether to keep taxes from rising, decrease the rate of unemployment, or revitalize the state's economy.

REELECTION CHANCES AND RAISING TAXES

One asset of being a governor today is likely reelection. At least in recent years about two-thirds of the governors who sought reelection have won, even when they faced serious economic problems. Most elections for governor are now scheduled for nonpresidential election years (for example, 1990 or 1991). Reformers have successfully argued that presidential and gubernatorial elections should be separate so that governors are not subject to the tides of national politics.

But not everyone is reelected; incumbents often believe that to run after four years of making tough and often controversial decisions and thereby gaining opponents is no advantage at all. Occasionally a governor who loses reelection attributes the defeat to an increase in state taxes. Sometimes the loss is related to a depressed state economy or, as in the case of former Governor Edwin Edwards of Louisiana in 1987, to a combination of economic problems and allegations of wrongdoing. A few governors, such as Clinton of Arkansas or Dukakis of Massachusetts, were defeated as much because of overconfidence as anything else. Both won reelection a term later.

Although most politicians believe that a governor who proposes new taxes will face defeat in the next election, studies by political scientists cast doubt on this proposition. As voters do indeed reward frugality and sometimes punish elected officials for tax increases, most governors will go to great lengths to avoid having to raise taxes. Still, circumstances often dictate what a governor can or cannot do. The health of the state's economy and the mood of the public toward the need for new programs and new revenues are critical factors in determining what a governor must do. A governor who does not propose new initiatives to improve the state's transportation or educational systems may face opponents in the next election who can win precisely because the governor failed to lead in these areas. Voters and the legislature will often go along with governors who can make a compelling case for new revenues and new investments.

An examination of governors throughout the last decade makes it clear that a gubernatorial call for tax increases in general is not likely to be successful. Yet when governors request a tax increase targeted for a specific worthy cause (for example, improving the schools), voters generally will support them. This is especially true if "political leaders are candid about why they need the money, sensible and fair in how they intend to spend it and courageous enough to lead the fight themselves."[3] Governors in Indiana, Virginia, Tennessee, and Arkansas all proposed and campaigned for "investment taxes" and generally became more popular because of their efforts. "Americans are neither selfish nor short-sighted on taxes— they just want assurance that their money will be spent wisely."[4]

A Governor's Formal Powers and Influence

"The executive power," says the Constitution, "shall be vested in the President of the United States." Compare this statement with its counterpart in a typical state constitution: "The executive department shall consist of a Governor, Lieutenant Governor, Secretary of State, Treasurer, Attorney General," and perhaps other officials. Unlike the president, the governor shares executive power with other elected officials. Most state constitutions go on to say that "the supreme executive power shall be vested in the Governor, who shall take care that the laws be faithfully executed." Thus it is the governor to whom the public looks for law enforcement and the management of sprawling bureaucracies.

Governor Samuel W. Pennypacker, Pennsylvania's chief executive from 1903 to 1907, once told how he had come to office eager to ensure that the laws of the state were faithfully executed. Looking around to see what tools he had to carry out this responsibility, he discovered that the only people to whom he could look for help were his secretary, the janitor, and his chauffeur. The prosecutors and police, locally elected and locally controlled, were subject to little or no gubernatorial supervision. The attorney general was elected independently by the voters and was not responsible to the governor. Of course, the governor could call out the National Guard, but this is a clumsy way to enforce the law. "So," said Governor Pennypacker, "I created the state police." Today all states have a police organization. In some states the governor has been given authority to supervise the activities of local prosecutors. Even so, most governors must rely on a variety of formal, informal, and ad hoc powers to see that "the laws be faithfully executed."

It is difficult to specify exactly the powers of a typical governor, because they vary widely from state to state (see Table 5–2). In most states constitutional changes have centralized more formal constitutional authority in governors. But governors' actual power and influence depends on their ability to persuade. This, in turn, usually depends on their reputation, popularity, knowledge of what should be done, and, of course, their ability to communicate. They must have political

TABLE 5–2
Rankings of States According to the Formal Powers of the Governor

STRONG	MODERATE		WEAK
Alaska	Alabama	Nebraska	Florida
California	Arizona	Nevada	Mississippi
Hawaii	Arkansas	New Mexico	New Hampshire
Idaho	Colorado	North Dakota	North Carolina
Illinois	Connecticut	Oklahoma	South Carolina
Iowa	Delaware	Oregon	Texas
Maryland	Georgia	Rhode Island	
Massachusetts	Indiana	South Dakota	
Michigan	Kansas	Vermont	
Minnesota	Kentucky	Virginia	
Missouri	Louisiana	West Virginia	
New Jersey	Maine	Wisconsin	
New York	Montana		
Ohio			
Pennsylvania			
Tennessee			
Utah			
Washington			
Wyoming			

Source: Adapted from Thad L. Beyle, "Governors," in Virginia Gray et al., eds., *Politics in the American States* (Scott, Foresman & Company, 1983), p. 202.

Note: Rankings are based on budget powers, appointive and organizational powers, tenure potential, and veto powers.

skills as well as constitutional authority if they are to provide leadership. To supplement their formal powers, most governors these days hold town meeting forums around their state, appear monthly on radio and television talk shows, and invite legislators and other influential party and policy leaders to the executive mansion for lobbying and listening sessions.

Remember, however, that not all states have powerful governors, and the powers of a governor are not necessarily constant; they may be decreased. On occasion, in fact, they are decreased by capable state legislatures.

Most governors have the following powers:

1. Appointive powers
2. The power to prepare the state budget
3. The opportunity to help establish the legislature's agenda
4. Ordinance-making power or executive order powers
5. The power to command the state National Guard
6. The power to pardon or grant clemency
7. The right to veto legislation and item-veto appropriations measures.

Let us look briefly at some of these powers.

APPOINTIVE POWERS

Perhaps a governor's most important job is to recruit talented leaders and managers to head the state's departments, commissions, and agencies. Governors now have a cabinet of advisors and senior administrators. Through recruitment of effective persons and prudent delegation to them, a governor can provide direction for the state government. Some governors can appoint hundreds of key officials; others, such as those in Mississippi, South Carolina, and Texas, have severe restrictions on their appointive powers. In most states the governor is still one executive among many, with only limited authority over *elected* officials, whom the governor can neither appoint nor dismiss. And if these officials are political enemies of the governor, they will not accept the governor's leadership. Governors have greater, but still limited, power over *appointed* administrative officials.

Further, in most states governors must share the appointive power with the state senate and may remove people only when they have violated the law or failed in their legal duties. The growing professionalism of state administrators whose programs are supported in part by federal funds is giving them a measure of independence from the governor as well as greater loyalty toward their counterparts at the national level than toward other state officials.

Governors face other problems as well. First, salaries are low in many states, especially in the smaller ones, and it is often hard to get people to leave better-paying jobs in private industry. The situation is even worse when the state capital is in one of the more remote or rural sections of the state. Second, leaders in some state legislatures often demand that their friends be appointed to certain top posts in the state's executive branch, and they will threaten to be uncooperative if the governor does not go along with some of their "suggested" nominees. Finally, turnover is relatively high in many state positions, and this often hampers a governor's efforts to carry out programs.

FISCAL AND BUDGETARY POWERS

A governor's fiscal and budgetary powers are usually a key weapon in getting programs passed. In most states the governor now has nearly full responsibility to prepare the budget and present it to the state legislature. The art of budget making involves assessing requests from various departments and agencies and balancing them off against scarce resources. Governors and their staffs have to calculate costs of existing and newly proposed programs and weigh these costs against estimated revenues or income for the state. The final budget document is presented to the legislature for its adoption as an appropriations measure. State monies cannot be spent without legislative appropriations.

Legislators can, and usually do, make a number of alterations in a governor's budget. In theory, a legislature controls all state activities and the overall budget process because it has the final say in approving the budget. In practice, however, most legislatures do not review every budgetary item but often trim or make additions only at the margins. Hence, budgets usually reflect the policy views of those responsible for their preparation—namely, the governor and the governor's budget office.

Plainly, a governor who has control over the budget and uses this power effectively has an important asset. This is somewhat more true where governors have the power of the **item veto,** a provision that permits governors to veto individual items in an appropriations bill while signing the remainder of the bill into law.[5] Here they can influence the flow of funds to the executive departments and thus shape the latter's activities. However, this is less true for agencies headed by elected officials. Purchase, fiscal, and personnel matters, moreover, are frequently centralized under the governor. When implemented by a strong staff and backed by a strong political base, a governor's fiscal powers are extremely important.

The governor's political power to make budget recommendations stick varies from state to state and from time to time. In the early 1980s in most states, taxpayer revolts—almost rebellions in some states—became intense. Taxpayers made it clear that they did not want to pay more in taxes, but they also did not want a reduction of state services. At the same time that governors were faced with taxpayer resistance, they saw federal funds being cut.

Most states spend at least 40 percent of their state's budget on education. Social assistance, transportation, prisons and criminal justice programs, health and rehabilitation efforts, and state parks and recreations consume other large portions of the budget. Fifty percent of the state's revenue usually comes from taxes; another 20 to 25 percent comes from federal sources. Charges for goods and services or users' fees account for perhaps 15 percent of the revenues. Governors have to strike some kind of balance.

Governor Mario Cuomo of New York believes you have to tax selectively and cut selectively to make the process work. Cuomo says he is always running into people who want him to increase spending. For example, someone will come up to him and say her daughter is in a state institution and it's awful. "They only change the sheets twice a day. Can't you do something—can't you have them change the sheets at least three times a day?" Cuomo says sure, he can have them changed three times a day. But then he looks them in the eye and says: "Now what are you going to give me so that I can pay for it? Do you want to wait longer in line at the Motor Vehicle office to get your license renewed? Do we stop paving the road in front of your home? Do you mind if we plow the snow less often?" Typically, of course, he hears that the people requesting the additional new spending don't want to forgo any of those things, which prompts the governor to say, "Well, then, I don't understand. Where do I get what I need to do what you want?" His point is simple. Given limited resources, choices must be made by elected officials. They cannot afford to do everything everyone would like to have provided by the state. Politicians are elected to negotiate the tradeoffs. You must "give to get."[6]

VETO POWERS

In all states except North Carolina, governors have relatively strong veto powers. To override a governor's veto, both chambers of state legislatures have to obtain a two-thirds majority vote. In all but seven states the governor has, in addition to the regular veto of entire bills, the power to veto individual items in appropriations measures. In a few states the governor can even reduce a particular appropriation. Both the *item veto* and the **reduction veto,** like all vetoes, can be overridden by the legislature (the former usually by a two-thirds or three-fifths vote in both chambers; the latter by a majority vote). But in many states most new laws and appropriations measures are sent to the governor after the legislature has adjourned.

To reassert their roles vis-à-vis the governor, many state legislatures have adopted measures to allow the legislature to call itself into special session to reconsider a governor's vetoes. Moreover, many state legislatures have adopted some kind of "legislative veto" of executive-branch administrative and regulatory decisions. Several states have even established a veto session—a short session following adjournment so that the legislature can reconsider all measures vetoed by the governor.

Amendatory or *conditional vetoes* (found in about seventeen states) allow governors to return a bill to the legislature with suggested changes or amendments. The legislators must decide whether to accept the governor's recommendations or attempt to pass the bill in its original form over veto.

EXECUTIVE ORDERS

One longstanding power of governors is their authority to issue executive orders that have the force of law. Even though these executive orders differ from statutes or formal acts passed by the legislature, they have almost the same binding effect.

Governors can issue executive orders as a result of specific constitutional grants, laws passed by their legislatures, or their implied powers as chief executive of the state. Governors have been given this quasi-legislative power because state legislatures often pass highly general—some would say vague—laws. Sometimes the executive ordinances supplementing a law are both more detailed and more important than the general guidelines contained in legislation. Recent governors have issued executive orders during such emergencies as natural disasters or energy crises, in compliance with federal rules and regulations, or to create advisory or coordinating commissions.[7]

But just as Congress has become more assertive in recent years, state legislatures have also increased their supervision over the rules and regulations issued by executive agencies. They want to ensure that what is done is actually what they intended.

COMMANDER IN CHIEF OF THE NATIONAL GUARD

Emergencies add to the authority of an executive because they call for decisive action. As commander in chief of the state's National Guard when it is not in federal service, the governor may use this force when local authorities are inadequate—in case of riots, floods, and other catastrophes, for example. Hardly a year goes by in which the National Guard of some state does not see emergency duty. In most states the state police are also available for emergencies.

THE PARDON POWER

In half the states, governors may pardon violators of state law; in the other states, they share this duty with a pardoning board. The governor may—except in cases of certain specified crimes or in cases of impeachment—pardon the offender, commute a sentence by reducing it, or grant a reprieve by delaying the punishment. The governor is normally assisted by pardon attorneys or pardon boards who hold hearings and sift the evidence to determine whether or not there are reasons for a pardon. A Tennessee governor caused considerable controversy and sparked federal investigation because he pardoned or paroled several dozen convicts just before leaving office in early 1979. Critics charged that some allegedly "purchased" their releases. Seldom, however, is the pardon power the subject of such controversy, presumably because it is generally administered with appropriate care.

POLICY-MAKING INFLUENCE

How much policy-making influence do governors have? Although their constitutional authority varies from state to state, their actual ability to influence legislation varies even more widely than a reading of the state constitutions might suggest.

Obviously, governors may send messages to their legislatures and argue for their programs. In some states they can trade appointive jobs for legislative support. They may also use their veto powers to trade for votes. They can usually attract more public attention to their views than any single legislator. Yet being the spokesperson for policy does not guarantee success. Much depends on a governor's ability, political base, and personal popularity, as well as on the political situation in which he or she operates. Some states have a long tradition of strong executive leadership. When governors have the support of powerful political organizations, they can guide policy. The governors of Michigan and Illinois, for example, have strong constitutional positions, and they are also likely to have party organizations behind them as well as close ties with followers in their respective legislatures.

But even in states in which they are less likely to be national figures, governors may derive power from a large popular following or strong party organization. The governor of Mississippi has much less formal power than the governor of Illinois, and carries less weight on the national political scene, yet within the state the former's control over minor jobs, contracts, and patronage may make this governor an important figure. The governor of New York must operate through more formal machinery in a complex state containing many power sources able to compete on the governor's own terms. Few governors of New York have ever been able to dominate their state legislatures to the same extent as some of the formally weak but politically powerful southern governors have been able to dominate theirs.

Balanced against all these formal powers are great obstacles. These may include a hostile legislature, cutbacks in federal funding, a depressed state economy, corrupt party or administrative officials, regional tensions in the state (downstate versus upstate, or urban versus rural splits), special interests and lobbyists, a cynical press, an indifferent or apathetic public, the sheer inertia of what critics call "the vast immovable inherited bureaucracy of government," antique civil service systems, and the reluctance of most citizens to get involved.

Some governors claim they are handicapped and that their programs are sacrificed because the opposition party is in control of the legislature. Others blame what they allege to be narrow-minded state lobbyists or an unfair press. One western governor complained that many of his state's problems—and many of the natural resource and social problems in western states—are caused by out-of-state, absentee landlord businesses or the national government, who together control much land in the West. The federal government owns at least half this land, a landmass, in fact, larger than western Europe. The land is managed, regulated, and overseen by a score of federal agencies, such as the National Park Service, the Forest Service, the Bureau of Land Management, the Fish and Wildlife Service, and the Department of Defense.

Still, governors are the most important policy leaders in the states. Observers differ, however, over how much these officials can actually do. Some claim that social and economic conditions really determine both how much money is available and how it is spent. In fact, they say, governors have little leeway in budget and policy determination. Even though governors often come into office hoping to begin new programs, they may spend most of their time raising money just to keep things going, and hence they are viewed by some observers as merely budget balancers rather than public policy leaders or shapers of a state's future. Some leading scholars, however, dispute this. Their research shows that a governor's ability to provide political leadership does affect the quality and implementation of public policy. The governor's role as leader of his or her political party also has an important impact on policy. The coalitions that governors form within their political parties help them put into effect the policies that they desire.[8] A governor's role increases in a state that has a competitive two-party system. In such a state, legislators of the governor's party are likely to work more closely with the governor to produce a successful legislative record.

In recent years, we have witnessed the election of a new breed of well-educated and able governors who have been effective in enlarging their policy-making roles. They are now able to appoint more and better state officials; most states now have some kind of cabinet system. Many contemporary governors come to office with impressive legislative and administrative experience. They are more likely to be real executive heads of government—not just figureheads. In short, many of the institutional barriers have been greatly diminished. The new governors are in a position to use their appreciable talents and to work to reshape public policy priorities in their states.[9] Because states will be playing a larger role in planning and administering a wide range of social and economic programs, the managerial and planning ability of each governor is clearly important.

Managing the State

Some governors come to office with no broad philosophy of management. Many are practicing attorneys or former state or national legislators and are used to handling each issue as it comes up, deciding it on its merits, and then delegating the administrative responsibilities to staff or department heads. Together, governors and their senior staffs must perform a variety of functions including the following:

Changing or initiating policy
Maintaining a policy or a position under pressure
Settling disputes among different agencies or factions within agencies

TABLE 5–3
How Governors Say They Spend Their Time[1]

ACTIVITY	TIME SPENT (PERCENTAGE)[2]
Managing state government	29%
Working with the legislature	16
Meeting the general public	14
Performing ceremonial functions	14
Working with press and media	9
Working with federal government	7
Working with local governments	7
Carrying out political activities[3]	6
Recruiting and appointing	6
Doing miscellaneous activities (staff, interstate, reading, phoning)	16

Source: Thad L. Beyle, "The Governor as Chief Legislator," State Government (The Council of State Governments, Winter 1978), p. 3.

[1] Totals do not add to 100 percent but are averages of the governors' estimates of the time they devoted to the particular activities.

[2] Percentages based on responses from those scheduling gubernatorial time in forty states.

[3] Plainly, some governors understate time spent campaigning for reelection.

Promoting the state (attracting tourism, exports, investments)

Recruiting top state administrative and judicial officials

Proposing budget priorities

Improving the quality of services rendered to the taxpayers

Settling disputes with the federal government and with nearby states

Many governors consider their managerial duties to be the least glamorous of their responsibilities, but they can hardly ignore their functions as their states' chief executive. Voters expect them to make programs run more efficiently, modernize the governmental structure, and be responsible for their part of the 3.5 million state employees throughout the nation. Of course, style and quality of leadership vary from governor to governor and from state to state. Management can also vary greatly from one agency to another; in addition, different kinds of programs demand different kinds of management.

A study of the Massachusetts governor's office differentiates four kinds of state agencies in Massachusetts according to the ways in which a governor deals with them.[10]

1. Those agencies requiring constant scrutiny, such as departments of corrections and public welfare
2. Those agencies that receive constant scrutiny because of the personal preferences of the governor, such as the department of mental health

3. Those agencies that receive gubernatorial attention because of a single crisis, such as the department of community affairs

4. Those agencies the governor leaves alone, such as housing and finance agencies

Governors have also had to become more involved in grantsmanship and in the planning and coordinating of federal grant-in-aid programs. The national government has passed much legislation that specifically designates the governor as the chief planning and administrative officer in the state. This role has led both to more flexibility *and* to more headaches for governors. On the one hand, to the extent these federal funds are still available, governors now have a form of patronage—services and programs for influential professionals and local communities. On the other, this new intergovernmental relations role requires more time, more staff, and constant negotiations both with the "feds" and with local and interest group leaders vying for the money or services involved.

One governor found that in his first few cabinet meetings when he would say, "Why don't we do X?" everyone would agree. But a month later, X would not have been done. He says he learned the hard way that "everybody does nothing." So he developed a new procedure using a metaphor to focus responsibility. Former Governor Lamar Alexander of Tennessee explains his procedure:

> When something was important, some *one* went "up the flagpole." For example, I remember saying, "We need fifty-one votes for the bill to reorganize all the technical institutes, community colleges, and vocational schools and put them under the boards of regents so we can deliver better job training for adults. Granville Hinton, you're on the flagpole." There was a big laugh, but everyone, especially Granville, knew that if we came up one vote short, it was his fault. Of course, we all would pitch in to help. But we knew, on that issue, Granville was in charge.[11]

INFLUENCING STATE AGENCIES

Understandably, senior public servants in a state usually look upon governors as important managerial and policy-making influences on their agencies. But state legislatures and interest groups also have significant power (see Tables 5–4 and 5–5).

Plainly, some agencies are not very responsive to their governors. Public agencies exist in a political climate; sometimes they are more responsive to interest groups, the legislature, or their own definitions of the public interest. Some reformers have long thought that all agencies should be accountable to the governor all the time. Others believe we should examine the given tasks of an agency and ask: "How far should it be removed from having to respond instantly to public opinion or to a governor's perception of public opinion? What questions should be left in the hands of the political system, the electorate, and the governor to

TABLE 5–4
Gubernatorial versus Legislative Influence on Agencies

	GOVERNOR	LEGISLATURE	EQUAL
Who exercises greater control over your agency?	46%[1]	26%	26%
Who exercises more detailed review of agency budgets?	34	31	31
Who is more likely to reduce your budget requests?	30	41	23

Source: Adapted from Deil Wright, David Kovenock, and Associates, *Assessing the Impacts of General Revenue Sharing in the Fifty States: A Survey of Administrators* (Chapel Hill: Institute for Research in Social Science, University of North Carolina, 1975). But see also Glenn Abney and Thomas Lauth, "The Governor as Chief Administrator," *Public Administration Review* (January–February 1983), pp. 40–49.

Note: N = 1581.

[1] Percentages based on the responses of state administrators surveyed.

be 'managed,' and which ones should be delegated to professional managers who are not directly accountable to any part of the political system?"[12]

MODERNIZING STATE GOVERNMENT

Another key development giving the governor more control over state government is the application of modern management techniques to state administration, for example, planning, systems analysis, and sophisticated computer and budgeting systems. In fact, the modern system of professional management is gradually replacing the old back-scratching or buddy system.[13]

There has been a trend toward increasing governors' involvement and control of the administration and streamlining of executive departments. In urban states with competitive party systems—such as New York, Illinois, New Jersey, Pennsylvania, Washington, and California—governors have considerable formal constitutional authority to organize their administrations as they see fit. Even in more rural

TABLE 5–5
Comparison of Various Influences on Agency Decisions

	GOVERNOR	LEGISLATURE	INTEREST GROUPS
High	50%[1]	32%	9%
Moderate	29	43	41
Slight	12	18	37
None	6	5	10

Source: Adapted from Deil Wright, David Kovenock, and Associates, *Assessing the Impacts of General Revenue Sharing in the Fifty States: A Survey of Administrators* (Chapel Hill: Institute for Research in Social Science, University of North Carolina, 1975).

Note: N = 1581.

[1] Percentages based on the responses of state administrators surveyed.

Being Governor: The Most Difficult Aspects

1. Coping with interference with family life
2. Working with legislature
3. Performing ceremonial duties
4. Keeping long hours
5. Making tough decisions
6. Accepting loss of privacy

7. Dealing with squabbles among government agencies
8. Working with federal government
9. Building and keeping staff
10. Working with the press

Source: Adapted from Thad Beyle, "Governors' Views on Being Governor," in Thad L. Beyle and Lynn R. Muchmore, eds., *Being Governor: Views from the Office* (Duke University Press, 1983), p. 25.

---

places, such as South Dakota, hundreds of agencies have been consolidated into a few comprehensive units as the result of executive orders from the governors.

A wave of state reorganizations that followed World War I and was repeated after World War II has continued. Attempts to reorganize state governments have not received universal praise, however. In some states reorganization commissions submit reports that are filed away and forgotten. Groups that profit from the existing structure—for example, those who have a pet bureau under their influence—can be counted upon to resist changes. So too can officials who fear loss of job or prestige. Also, legislators are often reluctant to approve recommendations that might make the governor too powerful.

Other critics oppose not so much the idea of reorganization as the basic principle of *executive power and responsibility*, which has dominated the reorganization movement. During the past several decades reorganizers have urged that the governor be made the manager of the executive branch. The following principles of reoganization have been suggested:

1. Agencies should be consolidated and integrated into as few departments as possible, so that similar functions will be grouped together and the governor will be able to exercise real control.
2. Lines of responsibility should be fixed and definite.
3. Single executives are preferable to boards and commissions.
4. The governor should have power to appoint and remove subordinates, including officers now elected, with the possible exception of the auditor.
5. The governor should have control over budgeting, accounting, reporting, purchasing, personnel, and planning, and should have the staff necessary to do these jobs.

Although they agree that centralized budgeting, purchasing, and the like are all good objectives, critics contend that conditions differ in each state and that no one pattern will fit all conditions. Often, they argue, there is little evidence to support the adoption of these reforms. What evidence do we have that the people will hold the governor accountable and that the governor will devote time and energy to administrative matters? Most governors are chiefly interested in legislative problems and public relations, and often they are not judged on their executive abilities. There is a real danger that the reorganizers are overlooking basic values in their concern with saving money. Reformers who design programs that promise efficiency and economy for a state often fail, some critics say, to warn their clients of the risk involved in creating a powerful chief executive where no effective party or legislative opposition exists to keep a strong governor in check.

Reorganizers agree it is ridiculous to make changes without regard to local conditions and problems. However, they maintain that the basic ideas—integrated authority, centralized direction, simplified structure, clear responsibility—are sound, carrying little danger of dictatorship. In fact, it is more likely that persons or special interests not responsible to the voters will take over government when the administrative structure is cumbersome, confusing, and too spread out. The legislature can more effectively supervise an administration integrated under the governor's control than one in which responsibility is split.

EFFECTS OF REORGANIZATION

Some observers say a half-century of strengthening the governors has not given us more efficient or democratic government. Others say it has. Still others say there is little evidence one way or another. Often the reorganizations change only organizational charts—with little impact on actual operations. Although large savings have been realized through centralized purchasing and the adoption of modern money-management practices, it is difficult to measure the results of consolidating departments, creating a governor's cabinet, establishing the office of **ombudsman,** or strengthening the governor's control over the executive branch. At the same time, the best-governed states do seem to be those in which the administrative structure has been closely integrated under the governor.

The reorganization of state administrative procedures is almost always justified in terms of efficiency and economy; and few would deny the importance of saving money. However, it is doubtful that the costs of operating state governments can be substantially reduced except by reducing their functions. Thus, we must ask: reorganization for what?

Overall formal reorganization is not the only way states modify and modernize their governmental structures. Often they change in stages, copying innovations from other states. Certain states, in fact, serve as exporters of innovations. So does the federal government. When it creates a department of housing and urban development, states often respond by creating departments of community affairs; when the federal government establishes a department of transportation, so do several of the states; and when the federal government created a special White

House-level office for trade, it was not long before many governors set up their own offices for trade and export responsibilities.[14]

Other Statewide Elected Officers

In many states other executive officials elected by the people include the lieutenant governor, secretary of state, attorney general, treasurer, and auditor (see Table 5–6).

The job of the *lieutenant governor*, like that of the vice-president, depends very much on the mood of the governor (except in Texas, where the lieutenant governor is sometimes as politically powerful as the governor). In some states a lieutenant governor presides over the senate and acts as a cabinet officer or even as a coordinator of several departments and agencies.[15] In almost every case the lieutenant governor becomes governor or acting governor in case of the death, disability, or absence of the governor from the state. Doubtless for this reason, more governors have sprung from this office than from any other.

Because the lieutenant governor sometimes leads a party faction different from that of the governor—and is occasionally even a member of the opposition party—he or she may become a thorn in the side of the chief executive. Thus, twenty-three states now provide for the election of the governor and lieutenant governor as a team—the same way that candidates for president and vice-president run in national elections. "The advent of team election, coupled with the assignment of weighty administrative tasks and larger salaries and budgets, has considerably

TABLE 5–6
Elected Executive Officials
in the States

Governor	50
Attorney general	43
Lieutenant governor	42[1]
State treasurer	38
Secretary of state	36
State auditor	25
Superintendent of education	16
Agriculture commissioner	12
Public utilities commissioner	12
Controller	10
Insurance commissioner	8

Source: The Book of the States, 1988–89 (Council of State Governments, 1988). Copyright by the Council of State Governments. Reprinted with permission.

[1] In the state of Utah one elected official serves as both lieutenant governor and secretary of state.

Separately Elected Officials by State

STATE	NUMBER	STATE	NUMBER
Alaska	1	Alabama	9
Maine	1	Georgia	9
New Jersey	1	Kentucky	9
New Hampshire	2	Nebraska	9
Tennessee	2	New Mexico	9
Hawaii	3	South Carolina	9
Virginia	3	Texas	9
Maryland	4	Washington	9
New York	4	Mississippi	10
		North Carolina	10
(Most states elect		Louisiana	11
five to eight officials.)		North Dakota	12

Source: Based on data from *The Book of the States, 1988–89* (Council of State Governments, 1988), pp. 51–52.

strengthened the oft-maligned office of lieutenant governor."[16] Still, many lieutenant governors have no statutory duties. In several smaller states, being lieutenant governor is a part-time job. A recent Nevada lieutenant governor, for example, practiced law nearly full time in Las Vegas and was paid $8,000 a year. He joked: "Heck, [presiding over the State Senate when it is] in session is the only thing I do—and check on the obituaries to see if I should be in Carson City [the capital]."

Are lieutenant governors really necessary? Eight states have done without them. The job they perform best is assuming the governor's job in case of death, resignation, or impeachment. Yet critics think the job is not needed if this is all lieutenant governors really do. Moreover, in many states the savings from not having to provide salaries, fringe benefits, and staffing for them would be considerable. The succession or replacement function could be performed by a state's attorney general, secretary of state, or the ranking member of the governor's party in the state legislature. Some have suggested that replacing a governor would be important enough to call a special election so that the people of the state could truly participate in the selection of their governor. Plainly, few people who cast their votes for governor consider that person's running mate. An interim governor could be designated by a state legislature during the sixty or ninety days leading up to the special election.

Although the position of lieutenant governor has worked out well in some states, the view persists that lieutenant governors are often in search of both a definition of their job and assignments that make them look important. The staffs and cabinets that are growing up nowadays around governors make the governor's chief of staff more of a deputy governor than most lieutenant governors. Then too, many candidates for lieutenant governor appear to seek the post for the name recognition and "the credential" to advance their political careers as they await forthcoming elections. The office is so unfulfilling that within the last few years both the lieutenant governors in Illinois and New York resigned right in the middle of their terms. In sum, the value to the state of the obscure office of lieutenant governor is debatable.

The *attorney general*—or state's lawyer—gives advice to state officials, represents the state before the courts, and supervises local prosecutors. Some attorneys general have real authority over local prosecutors and may prosecute cases on their own initiative. More and more these days attorneys general have made political capital out of investigating the state administration or launching proconsumer litigation efforts. The office is often a steppingstone to the governorship.

The *secretary of state* publishes the laws, supervises elections, and issues certificates of incorporation. In some states the secretary issues automobile licenses and registers corporate securities. A number of secretaries of state have jurisdiction over state cultural agencies and activities. This office is often the dumping ground for jobs that do not seem to belong to any other office and are not important enough to justify setting up a new agency. Yet several secretaries of state in recent years have begun modernization efforts in voter registration processes or have sponsored campaign finance and disclosure reforms.

The *treasurer* is the guardian of the state's money. Although in some states the job is largely ministerial, state treasurers generally have the vital responsibility of ensuring that cash is available to meet the obligations of the state and that all available funds are invested to maximize return.

The *auditor* has two major jobs: to authorize payments from the treasury and to make periodic audits of officials who handle state money. Before money can be spent, the auditor must sign a warrant certifying that the appropriation is authorized by law and that money is available in the treasury. This is the *preaudit,* which many observers believe should be given to a comptroller appointed by and responsible to the governor. The auditing *after* the money has been spent, however, is a job that most believe should be given to an officer responsible to the legislature. Even the most extreme advocates of centralized administration believe the auditor should not be responsible to the governor.

As part of the trend toward integrated administration, the duties of elected state officials have generally been limited to the functions specified in the constitution, and the more important functions given to officials appointed by the governor. In many states the budget directors and agency chiefs under the governor have more important roles than the state treasurer or the secretary of state. Yet elected officers can often control patronage, attract a following, and thus develop a political base from which they can attack the governor's program and administration.

Disputes between attorneys general and governors can be partisan (different parties or conflicting ambitions), but they also can be issue oriented. Thus governors in many states have their own staff lawyers or hire lawyers to represent them in fights with the states' attorneys general.

Sometimes progressive and controversial initiatives in the state governments come from these other statewide elected officials. An attorney general in Texas helped design and pass the Texas Open Records Act, one of the broadest and most strictly enforced freedom-of-information statutes in the country. A secretary of state in Massachusetts has modernized election laws, helped enact campaign finance laws, and championed conflict-of-interest reforms. A state treasurer in Colorado battled to transfer some of his state's revenue deposits from a few large Denver banks to smaller banks around the state and devised incentives for these banks to stimulate lending for student and small business loans and for low-income housing and family farms.

The Rewards of Being a Governor

Can anyone really succeed as governor? Some do not. Yet some, like Robert Ray of Iowa, Bob Graham of Florida, Thomas Kean of New Jersey, Dan Evans of Washington, Bill Clinton of Arkansas, and Richard Riley of South Carolina, became popular despite the political "heat" and the need to make tough decisions. In a sense governors don't have accomplishments; the people do. "A governor achieves his personal best by being honest and by staying in touch with the people who elected him to serve them," says former Governor Lamar Alexander of Tennessee.[17] Former Governor Tom Kean of New Jersey echoed similar thoughts when he reflected that, "When our common values are tapped and their energy released, we can do anything." Kean added, "I have tried to show during my political career, and especially my years as governor, that responsible government can meet people's needs and bring them together, that government can make a difference in the way we live."[18]

Who are the best governors? A popular former governor of Utah, Scott Matheson, maintains that they have been the men and women who have the right combination of values "for quality service, the courage to stick to their convictions, even when in the minority, integrity by instinct, compassion by nature, leadership by perception, and the character to admit wrong, and when necessary, to accept defeat."[19]

In sum, to a larger extent than we appreciate, the effectiveness of a governor is dependent upon the public support he or she is given. Although we should criticize them when they are wrong, misguided, or abuse the public trust, we have an equal obligation to applaud them when they are right, join in their coalitions when they are taking on tough yet desirable goals, and become public lobbyists when they need extra clout with the legislature or to overcome the veto power of some special interest. In a very real sense, our governors can only be impressive to the extent that we elect good ones, insist on their integrity, and vigorously support them when they make the right decisions.

Summary

1. One of the strengths of the federal system is that the states can act as laboratories of democracy, testing ideas which—if successful—can be copied on the national level. The states are also the testing place for many of our national leaders.
2. The job of governor is one of the most difficult tasks in American politics. Governors are usually male, lawyers in their 40s or 50s. Their chances for reelection are good, but their chances for accomplishing what they set out to do are nearly always overestimated by everyone—themselves included.
3. Today a governor is expected to be the state's chief policy maker, the architect of the state budget, the chief manager of the state administration, and the political and symbolic leader in the state. The governor also plays an increasingly complex role as the crucial link between the national and local governments. In short, governors are asked to accomplish miracles in this era of scarce resources and rising demands.
4. Governors have many formal powers. The most important are their budgetary and appointive powers. But a governor's formal powers mean little if he or she is not a persuasive communicator with good judgment and the capacity to think clearly.

Further Reading

GLENN ABNEY and THOMAS P. LAUTH. *The Politics of State and City Administration* (State University of New York Press, 1986).

LAMAR ALEXANDER. *Steps Along The Way: A Governor's Scrapbook* (Thomas·Nelson Publishers, 1986).

THAD L. BEYLE and LYNN R. MUCHMORE, eds. *Being Governor: Views from the Office* (Duke University Press, 1983).

MALCOLM E. JEWELL. *Parties and Primaries: Nominating State Governors* (Praegar, 1984).

THOMAS H. KEAN. *The Politics of Inclusion* (Free Press, 1988).

CHARLES KENNEY and ROBERT L. TURNER, *Dukakis: An American Odyssey* (Houghton Mifflin Co., 1988).

ROBERT S. MCELVAINE. *Mario Cuomo: A Biography* (Scribner's, 1988).

DAVID OSBORNE. *Laboratories of Democracy* (Harvard Business School Press, 1988).

ALAN ROSENTHAL. *The Governor and the Legislature* (Eagleton Institute of Politics, 1988).

LARRY SABATO. *Goodbye to Good-Time Charlie: The American Governor Transformed*, 2d ed. (Congressional Quarterly Press, 1983).

JACK M. TREADWAY. *Public Policymaking in the States* (Praeger, 1985).

ROGER VAUGHAN et al. *The Wealth of States: Policies for A Dynamic Economy* (Council of State Planning Advisers, 1984).

See also various special issues of the quarterly *State Government*.

The National Governors' Association publishes a variety of surveys, reports, and studies including a weekly *Governors' Bulletin* and the *Proceedings of the National Governors' Association* annual meetings. These and related documents can be purchased by writing to the National Governors' Association, 444 N. Capitol Street, NW, Washington, D.C. 20001.

Notes

1. See Keith J. Mueller, "Explaining Variation and Change in Gubernatorial Powers, 1960–1982," *Western Political Quarterly* (September 1985), pp. 424–431.

2. Three of the best general treatments of governors are Thad Beyle and Lynn Muchmore, eds., *Being Governor: Views from the Office* (Duke University Press, 1983); Coleman Ransone, Jr., *The American Governorship* (Greenwood, 1982); and Larry Sabato, *Goodbye to Good-Time Charlie: The American Governor Transformed*, 2d ed. (Congressional Quarterly Press, 1983).

3. Fred Branfman and Nancy Stefanik, "Who Says Raising Taxes Is Political Suicide?" *The Washington Post National Weekly Edition* (February 13–19, 1989), p. 24.

4. Ibid., p. 24. See also the excellent case studies of governors in Michigan, Massachusetts, Pennsylvania, Arizona, and elsewhere who pushed through economic development programs in the 1980s in David Osborne, *Laboratories of Democracy: A New Breed of Governors Creates Models for National Growth* (Harvard Business School Press, 1988).

5. But see G. Abney and T. P. Lauth, "The Line-Item Veto in the States; An Instrument for Fiscal Restraint or an Instrument for Partisanship?" *Public Administration Review* (May–June 1985), pp. 372–77. See also David C. Nice, "The Item Veto and Expenditure Restraint," *Journal of Politics* (May 1988), pp. 487–499.

6. This story is adapted from Robert S. McElvaine, *Mario Cuomo: A Biography* (Scribner's, 1988), pp. 337–338.

7. E. Lee Bernick, "Discovering a Governor's Powers: The Executive Order," *State Government* (Summer 1984), pp. 97–101.

8. Sarah McCally Morehouse, *State Politics, Parties and Policy* (Holt, Rinehart & Winston, 1981), and David Osborne, *Laboratories of Democracy*.

9. Sabato, *Goodbye to Good-Time Charlie*, and McElvaine, *Mario Cuomo*.

10. Martha W. Weinberg, *Managing the State* (MIT Press, 1977), p. 24.

11. Lamar Alexander, *Steps Along the Way: A Governor's Scrapbook* (Thomas Nelson Publishers, 1986), p. 108.

12. Weinberg, *Managing the State*, p. 227. For a study of a charismatic state bureaucrat who achieved notable independence from several governors as well as from the state legislature in New York, see Robert A. Caro, *The Power Broker: Robert Moses and the Fall of New York* (Knopf, 1974). See also *Governing the American States: A Handbook for New Governors* (National Governors Association, 1978).

13. See, for example, Lynn Muchmore and Harley Duncan, "The Kansas Balanced Base Budget System," *State Government* (Summer 1982), pp. 106–9.

14. For some general observations on the patterns of state reorganization, see James L. Garnett, *Reorganizing State Government: The Executive Branch* (Westview, 1980). See also Donald C. Stone, "Orchestrating Governor's Executive Management," *State Government* (Spring 1985), pp. 33–39, for a look at the growing staffs that work with governors.

15. Gail B. Manning and Edward F. Feigenbaum, eds., *The Lieutenant Governor: The Office and Its Powers* (The Council of State Government, 1987). See also Kathleen Sylvester, "Lieutenant Governors: Giving up Real Power for Real Opportunity," *Governing* (February 1989), pp. 44–50.

16. Sabato, *Goodbye to Good-Time Charlie*, p. 74. See also Eugene Declerq and John Kaminski, "A New Look at the Office of Lieutenant Governor," *Public Administration Review* (May–June 1978), pp. 256–61.

17. Lamar Alexander, *A Governor's Scrapbook*, p. 141.

18. Thomas H. Kean, *The Politics of Inclusion* (Free Press, 1988), p. 248.

19. Scott Matheson with James Edwin Kee, *Out of Balance* (Peregrine Smith Books, 1986), p. 186.

6

Judges and Justice in the States

Do you know the name of the chief justice of your state supreme court? You should. Although you hear more about the activities of federal judges than about their state counterparts, the 28,000 state and municipal judges conduct most of the judicial business. They preside over most criminal trials, settle most lawsuits between individuals, and administer most estates. Furthermore, they interpret state laws and play a vital role in determining who gets what, where, when, and how. Thus they have a crucial role in making public policy.

State judges have the final say—most of the time. Through petitions of **habeas corpus,** criminal defendants may occasionally get federal district judges to review the actions of state courts. And if, in disposing of a case, state judges have to interpret the meaning of the national Constitution, a national law, or a national treaty—that is, if the case raises a *federal question*—the losing party may request the United States Supreme Court to review the decision of the highest state court to which it may be taken under state law. Of the hundreds of thousands of decisions decided by state judges each year, however, only a handful reach the Supreme Court.

In recent decades state courts have become even more prominent in the political life of their state. In addition to the **new judicial federalism** in which state judges have started to apply the bill of rights in their own state constitution more rigorously, there has been a revolution in state **tort law.** This revolution has opened state courts to more people to sue more often about more things; for example, product liability suits brought by people who believe they have been injured as the result of faulty products. As state courts have become more active, state judges have become embroiled in visible controversial issues and have antagonized substantial interests. And as the public has grown sophisticated about the importance of judges as policy makers, judicial politics has become a significant feature of the political landscape.

The Shape of State Courts

Each state has its own court system. Because the fifty systems vary, it is difficult to generalize about them.[1] For convenience we may categorize state courts as follows: minor courts of limited jurisdiction, trial courts of general jurisdiction, and appellate courts.

MINOR COURTS

Minor courts handle misdemeanors, the less serious violations of state and local laws, traffic cases, and civil suits involving relatively small amounts of money. In some places they also hold preliminary hearings and set bail for more serious charges. Decisions of these courts may be appealed and in most instances tried *de novo*; that is, tried all over again without reference to what happened in the minor court. In most places these courts are financed and administered by the local unit of government: the township, the city, or the county.

In cities minor courts are known as municipal courts and are often divided into traffic courts, domestic relations courts, small claims courts, and police courts. Paid magistrates trained in the law preside over most of these courts.

In a few states, especially in rural areas, the justice of the peace system still survives. Justices of the peace are elected for short terms, they need not be trained in the law, and they usually serve from two to six years. Their authority is limited to performing marriages, notarizing papers, handling traffic violations, and hearing misdemeanors—usually those involving fines of less than $200. They also hear minor civil disputes. Because plaintiffs often can choose among several justices of the peace in a county, they may pick the one most likely to decide in their favor. Thus it has been said that JP stands for "Judgment for the Plaintiff."

Nowadays most minor court magistrates are salaried and legally trained. Most people accused of a crime have legal assistance. Yet court calendars are often so crowded that cases are "processed" with little time for individual attention. While many critics of the legal system contend that judges are too lenient and those accused of crime are "back on the streets" too quickly, others charge that poor and ignorant defendants often spend days in jail waiting for their cases to come to trial.

A new and apparently effective reform is the establishment of "court-watching" groups. In some cities these groups are sponsored by such organizations as the American Civil Liberties Union, which tries to ensure that our courts treat those charged with crimes fairly. In other cities the groups are sponsored by organizations concerned that judges may be too easy on defendants. Prosecutors, public defenders, and judges, it is alleged, too often become a comfortable "work group," with little or no public scrutiny. Court watchers make these professionals more sensitive to the views of the general public.

TRIAL COURTS OF GENERAL JURISDICTION

Trial courts with complete original jurisdiction are called county courts, circuit courts, superior courts, district courts, and common pleas courts. They administer equity, criminal, common, and statutory law. Some states maintain separate courts for criminal and civil matters. States commonly also have special probate courts to administer estates and handle related matters. Decisions of the general trial courts may be reviewed by appellate courts; however, most decisions of trial judges are not reviewed and become final.

APPELLATE COURTS

In a few states—Mississippi, Montana, Nebraska, Nevada, North Dakota, Rhode Island, West Virginia, and Vermont—appeals from trial courts are carried directly to the state supreme court. Most states, however, have intermediate appeals courts that fit into the system in much the same way that the United States courts of appeals fit into the federal structure.

The court of last resort is usually called the supreme court. (In Maine it is called the Supreme Judicial Court; in Maryland and New York, the Court of Appeals. And, if that is not confusing enough, in New York the trial courts are called Supreme Courts. Texas and Oklahoma have two courts of last resort—a Supreme Court that handles civil matters and a Court of Criminal Appeals.) Unless a federal question is involved, these state supreme courts are the highest tribunal to which a case may be carried. State courts of last resort have from three to nine judges; most have seven.

In all states judges have the power of judicial review and may refuse to enforce, and may restrain state officials from enforcing, state laws on the grounds of a conflict with the state or national constitution. All state judges take an oath to uphold the supremacy of the federal Constitution, and may declare federal laws unconstitutional, subject to final review by the United States Supreme Court.

STATE COURTS AND STATE POLITICS

State courts play a somewhat different role than do national courts:

1. State courts are "more deeply and more often into the affairs of the coordinate branches of government than is the Supreme Court."[2]
2. State judges are unconstrained by the doctrine of federalism.
3. State judges are much less constrained by the standing to sue requirement and limitation on taxpayer suits. In fact, in nine states the state supreme

"I hope you're not going to make a big
issue of this."

*Drawing by Modell; © 1986 The New Yorker
Magazine, Inc.*

court can set aside the case or controversy requirement and give advisory
opinions.

4. State judges feel much less need than do most federal judges to exercise
judicial restraint or to argue they are doing so. Unlike federal judges, most
state judges are subject to direct political accountability. In most states judges
serve for limited terms and stand for election. They too can claim to be
representatives of the people. "As elected representatives, like legislators,
they feel less hesitant to offer their policy views than do appointed judges."[3]
In addition, if there is dissatisfaction with a decision of a state supreme
court, it can be more readily set aside than can a decision of the national
Supreme Court. Most state constitutions are much easier to amend than
the United States Constitution is.[4]

What all this amounts to is that "state supreme courts rarely have the last
word on state law. The people can always claim that prerogative by tossing out
the judges, passing a new law, or amending the state constitution to correct a
judicial misstep."[5] "A California judge once said that he never forgot there was
'a crocodile in our bathtub,' for in most states the people can vote judges out of
office."[6]

How Judges Are Chosen

Judges are selected in four different ways:

1. *Popular election* is used in nearly half the states, some of which, mostly in
the West and upper Midwest, hold nonpartisan primaries for nominating
judicial candidates and elect them on nonpartisan ballots. That a nonpartisan
ballot is used does not necessarily mean that political parties are unimportant.

Method for Selection of Judges of the Court of Last Resort

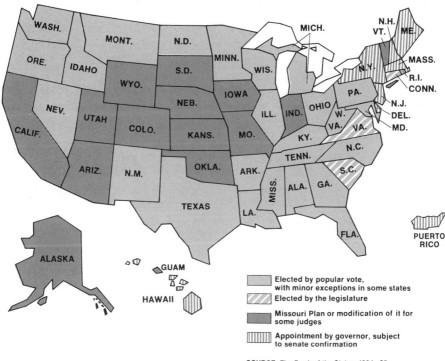

SOURCE: *The Book of the States, 1984–85.*

In at least half the states that hold nonpartisan elections, parties actively campaign in behalf of candidates.[7] Some states try to isolate judicial elections from partisanship by holding them on separate days from other elections.

Until recently, interest in judicial elections was often not intense, and voter turnout tended to be low. This lack of attention to judicial politics is beginning to change, and judicial elections are becoming increasingly contested. "More than half the state judges in the United States now face some form of election to either win or retain a seat on the bench."[8] It is still true, however, that few voters pay much attention to many judicial elections. Voter interest tends to be high when judges are part of contested elections on the same partisan ballots as presidents, governors, or senators.

It is interesting to note, however, that "a majority of the judges serving in states utilizing an elective judiciary . . . are in fact initially appointed by the governor to fill mid-term vacancies, usually occasioned by the retirement or death of sitting judges . . . and these appointed judges are overwhelmingly favored in their first electoral bids following appointment."[9]

2. *Appointment by the governor* with confirmation by the state senate is used in Delaware, Maine, and New Jersey, and with confirmation by a council in Massachusetts and New Hampshire. (In Delaware and Massachusetts governors have chosen to restrict their appointments to those whose names are submitted to them by judicial nominating commissions.)

3. *Election by the legislature* is the constitutional practice in Connecticut (nominated by the governor from merit selected panel), Rhode Island, South Carolina, and Virginia.

4. Many states use a modified appointment plan, known as the *Missouri Plan,* for some courts.[10]

THE MISSOURI PLAN

The **Missouri Plan** provides that whenever a vacancy occurs in a court to which the plan applies, a special nominating commission (composed of three lawyers elected by the bar, three citizens appointed by the governor, and the chief justice) nominates three candidates. The governor selects one, who then serves as a judge for at least a year. At the next general election the voters are asked: "Shall Judge X be retained in office?" If a majority agrees, the judge serves a full new term; if not, another person is selected by the same procedure. At the end of his or her term, a judge does not have to be renominated and reappointed. Instead, the judge merely certifies a wish to have his or her name placed on the ballot, and the voters are asked whether they want to retain that judge in office.

In California the governor makes the initial selection with the approval of a commission, instead of choosing among names submitted by a special nominating commission. After a period of service the judge runs in the next general election against his or her own record. Because of this modification of the Missouri Plan (or vice versa, because in fact California adopted its system first), some observers classify the California Plan as a separate entity.

Retention elections usually generate little interest and low voter turnout.[11] In some states citizens groups are beginning to provide information about judicial performance, and in 1988 Colorado became the first state to legislate a system of "evaluating judicial performance to provide persons voting on the retention of justices and judges with fair, responsible, and constructive information about judicial performance."[12] In all, fewer than forty judges out of more than two thousand judges have been removed as the result of retention elections. Occasionally, however, state supreme court judges are challenged in retention elections, especially when their opinions vary appreciably from the mainstream of public opinion and their decisions have aroused the hostility of significant special interests. (As one observer commented, "You can take the opposing candidate out of elections, but you can't take the elections out of the political arena."[13])

In recent years one of the more celebrated contested retention elections was that of Justice Hans Linde of the Oregon Supreme Court. Justice Linde has been a champion of an active role for state supreme courts in applying their own state constitutions to protect civil liberties. In 1985 he retained his seat against an active challenge that he was "soft on crime," yet it was close.

The 1986 retention election for Chief Justice Rose Elizabeth Bird and two of her associate justices of the California Supreme Court rivaled the gubernatorial election in terms of public interest and dollars spent. In fact, the Bird retention election was very much an issue in the gubernatorial contest between Republican George Deukmejian and Democrat Tom Bradley. It was alleged that under Bird's leadership the California Supreme Court had failed to apply the death penalty provisions of the California Constitution, and that she had allowed her own personal values to override her obligations as a judge. Her defenders argued that the attack upon her undermined the integrity of the courts, compromised judicial independence, and made judges too responsive to public opinion. She and the two associate justices were defeated.[14] As a result the governor appointed more conservative justices and the California Supreme Court has taken a more conservative stance.

THE APPOINTIVE VERSUS THE ELECTIVE SYSTEM

For two hundred years observers have debated the merits of the appointive versus the elective system for the selection of judges. Those who favor the appointive method argue that voters are uninformed about candidates and are not competent to assess legal learning and judicial abilities. Popular election, they assert, puts a premium on personality, requires judges to enter the political arena, and discourages many able lawyers from running for office. Finding the entire system irrational, one candidate for judicial office wrote: "I got used to people saying they would vote for me because 'you look like a judge.' " He stated: "There are ordinarily almost no issues in a judicial campaign upon which one can take a stand, and fewer still that strike any real sparks. . . ." In a community of any size, "there is no way for a judicial candidate to communicate relevantly with the electorate. This circumstance alone renders fraudulent the suggestions that judges are popularly elected: substitute 'blindly' for 'popularly.' "[15] Because of the lack of issues in some states, what counts is a popular name. In Ohio, for example, "Browns have run against Browns (in one Supreme Court race three Browns were running) and O'Neills against O'Neills."[16]

Proponents of the appointive system also contend that the elective process conceals what is really going on. Most voters, they say, have so little information about the merits of the candidates that judges are in reality picked by party insiders. In fact, because many vacancies are created when a sitting judge retires or dies, it is often the governor who selects the judges. The governor makes an interim appointment who serves until the next election; this individual usually wins the election.

What are the arguments of those who oppose the appointive system and favor the elective method? Judges, they argue, should be directly accountable to the people. When judges are appointed, they contend, they are apt to lose touch with the general currents of opinion of the electorate. Moreover, the appointive process gives governors too much power over judges.

Interest in judicial reform is once again heating up. Reform was an issue in the 1988 Texas election for supreme court justices, and that election triggered continued debate over the propriety of judicial candidates taking so much money from so few people. Over $7 million was spent by judicial candidates for six of the nine seats on the state supreme court; most of it was contributed by a small group of lawyers.[17] Pennsylvania is another state where allegations of special interests buying favoritism through campaign donations to judicial candidates have stirred up pressures for adoption of the Missouri Plan.[18]

In general, bar associations, corporate law firms, and judges tend to favor some kind of merit selection system, while plantiffs attorneys, and leaders of minority organizations, women's associations, minorities, and women's and labor groups are skeptical or opposed. In many states that continue to elect judges, it is increasingly clear that judicial candidates are dependent on a small number of law firms or special interests for their campaign funds. This reality encourages pressure for "reforming" the judicial selection process in those states.

WHAT DO WE KNOW?

Which system produces better judges?[19] The first problem is to define a "good judge." Most people take this term to mean a judge who makes decisions they like. Even when we describe desirable features more precisely—the ability to maintain neutrality between parties, a good knowledge of the law, writing ability, personal integrity, good physical and mental health, and the ability to handle judicial power sensibly—we are naming factors that are hard to measure.[20]

Are judges selected by one method more likely to make decisions of a certain kind than are judges chosen by other methods? Even this is difficult to determine. We do have some studies, but most of them cover a relatively brief period in only a few states. Nevertheless, several tentative conclusions are emerging.[21]

1. "Elected and appointed judicial systems do not differ as much in their results . . . as the debate literature would have us believe. . . ."[22]
2. One study found: "Judicial elections . . . have a built-in bias for men. . . . Quite simply, few women, blacks, Hispanics, or Asians have the political connections, financial resources, and campaign sophistication to overcome the stereotype that has the blindfolded woman holding the scales of justice, but a white man sitting at the bench dispensing it. . . ."[23] Other studies show that "more women are chosen by gubernatorial appointment and merit methods, but that blacks fare as well in judicial elections and nearly as well in legislative. Another study found that "merit systems tend to produce higher proportions of Protestant judges" in contrast to Catholic and Jewish judges.[24] However, variations among systems are extremely small "and there is some question whether these variations are statistically significant."[25]

3. The Missouri Plan has not eliminated partisan politics in the selection of judges, but it has altered the nature of such politics. It has "taken the partisan aspects of judicial out of . . . local (politics) . . . and projected them into the political world of the highest public official in the state."[26]
4. There appears to be no difference between the kinds of decisions made by judges selected through the Missouri Plan and those made by judges elected to office.
5. Democratic judges tend to make more liberal decisions than their Republican colleagues do.[27]
6. Courts to which judges are nominated and elected on a nonpartisan ballot show less partisan division than those whose judges are nominated by party conventions and elected in partisan elections.
7. State court judges, compared with those of the national Supreme Court, tend to reach unanimous decisions. This phenomenon appears to be unrelated to the matter of judicial selection.

HOW JUDGES ARE JUDGED

Unlike federal judges, who hold office during "good behavior," most state judges are selected for fixed terms, typically six to twelve years. (In Massachusetts, New Hampshire, and Puerto Rico, judges serve to age 70; in Rhode Island they serve for life.) But it is the states—rather than the national government—that have taken the lead in establishing procedures to judge the judges.

Because impeachment has proved to be an ineffective means to remove judges, today each of the fifty states has a board, commission, or court to handle allegations of judicial misbehavior. Despite the objections of many judges, these commissions are most often composed of nonlawyers as well as lawyers. The commissions investigate complaints and hold hearings for judges who have been charged with improper performance of their duties or unethical or unfair conduct. Establishment of these commissions appears to have helped restore public confidence in the state judicial systems.[28]

The Judicial Reform Movement

In 1906, at a meeting of the American Bar Association in St. Paul, Minnesota, Roscoe Pound, a distinguished figure in the legal profession, made a now-famous speech on "The Cause of Popular Dissatisfaction with the Administration of Justice." Pound spoke about waste, delay, and obsolete procedures, and he inaugurated almost a century of judicial reform.

Many of the reforms Pound proposed—court unification, centralized management, state financing, merit selection—have been adopted, but many of the problems he outlined—waste and delay—continue to plague our courts. The tort "revolution" has encouraged our increasing tendency to sue each other as well as the government. We are, many charge, a "litigious society." Dockets are crowded, relief is costly, and inordinate delays are common. (Perhaps you watched Dickens's *Bleak House* on public television and saw a horrendous example of how "justice delayed is justice denied." We too have our "chancery courts.")

Although there is a "dissolution of the scholarly consensus about their efficacy,"[29] some of the reforms frequently urged by those concerned with improving the administration of justice include:

1. Judges should be selected by some kind of system, such as the Missouri Plan, that screens candidates in terms of their qualifications.
2. Judges should be paid adequately so they have the financial independence to concentrate on their work, and so that the more successful lawyers will be willing to serve on the bench. Judges are unable to earn anything beyond their salaries. They must be cautious about investments, in order to avoid conflicts of interest. In most states the salary paid to a judge is considerably less than the average salary of the practicing attorneys of the same age and experience.
3. Judges should serve for long terms. The arguments here are much the same as those for tenure for college professors: Judges should be able to make decisions without fear of losing their jobs. Although only a few constitutional changes have extended judicial terms, actual tenure for judges is often longer than it might appear from looking at constitutional provisions. Incumbent judges are ordinarily reelected. And some state constitutions have been amended to ensure that sitting judges merely run against their own records, which in effect gives them longer terms.
4. Alternative methods to decide disputes—such as neighborhood justice centers and arbitration and mediation forums—should be established. Through the Dispute Resolution Act of 1979, Congress has encouraged states and localities to develop alternative dispute-resolution mechanisms. A few states have done so.
5. Rule-making powers should be given to the state supreme court or its chief justice. This is being done in more and more states. It permits judges to adopt rules relating to procedural matters and codes of professional conduct. Some rules even require lawyers to continue their education by taking refresher courses.
6. Although no person should be appointed or elected to a court because of race or sex or ethnic background, our courts need to be more representative of the communities they serve.[30]

The judicial reform movement has been successful, but, like most reform movements, it has its critics and skeptics. Some observers suggest that court delay is not as serious a problem as has been charged, and that the remedies adopted may undercut our checks and balances system.[31] However one feels about the merits of the proposed reforms, clearly the problems at which they are aimed will require more than procedural changes. Delay, for example, often works to the advantage of defendants and their attorneys, who wish to postpone trials. At other times prosecutors want delays in order to put pressure on defendants to accept guilty pleas. Lawyers may seek delays so that they can accept more clients and make more money. Further, no matter how modernized the management of court business, the flow of legal business grows continuously. And this leads to another, somewhat more controversial, recommendation.

Some people propose that traffic violations, automobile injury cases, and victimless crimes should be handled by some procedure other than court trial. New York has led the way in removing from the courts minor traffic offenses that do not involve serious moving violations; other states are following this lead. No-fault insurance programs could reduce the large number of cases stemming from automobile accidents. When we realize that half the people in prison, as well as half the trials that are held, involve victimless crimes, we can see that "decriminalization" would substantially reduce the load on the courts. Six states, for example, have already repealed statutes on public drunkenness and now consider alcoholism a disease rather than a crime.

The reform of state judicial systems is enmeshed in partisan, ideological, and issue politics. Moreover, judges are but one part of the total justice system. Their operations are best studied in the context of the entire system.

The Justice System

THE JURY

Although most of us will never be judges or serve as professionals in the administration of justice, all adult citizens have an opportunity—even an obligation—to be jurors. Trial by jury in civil disputes is used less often these days; people either make settlements prior to trial or elect to have their cases decided by a judge alone or referred to a mediator or arbitrator. Furthermore, only a small fraction of criminal cases are actually disposed of by a trial before a jury. Still, jury trials, and the threat of them, remain a key feature of our justice system.[32]

We have moved from a jury system in which service was restricted to white male property owners to one in which jury duty is the responsibility of all adult citizens. Today more time and energy are spent in trying to persuade (or coerce) people to serve on juries than in trying to exclude them. Because jury service is time consuming and burdensome, many middle-class professionals and other busy people do their best to avoid serving. Judges are often willing to excuse doctors, nurses, teachers, executives, and other highly skilled persons who plead that their services are more needed outside the jury room. As a result, juries are often selected from panels consisting in large part of older people, those who are

What You See Depends on Where You Sit, or Things Are Always More Complicated Than They Look

Consider this chilling story:

A twenty-two year old male is arrested for burglary and assault with a deadly weapon, both felony offenses carrying maximum penalties of ten or more years. At arraignment the judge notes that the accused has a prior record. . . . He sets bail at $10,000. Unable to afford a bondsman's fee, the accused is sent to the county jail. Two months later the judge reduces the bond to $2500, and relatives of the accused scrape together the money. Three months and six court appearances later, he pleads guilty to a single count of criminal trespass . . . and receives a five-month sentence with two months credited for time served in pretrial custody.

Everyone involved agrees that this case is a problem.

The arresting officer . . . will point to the reduced bail and light sentence as evidence that the courts do not care.

The public defender . . . will point out that his client, presumed to be innocent until proven guilty, spent two months in jail solely because he is poor. . . .

The defendant's family is distraught because of the financial hardship. . . .

The prosecutor . . . is frustrated because she could not locate one key witness. . . .

The judge is irritated because the case appeared on his calendar eight times before it was . . . resolved. . . .

After several trips to court, the proprietor of the burglarized store feels twice victimized—not only did he lose money during the robbery, but he has now lost money every time he left his store in order to appear in court.

The one available witness . . . is indignant at the lack of respect accorded her by the prosecutor. . . .

The defendant claims that, finding the door to the drugstore open, he entered to see if anything was wrong. He might conclude that he got off easy or that (the public defender) had sold him down the river.

A first-time observer in the courtroom would not have understood what was going on. But, noting that the accused was black and that all those in a position to affect his fate were white, he might have drawn a conclusion of race discrimination. . . .

No one is satisfied.

Let us again consider the case. Although the accused was charged with possession of a deadly weapon, the police were not able to produce a gun. The only *evidence* about the gun is the statement by the (witness) who claimed to have seen and been hit by it when she encountered the accused in the doorway to the drugstore. . . . The police report . . . states that the (witness) . . . refused medical treatment and "seemed intoxicated." (Furthermore,) some details changed each time she recounted the incident. . . . Although the proprietor . . . reported the loss of several cameras and transistor radios, in addition to cash, the accused was quickly caught based on the key witness's identification. One of the items listed was never recorded, and the money involved was not large or identifiable. . . .

Was the court lenient? Although the defendant had a history of prior arrests, he had only two convictions, both on breach of peace, and had never done time . . .

Five months is above average for trespass cases. Harsh? Frustrated by reports of the failure of probation, drug and alcohol treatment programs, the judge feels he has no option other than to put the offender behind bars. But aware that violence and sexual abuse were commonplace in state prisons and impressed that the offender's family had stood beside him, the judge hopes that he will be safer in the local jail and that he will be better able to maintain ties with his family. Still, the judge, ambivalent about the sentence, expresses hope that the offender may be eligible for daytime work release after a month or so, unaware that this program has been eliminated in recent budget cuts.

Source: Malcolm M. Feeley, *Court Reform on Trial.* Copyright © 1983 Twentieth Century Fund, Inc. Reprinted by permission.

unemployed or employed in relatively low-paying jobs, single people, and others who are unable to be excused from jury service. Some states have reacted to these problems by making it more difficult to be excused.

Trials by jury take more time than bench trials (trials before judges). They also cost more. As a result, some states are using juries of fewer than twelve for many crimes, and a few are permitting verdicts by less than a unanimous vote. The Supreme Court has approved these practices for states, provided the juries consist of at least six persons.[33]

THE PROSECUTOR

As we have noted, only a handful of those accused of committing a crime actually stand trial. And only 10 to 15 percent of those who are convicted are declared guilty as the result of a formal trial before either a judge or a jury. Most people who go to prison or who have to pay a criminal fine do so because they have pleaded guilty. "Presiding" over this out-of-courtroom process is the prosecutor.

The 18,000 prosecutors in the United States are usually county officials, locally elected and subject to little, if any, supervision by state authorities. In Connecticut they are appointed by judges, in the Virgin Islands by the attorney general, and in New Jersey by the governor, with the consent of the state senate. A prosecutor has "more control over life, liberty, and reputation than any other person in America."[34] (Incidentally, the prosecutor is largely an American invention, one of the few governmental positions we did not inherit from England. To this day, the administration of criminal justice in Britain is based on the theory of private prosecution of criminals.)

When presented with a case by the police, the prosecutor must decide first whether to file formal charges. He or she may: (1) divert the matter out of the criminal justice system and turn it over to a social welfare agency; (2) dismiss the charges; (3) take the matter before a grand jury, which almost always follows the prosecutor's recommendation; (4) in most jurisdictions file an **information affidavit,** which serves the same function as a grand jury indictment.

The decision to charge or not to charge is "well nigh unreviewable in theory and even less reviewed in practice."[35] Of course, there may be political consequences. A prosecutor who decides not to charge a person accused of some notorious crime is likely to be subject to political pressure and public criticism. But for routine crimes the prosecutor is politically in a better position to dismiss a charge than are the police. Police are supposed to enforce every law all the time. Of course, it is impossible for them to do so, and they must exercise discretion. But officers who fail to arrest a person alleged to have committed a crime could well be charged with failing in their duty. The prosecutor, however, has more leeway. In fact, the prosecutor is less likely to be criticized for dropping a case because of insufficient evidence than for filing a charge and failing to get a conviction.

DEFENSE COUNSEL, PUBLIC DEFENDERS, AND OTHERS

Many defendants cannot afford the legal counsel to which they are constitutionally entitled. The **assigned counsel system** is the oldest system to provide such defendants with counsel, and it continues to be used, especially in rural areas. Judges appoint attorneys to help defendants who cannot afford them. Sometimes such attorneys are paid from the public treasury, but other times they are not. They are expected instead to do the work **pro bono**—for the public good. Seldom are they given funds to do any investigatory work on behalf of their clients. Often judges pick young lawyers just beginning their careers or old ones about to retire. Some less scrupulous lawyers make their living as assigned counsel and are quick to plead their clients guilty. They are known contemptuously as members of the "copout bar."[36] After looking at the assigned counsel system, one writer concluded, "It results in incompetence being more the rule than the exception."[37]

Dissatisfaction with the assigned counsel system has led to the creation of the **public defender** system, first started in Los Angeles in 1914 and now used in most big cities. Under this system the government provides a staff of lawyers whose full-time job is to defend those who cannot pay. The system provides experienced counsel and relieves the bar of an onerous duty. Critics—including some defendants—protest that because public defenders are paid employees of the state, they are not likely to work as diligently in behalf of their clients as they would if they were specifically assigned to them. But most observers consider the defender system superior to the assigned counsel method. Steps are being taken to increase the pay of public defenders, protect their independence, and see that they win the confidence of those they represent. Washington, D.C., Seattle, Washington, and Contra Costa County, California, have especially strong public defender programs.

VICTIMS AND DEFENDANTS

When we talk about our criminal justice system, we sometimes get so carried away with abstractions that we forget that the two most important parties in any criminal case are not the prosecutor and the defense attorney, but rather the victim of the crime and those accused of it.

In general terms, defendants are likely to be "younger, predominantly male, disproportionately black, less educated, seldom fully employed, and typically un-married. By the time the sorting process has ended, those sent to prison will consist of an even higher proportion of young, illiterate, black males."[38]

Victims, too—compared to the rest of the population—tend to be young, black or another minority, and uneducated. A substantial number of victims, either because of lack of knowledge of what to do or fear of doing it, never report crimes to police and prosecutors.

Our system puts the responsibility for prosecuting criminals on the government. In most instances victims have no role, perhaps, other than as witnesses.

They are not consulted about what the charge should be nor asked what they think might be an appropriate penalty. The matter is strictly between the state, represented by the prosecutor, and the accused, represented by an attorney.

Around 1980 the "Crime Victim" movement started. Initiated originally by liberals, chiefly feminists, concerned about the difficulty of winning prosecutions for rape and about the harsh treatment of women witnesses, the movement quickly gained the support of conservatives who consider the present system unfair to victims. In the 1984 Victims of Crime Act, Congress authorized federal funds to support state programs compensating victims and provide funds to some victims of federal crimes as well.

More and more states are adopting a "Victim's Bill of Rights." These bills of rights make it easier for victims to get back their stolen property held in police custody. They also establish procedures to notify victims and give them a chance to be heard when prosecutors file formal charges, when judges set bail and impose sentences, and when parole boards consider releasing prisoners. These victim's bills of rights are not without their constitutional problems. The United States Supreme Court has held that it violates the federal Constitution for a state to present to a jury during the sentencing phase of a capital murder trial a victim's statement describing the effect of the crime on the victim and the victim's family, or to set forth the opinions of victims and family members. Such evidence, said the Court, "creates a constitutionally unacceptable risk that the jury may impose the death penalty in an arbitrary and capricious manner."[39]

Almost all states now compensate victims and/or have strengthened the laws permitting victims and their families to sue for civil damages.[40] Winning these suits is easier than obtaining convictions. In a civil suit one merely has to prove that the accused "more probably than not" committed the act, not that he or she did so "beyond a reasonable doubt," as in a criminal trial. The problem is that defendants seldom have resources. Even if victims win the right to collect damages from the defendants, they often cannot do so. As a result, under the stimulus of federal matching funds, most states now provide a victims' compensation program. Thirty states and Congress have also adopted "Son of Sam laws" (named after multiple murderer David Berkowitz) that take from convicted criminals any financial proceeds they might earn from selling the rights to their stories and make these funds available to cover restitution for victims.

PLEA BARGAINING

A common practice is for the prosecution to offer to reduce the seriousness of the charge if a defendant will enter a plea of guilty to a particular crime. In many places "between 95 and 99 percent of felony convictions are by plea."[41] At one time this practice was universally condemned. Many people still believe there is something "dirty" about it, like bartering away justice, and that it does lead to "condemnation without adjudication."[42]

Critics argue that plea bargaining forces people to give up their rights; moreover, defendants often do not get off much more leniently for pleading guilty to lesser offenses than if they stood trial.[43] Defenders of plea bargaining argue that it works. It produces, they argue, "a result approximating closely, but informally and more swiftly, the results which ought to ensue from a trial, while avoiding most of the undesirable aspects of that ordeal."[44] Many—but not all—of the several commissions of experts and investigators who have recently looked into the matter have endorsed plea bargaining.

Plea bargaining offers something to all those involved. Prosecutors are able to dispose of cases quickly, avoid long, drawn-out trials, eliminate the risk of losing cases, and build up better "election-worthy" conviction records. The accused, by pleading guilty to lesser offenses, avoid the danger of being sentenced for more serious charges. Defense attorneys avoid "the dilemma of either incurring the expense of going to trial with a losing case or appearing to provide no service whatever to their clients."[45] By being able to handle more clients, they can also make more money. Judges are able to dispose of cases on their dockets more easily.

Once the bargain between the prosecutor and the defendant's attorney has been accepted, the matter is taken before a judge. The judge goes through a series of questions to the defendant: "Are you pleading guilty because you are guilty? Are you aware of the maximum sentence for the crime to which you are entering a guilty plea? Were you coerced into pleading guilty or offered anything in return for it? Are you satisfied with the representation afforded by your attorney? The appropriate response must be given . . . and then the plea is accepted."[46] As long as the defendants know what they are doing and enter into the bargain intelligently, by pleading guilty they waive their constitutional rights to trial and may not subsequently back out of the arrangement. Prosecutors also must live up to their side of the bargain.[47] The Supreme Court has upheld plea bargaining several times.

SENTENCING

Because police and prosecutors screen out a large proportion of the doubtful cases, most left to be dealt with by the courts are those in which there is no serious dispute over the guilt or innocence of the defendant. . . . This fact sets the tone for the process. . . . Everyone concerned—the defense lawyer, the prosecutor, the judge, the probation officer—becomes aware of the fact that he or she is involved in a process where the primary focus is on deciding what to do with the people who are in fact guilty.[48]

Early in our national history, retribution, deterrence, and protection of society were the primary purposes of sentencing. Then rehabilitation became the major goal, and many thought it was the more humane approach. The indefinite sentence became popular, motivated by the idea that each prisoner should be considered an individual suffering from an "illness." Each prisoner should be diagnosed; a course of treatment should be prescribed; and if and when a "cure" is certified by such experts as psychologists and social workers, the prisoner should be released.

Recently most political leaders and many scholars have become disillusioned about our ability to effect "cures." (Others are also disillusioned about the deterrent effect of imprisonment.[49]) A comprehensive study of rehabilitative efforts inside prisons, although rejecting the conclusion that "nothing works," nonetheless stated: "We do not know of any program or method of rehabilitation that could be guaranteed to reduce the criminal activity of released offenders."[50]

This disillusionment with rehabilitation, combined with growing concerns about "crime in the streets" and mounting criticism about alleged judicial leniency, has fueled legislative action for mandatory minimum sentencing requirements and for narrowing judicial discretion.[51] State after state has adopted mandatory prison-term statutes for more and more crimes.

Judicial discretion remains broad, however. Penal codes do not set very specific terms of punishment. Different judges issue different sentences to defendants convicted of the same crime.[52] To reduce such disparities, several reforms have been suggested: establish more precise legislative standards; create advisory sentencing councils; or adopt the British practice of allowing appellate courts to modify sentences.

Due process must be observed in sentencing, which takes place in open court. The prisoner must be present and represented by counsel. In many places, social workers are assigned to help the judge determine the proper sentence. The judge also receives recommendations from the prosecution (and in a few jurisdictions from the victim as well), hears the arguments of the defense, and then sets the sentence within the limits prescribed by the state.

PROBATION AND PRISONS

Today 284,000 guards, probation officials, and parole officers keep custody over more than 1 million persons on probation and over 580,000 people in 800 prisons.

Traditional Justifications for Imprisonment

1. *Retribution.* Society is entitled to punish those who commit crimes, and if the state does not do so, people will be tempted to take the matter into their own hands.

2. *Deterrence.* Putting those who commit crimes in prison warns others and keeps some who might otherwise violate the law from doing so.

3. *Protection of society through incapacitation.* Some persons are so dangerous to the life and property of others that the only thing to do with them is to lock them in prison.

4. *Rehabilitation.* By placing convicted persons in a protected and controlled environment, we can work to rehabilitate them so that they will eventually become law-abiding and productive citizens.

Although the prison population of the United States actually declined during the 1960s, public demands for tougher sentences caused it to climb once again after 1967. It has doubled since 1970 and continues to increase at a rate of 7 percent a year. It costs from $75,000 to $100,000 to build each cell, and on average $23,000 a year must be spent to guard and feed each prisoner.[53]

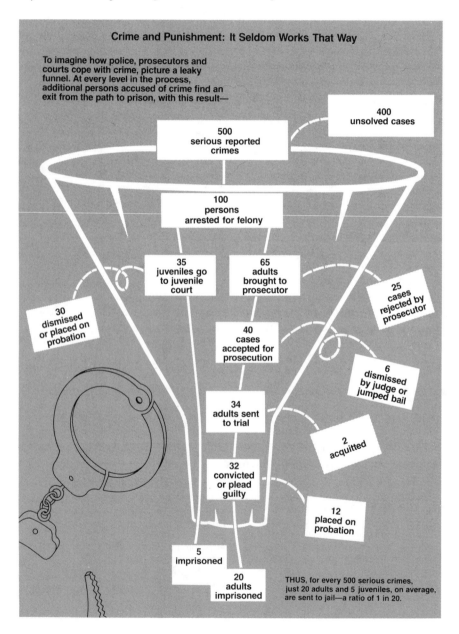

Crime and Punishment: It Seldom Works That Way

To imagine how police, prosecutors and courts cope with crime, picture a leaky funnel. At every level in the process, additional persons accused of crime find an exit from the path to prison, with this result—

400 unsolved cases

500 serious reported crimes

100 persons arrested for felony

35 juveniles go to juvenile court

65 adults brought to prosecutor

25 cases rejected by prosecutor

30 dismissed or placed on probation

40 cases accepted for prosecution

6 dismissed by judge or jumped bail

34 adults sent to trial

2 acquitted

32 convicted or plead guilty

12 placed on probation

5 imprisoned

20 adults imprisoned

THUS, for every 500 serious crimes, just 20 adults and 5 juveniles, on average, are sent to jail—a ratio of 1 in 20.

The increase in the prison population has resulted in serious overcrowding. In forty states conditions are so bad that federal judges have issued orders calling for either immediate improvement or the release of persons being held in situations that violate the Eighth Amendment's prohibition against cruel and unusual punishment.

Prisoners have very little political clout. Even so, because the overcrowding is so severe and the prison population is growing so fast, most states are responding to judicial intervention by spending millions to build new prisons and renovate old ones. The federal Civil Rights of Institutionalized Persons Act (1980) authorizes the Department of Justice to bring suits in behalf of persons being held under conditions that violate the Constitution, and the department has done so.

Relatively few people commit most of the violent crimes in our society. One out of every three persons let out of prison returns in three years. If we could identify these "career criminals" (**recidivists**) and keep them in prison, while at the same time releasing those offenders who are not likely to commit other crimes, we might be able to cut down on the overcrowding in the prisons and better protect the public. The trouble with this "throw-the-career-criminals-in-jail-for-a-long-time" theory is that it is not easy to determine in advance who are career criminals and who are not. For this reason some argue that we should require every criminal convicted of a second offense to stay in prison for five years, and that this practice would cut down the crime rate by 16 percent. To do this, however, would triple the present prison population, and would require billions to build new prisons, and $12 billion more each year to keep the additional prisoners.[54]

The high cost of corrections, in fact, is leading some states to rethink the wisdom of indiscriminate mandatory minimum sentence statutes and to reconsider the need to create for nonviolent offenders such alternatives as halfway houses, intensive probation work release, and other community corrections facilities.[55]

Courts in Crisis

The effectiveness of President Bush's attack on Governor Dukakis in the 1988 presidential campaign for his alleged "softness on crime" reflects the concern expressed by many Americans that "there has been a breakdown in the criminal justice system in America." A United States senator and a former federal prosecutor echoed this view. They charged that because courts are "overwhelmed by the huge volume of cases," "career criminals beat the system," defense attorneys "shop" for judges known for lenient sentences, prosecutors are "blackmailed" into accepting lenient plea bargains, and many career criminals "are given only a few months punishment."[56]

Critics agree that the system is in crisis but disagree on what the crisis is. There are at least two general models for thinking about our criminal justice system.[57] The *crime control model* considers criminals to be "inputs" into the system. If it worked properly, the system would "process" these inputs and produce results. Those who use this model are disturbed when they discover that the several parts of the criminal justice system operate with little relation to one another—that it is a "system" more in word than in fact. They are alarmed that the system is "jammed." The *due process model,* on the other hand, considers police, prosecutors, defense attorneys, judges, and correctional officials to be adversaries. Those who use this model tend to be more worried about an innocent person's being convicted or about the poor and minorities' being unfairly treated than about the system's not working efficiently. That it takes a long time to dispose of cases is of less concern than that the system might not be just.

Summary

1. State and local judges, prosecutors, juries, and correctional officials, along with the police, are key participants in our system for the administration of justice.
2. State and local courts are also important arenas for the making and carrying out of public policy.
3. For many years state and local courts operated with little public attention and not much public concern. Today, both as agencies for the making of public policy and as instruments for the administration of justice, they are the objects of many studies and the recipients of large sums of money. But the problems are difficult, especially because there is no agreement about what the problems are. As in every other field in which actions have important consequences, change is likely to be made incrementally, and it will come about as the result of the push and pull of political pressures.
4. Judges, together with jurors, prosecutors, and correctional officials, make up a loosely interrelated justice system. Many believe that this system is not properly dispensing justice to individual defendants or protecting the public from career criminals.

Further Reading

The American Judicature Society. *Judicature,* the journal of the American Judicature Society, published monthly (Chicago, Illinois).
PHILIP L. DUBOIS. *From Bench to Ballot* (University of Texas Press, 1980).
SUSAN P. FINO. *The Role of State Supreme Courts in the New Judicial Federalism* (Greenwood Press, 1987).
HENRY R. GLICK, *Courts, Politics, and Justice* (McGraw-Hill, 1988).
JOHN GUINTHER, *The Jury in America* (Facts on File Publications, 1988).
HERBERT JACOB. *Justice in America,* 4th ed. (Little, Brown, 1984).
MARY CORNELIA PORTER and G. ALAN TARR, eds. *State Supreme Courts: Policymakers in the Federal System* (Greenwood Press, 1982).
MICHAEL SHERMAN and GORDON HAWKINS. *Imprisonment in America* (University of Chicago Press, 1981).

CHARLES E. SILBERMAN. *Criminal Violence, Criminal Justice* (Random House, 1978).
G. ALAN TARR and MARY CORNELIA ALDIS PORTER. *State Supreme Courts In State and Nation* (Yale University, 1988).

N otes

1. Thomas A. Henderson, Randall Guynes, Carl Baar, and Neal Miller, *The Structural Characteristics of State Judiciaries* (Alexandria, Va.: Institute for Economic and Policy Studies, 1981).

2. Robert F. Williams, "In the Supreme Court's Shadow: Legitimacy of State Rejection of Supreme Court Reasoning and Results," *South Carolina Law Review* (Spring 1984), pp. 353 ff.

3. Hans A. Linde, "Observations of a State Court Judge," Robert A. Katzmann, ed., *Judges and Legislators: Toward Institutional Comity* (The Brookings Institution), 1988, p. 118.

4. Peter J. Galie, "The Other Supreme Courts: Judicial Activism among State Supreme Courts," *Syracuse Law Review*, vol. 33 (1982), pp. 731–93.

5. Elder Witt, "State Supreme Courts: Tilting the Balance Toward Change," *Governing* (August 1988), p. 38.

6. *Ibid.*

7. Herbert Jacob, *Justice in America: Courts, Lawyers, and the Judicial Process*, 4th ed. (Little, Brown, 1984).

8. Edwin Chen, "For Judges, the Stakes Are Rising," *Los Angeles Times* (March 4, 1988), p. 1.

9. Philip L. Dubois, "State Trial Court Appointments: Does the Governor Make a Difference?" *Judicature* (June–July 1985), pp. 20–21.

10. J. W. Peltason, *The Missouri Plan for the Selection of Judges* (University of Missouri Studies, 1945).

11. William K. Hall and Larry T. Aspin, "What Twenty Years of Judicial Retention Elections Have Told Us," *Judicature*, vol. 70, no. 6 (April–May, 1987), pp. 340–47; Susan B. Caron and Larry C. Berkson, *Judicial Retention Elections in the United States* (American Judicature Society, 1980).

12. Anne Rankin Mahoney, "Citizen Evaluation of Judicial Performance: The Colorado Experience," *Judicature*, vol. 72 (December–January 1989), p. 212.

13. Robert D. Raven, "Does the Bar Have an Obligation to Help Ensure the Independence of the Judiciary?" *Judicature* (August–September 1985), p. 67.

14. John T. Wold and John H. Culver, "The defeat of the California justices: the campaign, the electorate, and the issue of judicial accountability," *Judicature*, vol 70, no. 7 (April–May 1987), pp. 324–39.

15. Jon R. Waltz, "Some Firsthand Observations on the Election of Judges," *Judicature* (October 1979), pp. 186–87.

16. G. Alan Tarr and Mary Cornelia Aldis Porter, *State Supreme Courts in State and Nation*, (Yale University Press, 1988), p. 170.

17. Peter Applebome, "Rubber Stamp Is Gone In Texas Judicial Elections," *The New York Times* (October 21, 1988), p. B12; Anthony Champagne, "Judicial Reform in Texas," *Judicature*, vol. 72 (October–November 1988), pp. 146–68.

18. Paul M. Barrett, "Campaign Practices in Judges' Elections Spark Drive for Merit Appointments in Pennsylvania," *The Wall Street Journal* (December 9, 1988), p. A16.

19. Philip L. Dubois, *From Ballot to Bench: Judicial Elections and the Question for Accountability* (University of Texas Press, 1980), pp. 27–28.

20. Sheldon Goldman, "Judicial Selection and the Qualities of a 'Good Judge,' " *Annals* (July 1982), pp. 113–14.

21. Mary L. Volcansek, "The Effects of Judicial Selection Reform: What We Know and What We Do Not," in Philip L. Dubois, ed., *The Analysis of Judicial Reform* (Lexington, 1982), pp. 78–79.

22. Stuart S. Nagel, *Comparing Elected and Appointed Judicial Systems* (Sage Publications, 1973), p. 36; Susan P. Fino, *The Role of State Supreme Courts in the New Judicial Federalism* (Greenwood Press, 1987), p. 114.

23. John H. Culver, "Politics and the California Plan for Choosing Appellate Judges," *Judicature* (September–October, 1982), p. 158;

Henry R. Glick and Craig F. Emmert, "Selection Systems and Judicial Characteristics: The Recruitment of State Supreme Court Judges," *Judicature*, vol. 70, no. 4 (December–January 1987), p. 235.

24. Glick and Emmert, "Selection Systems," p. 235.

25. From Glick and Emmert, Ibid. p. 230, summarizing Henry et al., *The Success of Women and Minorities in Achieving Judicial Office: The Selection Process* (New York: Fund for Modern Courts, Inc., 1985).

26. Richard A. Watson and Rondal G. Downing, *The Politics of the Bench and the Bar: Judicial Selection under the Missouri Nonpartisan Court Plan* (Wiley, 1969), p. 353.

27. See Sheldon Goldman, "Voting Behavior on the U.S. Courts of Appeals Revised," *American Political Science Review* (June 1975), pp. 491–506, for a review of articles on the relationship between partisanship and judicial behavior.

28. Jolanta Juskiewicz Peristein and Nathan Goldman, "Judicial Disciplinary Commissions: A New Approach to the Discipline and Removal of State Judges," in Dubois, *The Analysis of Judicial Reform*, pp. 93–106.

29. Tarr and Porter, *State Supreme Courts*, p. 61.

30. Beverly Blair Cook, "Women Judges in the Opportunity Structure," in Laura L. Crites and Winfred L. Hepperle, *Women, The Courts and Equality* (Sage Publications, 1987), pp. 143–71.

31. Geoff Gallas, "Court Reform: Has It Been Built on an Adequate Foundation?" *Judicature* (June–July 1979), pp. 29–30; Raymond T. Nimmer, *The Nature of System Change: Reform Impact in the Criminal Courts* (American Bar Foundation, 1978).

32. John Guinther, *The Jury in America* (Facts on File Publications, 1988).

33. *Burch* v. *Louisiana*, 441 U.S. 130 (1979); *Ballew* v. *Georgia*, 435 US. 223 (1978). See Reid Hastie, Steven D. Penrod, and Nancy Pennington, *Inside the Jury* (Harvard University Press, 1983), for a study showing that nonunanimous verdicts are more likely to bring in convictions than those requiring unanimity. (Federal courts often use juries of less than twelve for civil cases, but for federal criminal trials the Court still requires both the common-law jury of twelve and unanimous verdicts.)

34. Robert H. Jackson, *Journal of the American Judicature Society* (1940), p. 28, quoted by Jack M. Kress, "Progress and Prosecution," *The Annals* (January 1976), p. 100.

35. Kress, "Progress and Prosecution," p. 109.

36. Charles E. Silberman, *Criminal Violence,*

Criminal Justice (Random House, 1978), p. 303.

37. Ibid.

38. Ibid., p. 218.

39. *Both* v. *Maryland*, 482 U.S. 496 (1987).

40. Robert Elias, *Victims of the System: Crime Victims and Compensation in American Politics and Criminal Justice* (Transaction Books, 1983); John R. Anderson and Paul L. Woodward, "Victim and Witness Assistance; New State Laws and the System's Response," *Judicature* (December–January 1985), p. 221; Peter Finn, "Collaboration between the Judiciary and Victim-Witness Assistance Programs," *Judicature* (December–January 1986), p. 192.

41. John H. Langbein, "Torture and Plea Bargaining," *The Public Interest* (Winter 1980), p. 48. See also Malcolm M. Feeley, *The Process Is the Punishment* (Russell Sage, 1979).

42. Langbein, "Torture and Plea Bargaining," p. 51.

43. Thomas M. Uhlman and N. Darlene Walker, "A Plea Is No Bargain: The Impact of Case Disposition on Sentencing," *Social Science Quarterly* (September 1979), pp. 218–34.

44. Thomas Church, Jr., "Plea Bargains, Concessions and the Courts: Analysis of a Quasi-Experiment," *Law and Society Review* (Spring 1976), p. 400. For a contrary view see National Advisory Commission on Criminal Justice Standards and Goals, *Report of the Task Force* (U.S. Government Printing Office, 1979).

45. Church, "Plea Bargains, Concessions and the Courts," p. 400.

46. Jonathan D. Casper, *American Criminal Justice: The Defendant's Perspective* (Prentice Hall, 1972), pp. 52–53. Abraham S. Goldstein, *The Passive Judiciary: Prosecutorial Discretion and the Guilty Plea* (Louisiana State University Press, 1981) is critical of judges for not supervising plea bargains more actively.

47. *Santobello* v. *New York*, 404 U.S. 257 (1971).

48. Edward Barrett, "The Adversary Proceeding and the Judicial Process," lectures to the National College of State Trial Judges, quoted in Lynn M. Mather, "Some Determinants of the Method of Case Disposition: Decision-Making by Public Defenders in Los Angeles," *Law and Society Review* 12 (Winter 1974), pp. 187–88.

49. Henry N. Pontell, *A Capacity to Punish* (Indiana University Press, 1985).

50. Lee Sechrest, Susan O. White, and Elizabeth D. Brown, eds., *The Rehabilitation of Criminal Offenders: Problems and Prospects,* Panel on Research on Rehabilitative Techniques of the

National Research Council (Washington, D.C.: National Academy of Sciences, 1979), pp. 3–6.

51. William B. Eldridge, "Shifting Views of the Sentencing Functions," *The Annals* (July 1982), pp. 104–11.

52. John Hagan and Kristin Bumiler, "Making Sense of Sentencing: A Review and Critique of Sentencing Research," in A. Bernstein, J. Cohen, S. Martin, and M. Tonry, eds. *Research on Sentencing*, vol. 2 (National Academy Press, 1983); Susan Welch, Michael Combs, John Gruhl, "Do Black Judges Make a Difference?", *American Journal of Political Science* (February 1988), pp. 126–35.

53. Gail S. Funke, "How Much Justice Can States Afford?" *State Legislatures* (July 1984), pp. 26–27.

54. Edna McConnell Clark Foundation, *Time to Build? The Realities of Prison Construction* (New York, 1985).

55. Barbara Fink, "Opening the Door on Community Corrections," *State Legislatures* (September 1984), pp. 24f.

56. Arlan Specter and Paul R. Michel, "The Need for a New Federalism in Criminal Justice," *The Annals* (July 1982), pp. 67–69.

57. Herbert Packer, "Two Models of the Criminal Process," *University of Pennsylvania Law Review* (November 1964), pp. 1–60.

7

Government at the Grass Roots

There are more than 83,000 units of local government in the United States (about 82,000 too many, some people feel). Illinois alone has over 6400; Pennsylvania has over 5300; Texas has nearly 4200; Rhode Island has 125, and Hawaii only 19. The average number of units per state is around 1600 (see Table 7–1). Counties, cities, school districts, townships, water control districts, park districts—all are crowded together and piled on top of one another. The Chicago metropolitan area alone has about 1000 units of local government. Average citizens live under five or six layers of government. They pay taxes to all of them—federal, state, county, municipal, and others—and they are supposed to help select all of their leaders.

Why do we have such a patchwork? The basic pattern was imported from England, as were so many of our governmental forms. As the years passed, new governments were created to take on new jobs when the existing units were too small or were not up to the task. Also, people kept moving to, or at least near, the large cities, and urbanization began to take hold. Decades of compromise and struggle among conflicting groups have given us our present system. It creaks and groans. It costs a lot of money. It is inefficient. But it is very much with us.

Local governments vary in their structure, size, power, and relation to one another. But in a constitutional sense they are all the same because they all live on power "borrowed" from states. The states are basically unitary governments; constitutionally, all power is vested in the state governments, and local units exist only as agents of the states and only exercise power expressly given to them by their respective state governments.

TABLE 7–1
Number of Governments in the United States

TYPE OF GOVERNMENT	1987	1982	1977	1972
Total	83,217	81,831	79,913	78,269
U.S. government	1	1	1	1
State governments	50	50	50	50
Local governments	83,166	81,780	79,862	78,218
County	3,042	3,041	3,042	3,044
Municipal	19,205	19,076	18,862	18,517
Township	16,691	16,734	16,822	16,991
School district	14,741	14,851	15,174	15,781
Special district	29,487	25,078	25,962	23,885

"Little Federalism": State-Local Relations

How does the *unitary* nature of state-local relations contrast with the *federal* nature of nation-state relations? The slicing up of governmental power among the various local units and the state government leads to many of the same problems we noted in the chapter on federalism. There is the same conflict between groups that want the state to do something and groups that fear an invasion of local rights. There is the same difficulty of constantly adjusting functions among the various units of government as economic and social conditions change. And there are the same disputes over whether a local majority or a statewide majority is to have its way. Yet there is also a crucial difference.

In the beginning, state legislatures were given almost unlimited constitutional authority over local governments, and they ran them pretty much as they wished. They granted, amended, and repealed city charters, established counties, determined city and county structure, set debt limits, and passed laws for the local units. But by the end of the nineteenth century, many state constitutions had been amended to forbid their legislatures to pass laws dealing with particular local governments. In place of legislative enactments, constitutional provisions determined the structure, and in some cases, even the process of local governments.

Because local governments are created by the state legislatures and have no constitutional authority in their own right, there are fewer obstacles blocking state interference in local matters than there are in national-state relations. State officers participate in local government to a much greater extent than federal officers do in state politics. When doubt has arisen about the authority of local governments, the courts have generally decided against them.

As in so many areas of politics, the difference between state-local and nation-state relations is one of degree rather than of kind. Moreover, during the past several decades home-rule amendments have been added to about half the state constitutions. These amendments authorize many cities and some counties to run their own affairs, and they limit the power of state officials to interfere. Thus, **constitutional home rule** in a small way introduces the federal principle into *state* constitutions.

The hedging in of the legislature's power did not end the enormous state influence over local governments. While the legislature's authority was being curtailed, the power of state administrative officials was being expanded. Problems once thought to be local came to be viewed as statewide. Many local governments lacked the money to do essential jobs. They could not afford specialists, and their administrative standards were notoriously low. Sometimes the states just took over a job previously handled by local people; sometimes the states offered local governments financial assistance, with certain strings attached. Gradually state officials were given more and more authority to supervise local officials. This tendency became especially evident in law enforcement, finance, health, highways, welfare, and election procedures.

The extent of state control over local units varies from state to state and, within each state, among the different kinds of local government. At one extreme, local officials merely have to file reports with specified state officials. At the other extreme, some state officials have the authority to appoint and remove some local officials, and thus exert considerable control over local affairs.

At present we are witnessing an acceleration of state grants of general authority to counties and cities, or what is known as **legislative home rule.** In Alaska, Montana, and Pennsylvania, general grants have been made to nearly all local jurisdictions.

Trends affecting state-local relations over the past twenty years can be summarized as follows:

States have lessened constraints and broadened authority of county and city governments.

Counties in particular have acquired more authority.

States have encouraged the reform of state and local fiscal systems, and many states have allowed local governments broader taxing authority.

State reforms in school finance have reduced fiscal disparities among school districts in their states.

Local governments have become more dependent on state and federal aid.

Most states have established state departments of community affairs or state-local relations commissions to increase consultation between state and local governments.[1]

Above all, state officials have generally acted as though they are genuinely conscious of local problems and have been performing more responsibly toward county and city governments. This heightened concern is acknowledged by such local officials as city managers, who regularly have to work with both state and federal officials. As we noted in our discussion of federalism, in recent years the direct ties between national and local officials, especially in the larger urban areas— ties that often ally them against state officials—have been weakened as the result of severe cutbacks in federal assistance. Many, or even most, city managers today report better working relations with state than with federal officials.[2]

Government by the People—County Style

Counties are usually the largest jurisdiction within a state, yet they are often over-looked, forgotten, or invisible. Only a few counties are more well known than the major cities or local municipalities that compose them. Thus Westchester County, New York; Montgomery County, Maryland; Bucks County, Pennsylvania; Marin County in northern California; and Orange County in southern California are nationally known, prominent jurisdictions. Of course, Dade County, Florida, which includes Miami, and Cook County, Illinois, which includes Chicago, are also celebrity counties. Most people don't know it, but some cities, such as Denver, Philadelphia, and San Francisco, are simultaneously cities and counties.

Until recently, counties in many states acted almost exclusively as functionaries for the state government, performing various state-mandated duties for the cities, towns, and residents within their borders. Counties were convenient subdivisions; they spent most of their time merely carrying out policies established elsewhere.

For those who live outside the city, the county and township (in Louisiana, the parish; in New England, the town) are the important units of local government. Although cities are not alternatives to county governments, but rather are additional layers, city people tend to look to City Hall as the place where community affairs are managed. Where there is no city hall, the county courthouse is often the center of politics.

States are divided into counties, although in Louisiana they are called parishes, and in Alaska boroughs. With a few exceptions (such as Connecticut and Rhode Island, where counties have lost their governmental function), county governments exist everywhere in the United States. There are more than 3000, and they vary in size, population, and functions. Loving County, Texas, for example, has less than 200 inhabitants, whereas Los Angeles County, California, has about $8\frac{1}{2}$ million.

There are two major types of counties: large urban ones like Los Angeles County, Cook County (Illinois), and Dade County (Florida) and nearly 2400 rural ones. The urban counties have many of the same structures as their rural counter-parts, but they are more intertwined with the problems of the urban centers. Our discussion centers primarily on county governments outside the large urban centers.

County governments are least active in New England states where the county is little more than a judicial district; county officials do a little road building, but not much else. Elsewhere the traditional functions of counties are law enforcement,

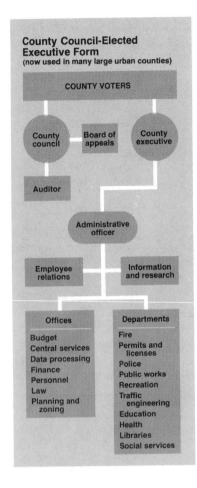

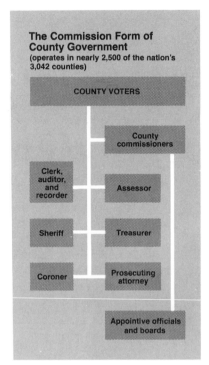

highway construction and maintenance, tax collection and property assessment, recording of legal papers, and welfare.

Despite the perception that the counties are dying governments, they have within recent years taken on more jobs than they have lost. Counties in a few states have given up some of their responsibilities, but in most other states, especially in the South, they are taking over from the states such urban functions as transportation, water and sewer operation, and land-use planning. Elsewhere certain cities are contracting with counties to provide such joint services as personnel training, law enforcement, and correction. Although Americans continue to move to the suburbs and rural areas beyond the city's border, they still want the services to which they have grown accustomed. More and more they expect the urban or suburban counties to provide urban functions and to secure a share of federal funds to support these functions.

COUNTY GOVERNMENT

How are counties organized to do their jobs? Counties, even more than municipalities, exist to enforce state laws and to serve as administrative units of state government. In general, most counties have little legislative power. The typical county has a group of officials who act in some fashion as the central governing body. These groups of officials comprise public agencies with various titles, but most frequently they are called a board of commissioners or supervisors. They vary in size from one to more than fifty members, yet the majority of boards have from three to seven members. They administer state laws, levy taxes, appropriate money, issue bonds, sign contracts on behalf of the county, and handle whatever jobs the state laws and constitution assign to them. In recent years, however, many states, in response to the growing awareness that many problems such as waste-disposal and transportation cannot be solved except on a regional basis, are beginning to give county-wide agencies major policy-making responsibilities.

County boards, as we shall call these agencies, are of two types. The larger boards are usually composed of township supervisors or other township officials; the smaller boards are usually, but not always, elected from the county at-large. At-large elections are being increasingly attacked for making it difficult for minorities to be elected to office. Minorities, especially when they live in large numbers in one or two sections of a county, can usually win more seats if there is a district rather than an at-large election system. County board members are often key political leaders, and in some states they control local affairs through their power over state patronage. They are much more important than a mere listing of their formal powers might suggest. Solving road problems and granting contracts to road contractors are frequently the major business conducted at board meetings.

The county board shares its powers with a number of other officials, most commonly the sheriff, the prosecutor or district attorney, the county clerk, the coroner, and the auditor. These are generally elected officials. Sometimes county treasurers, health officers, and surveyors are also found on the ballot. In general, counties are administered by an unwieldy collection of relatively independent agencies, and until recently there was seldom a single administrator or executive responsible for coordinating activities. However, today over 500 counties appoint a chief administrative officer who serves at the pleasure of the county commissioners. Approximately sixty relatively large counties now elect a county executive who is granted power over most administrative functions.

WHAT DO COUNTY OFFICIALS DO?

Sheriff Except in Rhode Island, where they are appointed by the governor, sheriffs are elected by the people of the county, usually for a four-year term. They are charged with enforcing the law and running the county jail. In addition, they are the officers of the county court. In some metropolitan counties in the North, and in rural counties in the South, sheriffs are active as law enforcement officers. But in most counties they let the city police do the job within the cities and the state police take charge in the rural areas. In some of the rural areas, however, the sheriff and deputies are the only ones to keep law and order. If sheriffs encounter serious trouble, they can summon local citizens to come to their assistance.

Prosecutor   The prosecuting attorney—sometimes known as county attorney, state's attorney, or district attorney—is commonly elected by voters of the county. Prosecutors, as discussed in the previous chapter, aid the grand jury in preparing indictments, and in some states they bring persons to trial by what is known as "information." They prosecute state law violators and represent the state and county in civil suits. Their discretion is wide, and they are often the sole decision makers about whether or not to prosecute in a particular case. The job is especially attractive to young lawyers, as it often serves as a steppingstone to a higher political office.

County Clerk   The office of county clerk exists in about half the states. In other states the *clerk of the court* often performs this job. The county clerk is secretary to the county board and has such miscellaneous duties as supervision of elections; issuance of hunting, fishing, and marriage licenses; and the granting of permits for the operation of amusement establishments outside city limits.

Who Governs at the County Level?   County governments are not always as headless as they might appear. As in all local jurisdictions, there is a politically active tier of county employees, those who hold elective office, and those who regularly lobby or do business with county officials. In some rural areas a "courthouse gang" can still be found. This may be an informal group who occasionally have breakfast or lunch together or who are members of the local Rotary or Kiwanis Club and regularly attend and run such civic events as the county fair or rodeo, Fourth of July and Memorial Day observances, and so on. The makeup of these networks varies from county to county, yet among their members are often a few of the county commissioners, the county executive, the local publisher, local lawyers involved in criminal and probate work, road contractors, a few developers, representatives of the home builders and real estate interests, and party and political officials who know how the system works and how things get done.

Some urban and suburban counties (of which there are an increasing number) still have political machines, often dominated by one political party. Democrats, for example, still control Cook County, Chicago, and the sprawling borough of Queens in New York, while Republicans are very much in control in Nassau County, Long Island, in suburban New York. These areas offer considerable patronage to those who win office; indeed, as investigations of the New York area have discovered, illegal kickbacks to party and elected officials are not uncommon.

The county is also an electoral district, and members of the state legislature are often graduates of county courthouse politics. Effective county politicians often run for higher office. U.S. Senator Alphonse D'Amato of New York served as a county executive in Nassau County before winning his senate seat. County executives in New Jersey, New York, and Michigan have recently run for governor. Moreover, the local chairperson of the Democratic or Republican county political organization may be a major influence on county and state politics.

In the recent past, a member of the courthouse elite was often recognized as the county boss, or simply as the boss around the county seat. This is less true today, yet there are people who can influence county decisions on certain issues; for example, the editor or owner of the local paper or television station, the president of the chamber of commerce or economic development board, the president of a local bank, the executive director of the farm bureau, or the leader of a union or civic organization. Occasionally, certain county officials—sometimes the presiding officer of the county board or commission—are recognized as having considerable political influence over what issues are discussed.

In general, however, the same types of interest and civic groups that organize to influence state legislatures and city halls can also be found in and around county governments. Politics may be less publicized at the county level, but if some nuclear waste site or community college controversy erupts, we suddenly see who are in positions of power and influence in the nation's counties. Even though they are frequently our least visible layer of government, counties are vitally important. After all, it is county governments that are embroiled in highly political decisions about who gets what, when, and at what price.

COUNTY PERFORMANCE

How well do counties do their job? It's a mixed picture. First, there are too many of them. It is not uncommon to have a county of 500,000 people with neighboring counties of 50,000 or even 20,000. When counties were first organized, the idea was to provide a county seat within a day's journey of everyone in that county. Farm families could pile into their wagons and head for the courthouse. While the farmers were attending to business, their families could shop and pick up the local gossip. And they could all get home in time to do the evening chores. Today, of course, a farmer can drive across a whole state in a day.

Second, the small area and population of many counties inevitably lead to inefficiency. Study after study has shown that money could be saved and services improved by consolidating counties. Although there is much talk about such action, few consolidations have taken place. County residents in rural America take pride in their counties and do not like to see them lose their identities. Officeholders, their families, and their friends do not want county jobs to disappear. Businesses at the county seat depend on officers, employees, and persons drawn to the city for much of their patronage.

Finally, although counties have often been the forgotten stepchildren of the state, their jurisdictional boundaries give them great potential for solving complex problems that are impossible to solve at the city level. In more and more states this fact is being recognized. Counties, once thought to be a dying level of government, are now thought to be well suited for policy and administrative leadership.[3]

The American City

Although several cities existed when the U.S. Constitution was written, the nation in 1787 was overwhelmingly rural, and seven out of ten people worked on farms. People clustered together, if at all, mainly in villages or small towns scattered throughout the thirteen states and neighboring territories. All this has changed; we are now a nation of over 19,000 cities, and although some cities have just a few hundred people, others have millions. Three of our supercities have populations larger than the total population of the Republic in the 1780s.

The villages and cities of the 1760s and 1770s were the indispensable workshops of democracy, the places where democratic skills were developed, where grand issues were debated, and, above all, where the people resolved their commitment to fight the British to secure our fundamental rights.

What does the word *city* call to mind? Bright lights, crowded streets, museums, slums, skyscrapers, and lots of people. To some of us the city may be Main Street, Courthouse Square, the old cannon down by the harbor or riverfront, and farm families shopping and talking on Saturdays. A city is not merely improved real estate. It is also people: men and women living and working together. Aristotle observed that people came together in the cities for security but they stayed there for the good life. The "good life" is defined differently by different people, yet it often includes these attractions:

Employment opportunities
Cultural centers, museums, performing arts centers, theatres
Diverse educational institutions
Entertainment and night life
Professional sports teams
Good restaurants
Diversity of people and lifestyles

Each city has two major functions. One is to provide government within its boundaries so that its citizens may maintain law and order, keep streets clean, educate children, purify water, create parks, and in other ways make the area a good place in which to live. Yet the city has a second function; as an instrument of the state, it carries out state functions. It is distinguished from a county in the greater amount of discretion given to local officials and the greater emphasis placed on local functions. A county is supposed to operate primarily as an administrative unit of the state. The distinction, of course, is one of emphasis.

Each city has its own *charter*. The charter is to the city what a constitution is to the national or the state government. It is not necessarily a single document, however; a city's charter outlines the structure of the government, sets the authority of the various officials, and provides for their selection.

LOCAL HOME RULE

European cities can do anything that is not expressly forbidden; American cities have only those powers expressly conferred on them. State legislatures still exercise a great deal of control over city affairs. In addition to drawing up charters for the cities, the legislature allots functions to local officials and withdraws them at will. In case of a conflict between a state and a local law, state law is almost always enforced.

About forty states have some form of home rule provision for their cities and towns. Some states have **legislative home rule** whereby the state legislature delegates authority over certain subjects so that the cities do not have to ask permission to deal with them. In about half the states, however, *the constitution*, not the state legislature, delegates to citizens of certain-sized cities (a few extend the power to all municipalities) authority that they may exercise *without the concurrence of the state legislature*. These are the *home rule states*. The people of the city may elect a group of citizens to draw up a charter. After the charter has been approved by local voters (in some states it must also be approved by the legislature or the governor, or both, to ensure that it will not conflict with the constitution), it becomes the city's basic instrument of government and may be amended by local citizens. Further, home rule cities have the general power to dispose of matters of local concern without special authorization from the legislature. Most cities of over 200,000 people, and about 40 percent of cities of 5000 or more, have some measure of home rule.

The independence from state legislature control of home rule cities, especially the smaller and medium-sized ones, should not be exaggerated.[4] These cities have some freedom in determining the general structure of their city governments, but home rule often only slightly increases their substantive powers. For when all is said and done, the state legislature and the governor often control most of the assets and much of the political clout. Still, some cities, such as those in Michigan, Texas, Connecticut, and North Carolina, have acquired significant substantive powers from home rule provisions.

Is home rule worth the struggle? Despite the small increase in local autonomy, and despite the fact that constitutional home rule introduces an element of rigidity into state-local relations and enhances the authority of state judges (who often have to determine which laws prevail), most reform groups favor it. It frees the legislature from having to deal with some local matters. It permits administrative flexibility (depending on how the flexibility is used and what side you are on, this may be desirable or undesirable). Perhaps home rule's chief importance is symbolic. Still, the symbol may have the effect of discouraging state legislatures from interfering in local affairs and of encouraging greater responsibility at the grass-roots level of government. It also gives the voters of a particular city the power to decide for themselves the general structure of their municipal government.[5]

FORMS OF CITY CHARTERS

Although formal charters are good sources of information for learning how the people in our 19,000 cities govern and are governed, city charters can be misleading. The actual constitutions—in the sense of the rules by which our cities are governed, in contrast to their legal charters—vary from the narrowest rule by the few to the widest participation by the many. Note that the varying structures are not neutral in their impact. The different forms encourage different kinds of participation and responsiveness. In short, power and clout and who gets what, where, and how, can definitely be shaped, in part, by a city's structural arrangements.

The Mayor-Council Charter The **mayor-council charter** is the oldest and most popular charter in the smallest and largest of cities. Under this type of charter the city council is usually a single chamber. The size of the council varies: a few have only two members, and some have as many as fifty. Seven members is the median size in cities with over 5000 people. Many methods are used to select the council members: nonpartisan and partisan elections, elections by small wards and large wards, or elections from the city at large. It is not uncommon for special local parties to participate in local elections, for example, the Citizens party, the Taxpayers party, and so on. How council members are chosen is an important factor in determining how power is distributed in a city. Large cities that elect members in partisan elections generally choose them by small districts

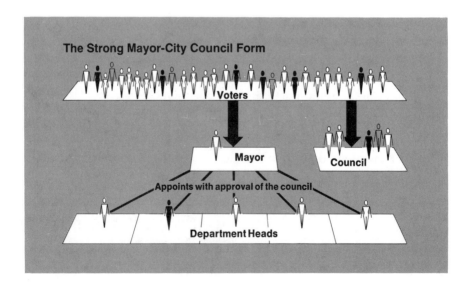

or wards rather than at-large. This combination tends to support strong party organizations. Nonpartisan at-large elections make party organization difficult. The larger the election districts, the more likely citywide considerations will be brought to bear in the selection of council members, and the greater the influence of citywide institutions such as the local newspapers.

The difference between at-large or large-district elections and elections based on small, single-member districts can be significant in terms of what racial and ethnic groups a city wants to have represented on its city council. Does it want the city's elite, white and black, to be on the council; or does it want the poor blacks, browns, or underclass as well as the middle class? From the standpoint of the poor and disinherited, the at-large system and the small council are of little help. The single-member district or ward system permits minorities a better chance for representation.[6]

Under the Voting Rights Act of 1965, the United States attorney general may keep a Southern city, subject to the limitations of the act, from adopting the at-large system if the effect will be to dilute the voting strength of blacks. But what of cities or counties that have long had such systems? Can they be forced to give them up because such elections ensure that blacks are never elected? The mere fact that no black is elected does not by itself establish a violation of the Fourteenth or Fifteenth Amendment. The Constitution forbids only practices adopted or maintained with the purposeful intent to discriminate.

When Congress debated the extension of the Voting Rights Act in 1982, civil rights advocates urged it to outlaw at-large systems in areas covered by the act. They contended it is impossible to show a discriminatory purpose. After all, not many city officials are so foolish as to admit that they favor the at-large system just to keep blacks from being elected. Others said cities should be free to adopt whatever election system they wished; after all, the Constitution guarantees that no person will be denied the right to vote because of race, not that those of your own race will win the election. But Congress, after specifically stating that the Act does not require proportional representation, said the following: In trying to determine whether or not an election procedure—including an at-large system— violates the Civil Rights Act, federal judges should look into the totality of the circumstances, including the results.

Moreover, the Supreme Court has made it easier to establish that at-large systems violate both the Constitution and the Voting Rights Act. Discriminatory intent need not be proved by direct evidence. Such intent may be inferred from the fact that (1) a city or county has had a past history of discrimination designed to keep blacks from voting; (2) blacks make up a large majority of the population; and (3) no black has ever been elected to office under an at-large system.[7]

The powers of the mayor vary from charter to charter (and even more widely from city to city and mayor to mayor). There are, however, two basic variations of the mayor-council form: **strong mayor-council** and **weak mayor-council.** Under the strong mayor-council form, the mayor is elected directly by the people and given fairly broad appointment powers. The mayor, often with the help of his or her own staff, prepares and administers the budget, enjoys almost total administrative authority, and has the power to appoint and dismiss department heads. The system obviously calls for a mayor to be both a good political leader and an effective administrator, traits not always found in the same person.

In weak mayor-council cities, mayors are often elected from among the membership of the elected city council, and not directly by the people, except insofar as they have first been elected to the council. The mayor's appointive powers are usually restricted, and the city council as a whole generally possesses the legislative and executive authority. The mayor in the weak mayor-council form must usually obtain the council's consent in all major administrative decisions. Often, weak mayor-council cities permit direct election by the voters of a number of department heads, such as police chief or controller. In weak mayor-council cities, no single administrative head exists for the city, and power is fragmented. The weak mayor-council plan was designed for an earlier era, when cities were smaller and government simpler. It is especially ill suited for large cities where political and administrative leadership is vital. Nineteenth-century political machines evolved under the weak mayor-council structure because its lack of administrative centralization was an open invitation for external direction.[8]

Tracing the office of mayor over the years and through various charters, we find a general trend toward an increase in mayoral authority. Like the presidency and the governorship, the office of mayor has grown in importance. Most cities have altered their charters in order to give their mayors power to appoint and remove heads of departments and investigate their activities, send legislative messages to the city councils, prepare the budgets, and veto council ordinances. In other words, the mayors have been given a share in policy making, and city administration has been centralized under the mayors' directions.

Many people believe the strong mayor-council system is the best form of government for large cities because it gives the cities strong political leaders and makes efficient administration possible. Further, by centering authority in the hands of a few individuals, it makes less likely the growth of "invisible government" by people who have power but are not publicly accountable for its use.

The Commission Charter In 1900 the city of Galveston, Texas, was flooded by storm-driven tides. Over 6000 people lost their lives, and property worth millions was destroyed. When the mayor and aldermen were incapable of action in the emergency, power fell into the hands of a group of businesspeople who had been discussing methods of improving the harbor. After studying the charters of several cities, they went to the legislature with what was then a somewhat novel proposal for a new charter. They asked that control of the city be vested in five commissioners. The legislature approved.

The idea of placing all governmental powers in the hands of five people flew in the face of the traditional doctrine of separation of powers. Many thought it was too dangerous to give a small group control over both administration and

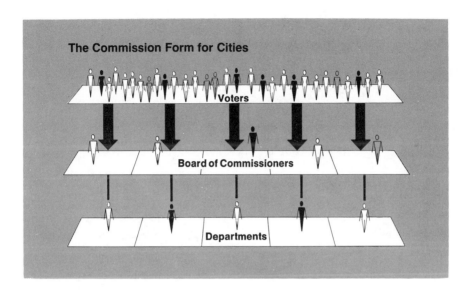

The Commission Form for Cities

Voters

Board of Commissioners

Departments

legislation. For this reason, another charter system known as the Des Moines Plan, included the **initiative, referendum, recall,** and nonpartisan ballots for primaries and elections. The plan became popular, and by 1917 over 500 cities were governed this way. Since that time the number has declined, although Portland, Tulsa, Mobile, and about 100 other cities with populations over 10,000 still have this kind of charter.

The commissioners, usually five, collectively constitute the city council; individually, they are the heads of the departments of city administration. Most commissioners devote full time to their jobs and actively administer the affairs of their particular departments. One of the commissioners is selected by the commission as mayor, but in most cities the mayor has little more power than the other commissioners.

The **commission charter** was widely heralded as introducing safe and sane business methods to city affairs. But after a brief wave of popularity, the new idea lost much of its glamour; the party bosses were suspicious and the city reformers disappointed. Certain critics say the commission plan was an upper-class struggle to wrest control of city hall from the lower class. And plainly this reform was enthusiastically backed by business interests. Although it provided for more integrated control than the old mayor-council system, the commission charter left the city without a single responsible administrative head; in effect, a commission city has five mayors. Moreover, commissioners chosen because they represent major groups within the city often leave something to be desired as administrators of departments.

For these reasons, many cities have turned away from the commission form to a system that provides for a strong mayor, or to the council-manager form. "Use of the plan is slowly disappearing today, with only 185 cities still clinging to it.'"[9] Larger cities usually shift to the strong mayor-council plan. Salt Lake City, for example, did so in early 1980, and Lawrence, Massachusetts, did so in 1986.[10]

The Council-Manager Charter   The **council-manager plan,** also known as the city-manager plan, was acclaimed at the turn of the century as "the latest word in municipal reform." It is indeed one of this nation's significant governmental innovations. In 1908 the small city of Staunton, Virginia, appointed a general manager to direct the city's work. Little note was taken of the step, but Richard Childs, an advertising man active in the short-ballot movement, became interested in the plan.

Childs was enthusiastic about the commission plan because it applied two basic ideas, *unification of power* and a *short ballot*, to city affairs. But it did not go far enough. Childs reasoned that if a chief administrative officer were added to this, the results should be even better.[11] The city manager plan soon became the darling of both reformers and the business elite. They liked the idea that the council would serve as a sort of "board of directors" in the business sense of setting broad policies, while a professional executive would see that these policies were carried out with businesslike efficiency.

Today about 2500 cities, located in every state except Indiana and Hawaii, operate under a council-manager charter. It has, in fact, become the most popular form of local government in medium-sized cities of more than 10,000 citizens. It is especially popular in California, where about 98 percent of the cities now use it. The largest cities operating under a city manager are Dallas and San Antonio; other cities using the plan include San Diego, Phoenix, Kansas City, Cincinnati, Oakland, Rochester, and Fort Worth.

Under the council-manager charter the council is usually elected in nonpartisan primaries and elections, either on a citywide basis or by election districts much larger than the wards in mayor-council cities. The council appoints a city manager and supervises the manager's activities. It makes the laws, approves the budget, and, although it is not supposed to interfere in administration, supervises city government through the manager. A mayor is expected to preside over the council and represent the city on ceremonial occasions, but many mayors in fact do a good deal more than this. Contrary to what some textbooks imply, the mayor in council-manager cities can sometimes be a strong policy and political leader as well as a dominant influence in exercising political power.[12]

The city manager advises the council on policy and supervises the administration of city business.[13] Because council-manager cities try to attract the best available persons, few of their charters require the councils to select managers from among local citizens nor do they prescribe detailed qualifications. Although city-manager charters seem to call for a nonpolitical city manager who merely carries out policies adopted by the council, and for council members who refrain from interfering with the administration of city affairs, in practice it is often difficult to distinguish clearly between making and applying policy.[14]

Most managers, especially in larger cities, are a major source of policies and programs. City managers are participants in the political process of their communities whether they play active roles by initiating policy, passive roles by merely drawing council attention to emerging problems, or neutral roles by refusing to commit themselves publicly on controversial questions.

City managers often serve as key leadership figures and policy innovators, but they seldom act solely as politicians. Usually city managers tread a middle ground between the two poles of politics and expertise. City managers, of course, vary in the way they interpret their responsibilities. Some consider themselves political leaders who should develop, propose, and seek to implement policies; others consider themselves professionals who should concentrate on housekeeping tasks and make sure they carry out policies proposed by the council. In practice, most city managers act somewhere in the middle between these two extremes.

Because of the unavoidable involvement of the manager in the politics of the community, managers are sometimes fired when there is a change in the control of the council. City managers serve at the pleasure of the council and can be let go by a simple majority vote. The dismissal of a manager is usually explained in other than political terms—lack of sufficient management ability, a personality conflict, and so forth. Or a manager may resign because of the council's meddling in administration. Such explanations, however, are often only thin disguises for heated political struggles in the community.

How has the city manager plan worked? In cities characterized by low social diversity and high consensus about community goals, the council-manager form has met with considerable success. Such cities have generally enjoyed improved standards of public employment, reduced costs, and better services. But some observers say it has also weakened political leadership in these cities and has confused citizens as to who really provides policy leadership.

Do structural reforms make any difference? That is, do council-manager cities with at-large, nonpartisan elections produce different kinds of policies because of their structural arrangements? One student of urban politics concludes that political structures do have an impact on public policies: "Reformed cities respond more pronouncedly to those pressures that tend to reduce spending; unreformed meaning mayor-council or commission cities respond more to those pressures that increase spending. If reformers wished to impose a middle-class efficiency ethos on city government, they were successful."[15] Exactly how and why these policy differences arise is not wholly clear. The fact that high incomes are associated with adoption of council-manager and nonpartisan election systems may be a factor.

But there is too much variation in American cities to label cities and their forms and predict policy outcomes. The more scholars examine the relationship between political attitudes or orientations and the structures of city government, the less they are convinced there are clear-cut cause-and-effect linkages.[16]

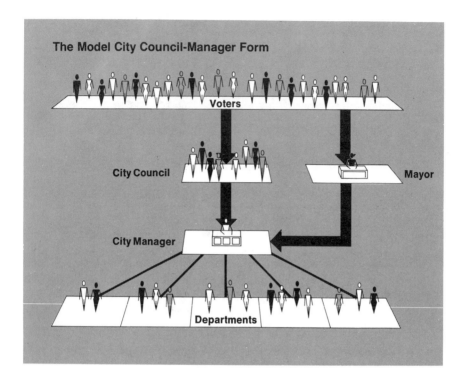

The Model City Council-Manager Form

Voters

City Council

Mayor

City Manager

Departments

Special Districts

Special districts are organized units of government usually established to provide one or more specific services, such as sewage disposal, fire protection, or pollution control, for a local area. They have tripled in number during the past thirty years. They are often created for financial reasons to enable an existing unit of government to evade established tax and debt limits, or to spread the tax burden over a wider area than individual existing municipalities or counties. Many smaller special districts are formed in suburban areas to obtain urban services without having to create a city government or be annexed to one. Many special districts have been created in response to federal aid programs such as pollution control, soil conservation, and urban renewal.

Although there is no consistent pattern in their organization and structure, special districts usually have governing boards appointed by officials of other governments or elected by the general public. Special districts are useful to deal with urgent problems that overlap boundaries of existing units of government.[17] Critics of the rapid increase of special districts claim their existence prevents comprehensive planning. Furthermore, the governing boards of these special districts usually enjoy low political visibility, and the typical citizen is generally uninformed about their decisions. Although many of these districts have only a few employees (and many have none at all and are of little importance), others are powerful bridge, highway, tunnel, or transit authorities that can become far removed from accountability to the public. These criticisms raise doubts about how responsive the special districts are to their constituents.

Despite these and other complaints, however, special districts are not likely to fade away. A large number of problems defy city and county boundaries, and the regional special district can offer an economies-of-scale approach that will continue to be an attractive alternative to officials at the grass roots.

Town Hall Democracy

North of the Ohio River, east of the Mississippi River (with minor exceptions), and outside of New England, the general practice is to subdivide counties into townships or boroughs. The township is gradually losing some of its functions to counties and cities. Oklahoma, after whittling down township functions to almost nothing, abolished them altogether. In Iowa, townships still exist formally, but they have lost so many of their functions that the Census Bureau has stopped counting them. Where they exist, townships often build and maintain roads, and sometimes they serve as districts for school purposes. In some states all the voters of the townships are entitled to attend an annual meeting to elect officers, levy taxes, and make appropriations. These meetings are, however, usually poorly attended.

NEW ENGLAND TOWN MEETING DEMOCRACY

Early settlers in New England in the 1660s adopted a community-meeting style of participation as they made common cause of survival in the new land. Doubtless they adapted certain of these practices from community meetings then popular in England. The town is the principal kind of rural or noncity government in New England. It is sometimes difficult for outsiders to understand that a New England town is a unit of government that includes whatever villages there may be, plus the open country. Except where a municipality has been incorporated, the town performs most of the functions a county does elsewhere. Connecticut, in fact, has abolished counties except for sheriff services. Maine has twenty-two cities, plus about 400 towns that use the town meeting system of democracy; Vermont has eight cities and over 200 towns using the town meeting process.[18] Many of these towns (especially those with populations under 20,000) still hold annual do-it-yourself town meetings open to all voters.

The assemblies at town meetings usually choose a board of executive officers, historically called selectmen, generally consisting of three to five members, who carry on the business of the town between meetings, are in charge of town property, grant licenses, supervise other town officials, and call special town meetings. A town clerk, treasurer, assessor, constable, and school board, as well as numerous other persons, are elected by the voters or appointed by the selectmen.

The New England town meeting has long been a celebrated institution. The picture of sturdy and independent citizens coming together to talk over public affairs and speak their minds is a stirring one. The New England town is sometimes pointed to as the one place in the United States where there is no elite and where participatory democracy really exists. And the town meeting is the most obvious example of direct democracy: The voters participate directly in making the rules, passing new laws, levying taxes, and appropriating money. Nonetheless, a veteran group of activists often provides political and policy-making leadership.

Many state and local officials in New England say the town meeting system is on the decline. Derry, New Hampshire, for example, held its last town meeting in 1985 and switched to a mayor-council system. The town meeting had served Derry well for most of its 158-year history, yet it had proved unequal to the challenge of rapid growth and an influx of people who commute long distances to work. In its heyday the New Hampshire town meeting was an all-day event combining community business and neighborly socializing.

> Held on the second Tuesday in March, it typically began with the election of officers and then took up such matters as road and building repairs. At midday everyone would retreat to the nearby church vestry or Grange Hall for a hearty meal before returning to the town hall to tackle any remaining issues.
>
> Things changed as people began commuting to work and could no longer afford to take a day off to conduct town business. Meetings were shifted to Tuesday night and then to Saturday in an effort to bolster attendance.[19]

When New England communities grow larger than is feasible for the "y'all come" type of town meeting, they often modify the system to a representative town meeting process. This means that they elect 200 or more town meeting members from the various town precincts, with staggered three-year terms; in other words, one-third of the members are selected each year. This is the system, for example, in Brookline and Milton, Massachusetts. Some of the modified systems move also to a town manager system, and others continue having the secretary to the Board of Selectmen or the town clerk handle most of the day-to-day management functions of the community.

Who Influences City Policy Making?

We like to believe every American citizen is at least potentially equal in having a say in local government. We know, however, that people like mayors or prominent local business leaders are often more influential than the rest of us. Nursing home residents, the unemployed, migratory workers, young drifters, and the indigent are unlikely to have much influence. In fact, probably neither the very poor nor the very rich influence what goes on at our local city halls. Participation in community affairs is far more likely a middle-class and upper middle-class practice.

Most of us, most of the time, leave the responsibility of running our cities and counties to local officials and those few hundred people willing and able to serve on the scores of community boards and in local civic organizations. The traditionally important people in city government are still the mayor, other elected representatives, senior public administrative officials, the district attorney, local judges, and state and national representatives. But if most people do not choose to be leaders in their communities, it does not mean they do not care about tax rates, the quality of life, and the availability of services in their cities. Hundreds of local people can be quickly mobilized if officials at the local city hall mishandle local affairs and make unpopular decisions.

Indeed, activism has increased; people now form groups to protect their communities from waste landfills, toxic dumps, shopping malls, and highways. With dogged perseverance and shoestring budgets, middle-class protest groups have often successfully taken on city halls or won victories for their neighborhoods in the courts. Typical interest groups active in local government are the following:

Neighborhood associations

Chambers of commerce

Local trade and manufacturing associations

Business leaders of major local concerns (bankers, department store owners, publishers, managers of local high tech or steel companies)

Small merchants associations (downtown merchants groups, Main Street associates, shopping mall owners)

Taxpayers associations

Council of civic associations

Utilities (power, electricity, and fuel companies)

Real estate and home builders associations

Local contractors

Local unions

League of Women Voters

Public employee groups (teachers, police, and fire fighters)

Civil and human rights groups (Urban League, NAACP, Hispanic and Asian-American groups)

Parents groups (PTA, Mothers Against Drunk Driving)

Environmental groups (Sierra Club)

Farmers' groups (Farm Bureau, Farmers Union)

Religious organizations

Ethnic and fraternal organizations

Single-interest groups (NIMBY—Not In My Back Yard; PUKE—People United for a Klean Environment; CARE; WATCHDOG; TRIM; SWAT)[20]

Not all of these groups are equally important. And the list of course grows longer in any specific community, taking into account that city's special problems and ethnic, class, and commercial interests. Ask yourself about your home community. Which groups or individuals appear to enjoy access and special influence at city hall? Can groups successfully fight city hall and get decisions modified or reversed? What groups have done this in recent years? Do minorities and the less privileged have to acquiesce to unfair or unreasonable decisions made by the city elites or is there considerable political equality in your home area?

A sure way to involve people in city government is to propose a new policy that threatens the values and safety of the homes of middle or upper-middle-class taxpayers. A suggestion that a correctional facility, a freeway, a new dump, or a toxic disposal site is coming to their neighborhood will swiftly mobilize citizens who are otherwise happy to be passive spectators in grass-roots America. Likewise, the firing of a popular school principal, the closing of a neighborhood school, or a major increase in the property tax will produce a rally of citizen protest that can change the policy-making process at city hall.

Above all, of course, voters and the mildly active or attentive citizens in a community help set the general tone of their community government. Elected and appointed officials regularly reach out and try to sense the mood of the local citizenry. They want to avert marches on city hall, recall elections, and citizen dissatisfaction. Their desire to be reelected at the next election keeps them reasonably accountable.

This does not mean that we rave about the quality of services in our local governments. A Gallup Poll suggests that although we generally respond favorably to the services we receive from city government and local public transportation agencies, we rate them less favorably than we do the services from commercial organizations that are in the consumer services business.

Despite low turnouts at city government hearings, town meetings, and local elections, and despite considerable public indifference to the decisions made at city hall, more people are probably involved in more local government activities today than ever before. In general, the middle class, the middle-aged, and the homeowners in a community are most likely to participate. Also, people usually have more influence when they form a group than as individuals, and a coalition of groups can often exercise considerable clout in city policy-making processes.

Grass-Roots Self-Help Movements

In contrast to the political participation within the formal structures of city or community government, we are also seeing countless people across the country coming together in their own neighborhoods to tackle mutual problems or to form neighborhood cooperatives. Sometimes this is simply to handle collective babysitting arrangements or organize charity runs or golf tournaments. Yet, it is also often utilized to supervise neighborhood crime watches and weatherization initiatives or to build bike paths or little league fields in one section of a community. Local nonprofit groups in New York have built award-winning apartment complexes amidst burned-out inner-city tenements. Other groups have mobilized to bring about storefront revitalization, street improvement, and area beautification programs by initiating farmers' markets, miniparks, and gardens.

The foundations of the contemporary grass-roots self-help groups are well established in America's past. The community often rallied when a neighbor's farm burned down; volunteer fire departments emerged out of this tradition. Local Grange and consumer cooperatives also reflect this impulse. But our country, which has become a highly mobile and an increasingly impersonal society, has tended to drift away from these traditions. Today most of the people in this nation shop at shopping centers rather than on Main Street or in the old village or downtown area. People resent the fact that public institutions designed to serve them have become remote and, perhaps, overly professionalized. Thus, people across the country sometimes join together to do in an informal and decentralized way what extended families or small villages of the past used to do. Simply, they come together and embark upon community improvements.

Just as most business innovations in America take place in small firms, so too are most social experiments and innovations generated in small neighborhood or community entities—not within the large, cumbersome, traditional governmental bureaucracies. In a way, these efforts are part of the "small is beautiful" trend. But they have also occurred because formal local governments have sometimes become remote and overly cautious. Many local groups seeking help from city hall or from county officialdom give up after running into the forest of building codes, zoning rules, and countless other regulations that inhibit innovation in local government. The alternative to despair is to do it yourself. And this is exactly what is happening in grass-roots America right now. The more successful experiments are being watched carefully by the professionals at city hall, and some of the "innovations" will be absorbed either by those in office or by new candidates. Some of these new candidates indeed will be products of these neighborhood groups and will, in fact, win election on the basis of these innovations.

Summary

1. Governmental forms at the grass roots in the United States come in a great variety of shapes and structures and perform various functions. However, they have in common the fact that constitutional power is vested in the states, and that counties, cities, and towns act as agents of the state.

2. The most common governmental form at the county level is the commission, although larger urban counties are moving to council-administrator or council-elected executive plans.

3. The most common governmental forms at the city level are the mayor-council or the council-manager (city-manager) plans. Mayor-council governments generally have a strong mayor as well as partisan city elections. They operate with a ward system and have reasonably short and simultaneous council terms. Council-manager cities generally select the mayor from the council, operate with at-large and nonpartisan elections, and have overlapping terms for council members. In general, city-manager cities are found in medium to large cities and in western, especially Sunbelt, cities.

4. Who influences grass-roots governments? Elected and appointed city officials and those whose lives are directly affected by what local governments do—city and county employees, business leaders, those who have or desire contracts with the local governments, and so on. Most people don't have the interest and the time to watch, not to mention fight, City Hall, unless there is a direct threat to something they have or want to have, such as a school or a quiet neighborhood.

5. Most local governments enjoy considerable stability and continuity. Governmental consolidations seldom take place, except for school districts that consolidate to take advantage of economies of scale. On the other hand, in the past few decades there has been tremendous growth in the number of special districts formed to provide special-purpose functions for several communities in an area. This trend is now slowing. We have also seen an increase in neighborhood self-help groups that are often at the cutting edge of creative problem solving and social innovation in grass-roots America.

Further Reading

BARBARA ACKERMAN. *You the Mayor? The Education of a City Politician* (Auburn House, 1989).

JAMES M. BANOVETZ, ed. *Small Cities and Counties: A Guide to Managing Services* (International City Manager Association, 1985).

RICHARD D. BINGHAM. *State and Local Government in an Urban Society* (Random House, 1986).

GEORGE S. BLAIR. *Government at the Grass Roots* (Palisades Publishers, 1981).

MICHAEL ENGEL. *State and Local Politics: Fundamental Perspectives* (St. Martin's, 1985).

GERALD L. HOUSEMAN. *State and Local Government: The New Battlefield* (Prentice Hall, 1986).

BRYAN D. JONES. *Governing Urban America* (Little, Brown, 1983).

DAVID R. MORGAN. *Managing Urban America*, 2d ed. (Duxbury Press, 1984).

JAMES H. SVARA. *Official Leadership in the City: Patterns of Conflict and Cooperation* (Oxford University Press, 1989).

BRUCE STOKES. *Helping Ourselves: Local Solutions to Global Problems* (Norton, 1981).

HARMON ZEIGLER, ELLEN KEHOE, and JANE REISMAN. *City Managers and School Superintendents* (Praegar, 1984).

See also *National Civic Review: The Journal of Community Problem-Solving*, published six times a year; and *The Municipal Yearbook*, published annually by the International City Management Association.

N otes

1. These related trends are documented in detail in Chapter 14, ACIR, Commission Report, *The Question of State Government Capability* (U.S. Government Printing Office, 1985). See also Joseph F. Zimmerman, *State-Local Relations: A Partnership Approach* (Praeger, 1983).

2. See Thomas J. Kane, Jr., "City Managers View Intergovernmental Relations," *Publius* (Summer 1984), pp. 121–33.

3. See Matthew Kauffman, "Counting on Counties," *New Jersey Reporter* (September 1984), pp. 25–30.

4. James M. Banovetz and Thomas W. Kelty, "Home Rule in Illinois: Image and Reality," in *Illinois Issues* (Sangamon State University, 1987).

5. See Doyle M. Buckwater, "State-Municipal Relations: Improving the Arch of Federalism," *State and Local Government Review* (Winter 1984), pp. 27–33.

6. Peggy Heilig and Robert J. Mundt, "Changes in Representational Equity: The Effect of Adopting Districts," *Social Science Quarterly* (June 1983), pp. 393–97. See also Theodore Robinson and Thomas R. Dye, "Reformism and Black Representation on City Councils," *Social Science Quarterly* (June 1978), pp. 133–41.

7. *Rogers* v. *Lodge*, 458 U.S. 613 (1982); and *Thornburg* v. *Gingles*, 478 U.S. 30 (1986).

8. David R. Morgan, *Managing Urban America*, 2d ed. (Duxbury Press, 1984).

9. Charles R. Adrian, "Forms of City Government in American History," *The Municipal Year Book 1988* (International City Management Association, 1988), p. 9.

10. Agnes S. Bain, "Lawrence in Transition." Paper presented at the New England Political Science Association, Hartford, Connecticut, April 1986.

11. On Childs's contribution in this area, see John Porter East, *Council Manager Government: The Political Thought of Its Founder* (University of North Carolina Press, 1965).

12. Nelson Wikstrom, "The Mayor as a Policy Leader in the Council-Manager Form of Government: A View from the Field," *Public Administration Review* (May–June 1979), pp. 270–76. See also James Svara, "Understanding the Mayor's Office in Council-Manager Cities," *Popular Government* (Fall 1985), pp. 6–11.

13. Len Wood, "Building City-Council–City-Manager Relations," in *Western City*, vol. 63 (July 1987).

14. Harmon Zeigler, Ellen Kehoe, and Jane Reisman, *City Managers and School Superintendents* (Praeger, 1984). For earlier studies, see Ronald O. Loveridge, *City Managers in Legislative Policies* (Bobbs-Merrill, 1970); and Richard J. Stillman, *The Rise of the City Manager* (University of New Mexico Press, 1974). See also *Handbook for Council Members in Council-Manager Cities*, 4th ed. (National Civic League Press, 1989).

15. William Lyons, "Reform and Response in American Cities: Structure and Policy Reconsidered," *Social Science Quarterly* (June 1978), p. 130.

16. Bryan D. Jones, *Governing Urban America* (Little, Brown, 1983).

17. See Robert B. Hawley, Jr., *Self Government by District: Myth and Reality* (Hoover Institution Press, Stanford University, 1976).

18. William Doyle and Josephine F. Milburn, "Citizen Participation in New England Politics: Town Meetings, Political Parties, and Interest Groups," in Josephine F. Milburn and Victoria Schuck, eds., *New England Politics* (Schenckman Publishing, 1981), p. 37.

19. Editorial Research Reports, "New England Town Meeting Reaching the End of the Road," *Today* (March 28, 1986), p. 12. See also Joseph Zimmerman, "The New England Town Meeting: Pure Democracy in Action?" in *The Municipal Year Book*, vol. 51 (1984).

20. Some of these are suggested in Glenn Abney and Thomas P. Lauth, "Interest Group Influence in City Policy-Making: The Views of Administrators," *The Western Political Quarterly* (March 1985), pp. 148–61. Others are suggested in Judith Feldstein, "More Citizens Battle City Hall," *The Times* (Trenton, N.J.) (April 7, 1986), pp. 1, 10.

8

Governing
the Supercity

Cities are far more than buildings, streets, and people; above all they are centers of civilization. How they develop, how they affect us, how they function politically, and how we can revitalize them as healthy, safe, and economically sound centers are critical and urgent concerns.

Today the metropolis, not the farm or the small town so beloved in American fact and fiction, is where most of us live. About 75 percent of the American people live on about 5 percent of the land. At least 70 percent live in metropolitan areas. Fifty-five percent of us live within sixty miles of coastal shoreline (Atlantic, Pacific, Gulf of Mexico, or along the Great Lakes or the St. Lawrence River).

The political, economic, and legal problems of our metropolitan regions are obviously interconnected. Policy makers at all levels of government constantly seek better ways to govern our metro areas, to achieve sensible economic growth and equity, and to ensure environmentally safe metro regions. There are no easy answers.

This chapter looks at the ways in which power is constrained in our central cities and metro regions, and the ways in which political leaders—especially a new breed of mayors—try to maximize political power in their attempts to govern and revitalize major urban areas. We also examine the suburbs and patterns of metropolitan regional cooperation.

Some observers consider the jumble of civic jurisdictions the main impediment to sound government in the sprawling supercities of America. They say the vast dispersal of power leads to fragmentation that discourages coherent policy planning. However, those people who want to control their local schools and determine how the land around them is used believe fragmented power prevents their urban government from becoming coercive—just as separation of power and divisions between state and national governments check and balance power in the larger jurisdictions.

Today's giant cities unquestionably face problems: congestion, slums, smog, tension, rootlessness, loss of community, unsafe streets, and unrestrained sprawl and visual pollution. Writers and critics since Thomas Jefferson have projected an unflattering image of the city as a cold, impersonal, and often brutal environment in which crime flourishes and people lose their dignity.

The big city is also contrasted with the "wholesome" small community. Less sophisticated critics appear to measure the modern city against a small town inhabited by Anglo-Saxons who speak with a New England or Middle Western accent and who spend their time sitting around the stove at the general store discussing local politics.

Supporters, on the other hand, contend the big city is not just a place of smog and sprawl; it is the center of innovation, excitement, and vitality. The city has social diversity and less community pressure to conform. The large community is a meeting place for talent from all over the nation and the world: dancers, musicians, writers, actors, and business leaders. Traditionally big cities have provided jobs and opportunities. New York City, for example, is called the Big Apple—the land of opportunity. People who like living in the city point out that fairly homogeneous smaller communities that retain some identity often exist within metropolitan areas. Some of the best known are Greenwich Village and Soho in lower Manhattan, Georgetown and Cleveland Park in Washington, D.C., the Russian Hill and Chinatown sections of San Francisco, and the North End and South Boston areas in Boston.

Some people continue to challenge the idea of an urban crisis. They contend most city dwellers live more comfortably and conveniently than ever before, with

Richest and Poorest Urban Communities

RICHEST	PER CAPITA INCOME	POOREST	PER CAPITA INCOME
Bridgeport, Conn.	$26,316	McAllen, Tex.	$ 7,001
San Francisco, Cal.	24,593	Laredo, Tex.	7,035
Bergen-Passaic, N.J.	23,040	Brownsville, Tex.	7,409
Middlesex, N.J.	22,783	Provo, Utah	8,870
Nassau-Suffolk, N.Y.	22,001	El Paso, Tex.	9,484
Washington, D.C.	21,539	Las Cruces, N.M.	9,578
San Jose, Cal.	21,510	Pascagoula, Miss.	10,231
Anaheim-Santa Ana, Cal.	21,444	Houma-Thibodaux, La.	10,582
Lake County, La.	21,432	Jacksonville, N.C.	10,668
West Palm Beach, Fla.	21,246	Bryan, Tex.	10,688

Source: Based on data from *Wall Street Journal* (May 5, 1989), p. C10.

more and better housing, schools, transportation, and so on. By any conceivable measure of material welfare the present generation of urban Americans is, on the whole, better off than other large groups of people have ever been anywhere. There is congestion, to be sure, yet many people find advantages as well as disadvantages.[1] Many cities, especially in the West and South, are in good shape, and Boston, Pittsburgh, Baltimore, and Indianapolis are now viewed as revived and vital, not decaying.

Cities survive. Throughout history cities have been threatened by political and environmental catastrophes. Urban decay, in one form or another, has always been with us. Cities that continued to thrive did so because they were able to respond effectively to crises not unlike those we are currently experiencing. Today the differences are those of scale, consequences, and speed of change.[2] How well the cities will survive, and with what mix of people, will depend on the tides of the national economy, the way we organize our regions, the way we design policies, and the vision and leadership individual cities can muster to build their own futures.

Interest-Group Democracy in the Cities

The stakes and prizes of big-city politics are considerable: appointments to city offices; tax considerations; regulation of businesses, professions, and other activities; and city contracts to provide such city services as education and sanitation. These—and a general interest in honest, efficient, and coordinated metropolitan government—encourage interest groups to mobilize as much influence as they can to deal with the urban government. Interest groups vary in size, solidarity, and effectiveness. City politicians must deal with the kind of interest groups found anywhere in an industrial society: organized workers, business leaders, neighborhood associations, professional associations, good government associations, home builders and developers, consumers, taxpayers, environmentalists, and various ethnic groups. Typically, these groups are much closer to city officials than they are to a governor or a president. The mayor of a big city constantly operates in the eye of a political hurricane. To a greater extent than a president or governor, the mayor must deal with highly specialized interest groups.

The most powerful groups in most large cities are typically various business groups. It is only a modest oversimplification to equate the interests of big cities with the interests of their employers who provide the economic base for taxes and for jobs. Mayors realize this and know they will be judged on how well they can promote the local economy. But today business groups have to share power and influence with others and on most issues cannot dominate politics without allies.

Cities also have so-called "problem groups," composed of people who share a concern over a particular city problem even though they have different economic interests. Groups concerned with halting highway construction, curbing the size of large office buildings, fighting toxic waste dumps, or developing parks or jogging trails can put a great deal of pressure on City Hall, especially when supported by the local media. Once the problem is solved or somehow disappears, however, the group may disappear with it.

Another special interest group is the good government or reform group. In some cities these groups have enjoyed such strong leadership and wide support that they have operated almost like political parties. But in most big cities, reform groups are simply one more pressure on City Hall, and they are often divided among themselves. Their activities range from trying to improve an entire metropolitan area, as the Citizens Leagues in Minneapolis-St. Paul and Baltimore have done, to simply collecting facts and figures.[3]

Also important are the unions of city employees. Police, firefighters, street cleaners, teachers, and other public employees have organized into unions, many of which are affiliated with the national AFL-CIO. These groups say they are concerned about the city as a whole, yet they are especially interested in such specific matters as pay, working conditions, and job security. Although in most states strikes by city employees working in vital services are prohibited by law, enforcement is difficult. Teachers and municipal workers use the strike or the threat of a strike to force cities to increase wages and provide better benefits. Such unions are often a major influence in larger cities. Mayors, liberals as well as conservatives, complain that public-employee unions are sometimes so powerful they make the old-fashioned political machine look tame.

INTEREST-GROUP TACTICS

Ordinarily, groups in a metropolis pursue the same activities as pressure groups anywhere; they put out press releases, hold meetings, write letters to the mayor and council, and generate all the pressure they can. Occasionally a local interest group is extremely effective. A few years ago, for example, the Kellogg Company threatened to halt its plans to build an expensive new headquarters building and even to move its 700-person office staff to some other city unless Battle Creek city (population 35,724) merged with nearby Battle Creek township (population 20,615). The famous cereal company, with long roots in the community, viewed a merger as the best means to cure the political division that was splintering the area's economic development efforts. Its bold plan worked: the two communities put aside differences and approved a city annexation of the township. Local residents, in both communities, feared the staggering economic consequences a Kellogg pullout would bring to their already depressed economy.[4]

Community organizations sometimes use the *initiative, referendum* and *recall* (the tools of populism we discussed in Chapter 26). Although the recall is employed only occasionally—usually in such western states as Oregon, Colorado, and California—there have been some notable recalls: mayors in Omaha and Atlantic City, and three city council members in Honolulu in 1985. Mayors of three larger cities—San Francisco, Seattle, and Cleveland—faced recall elections in the past decade, but all three mayors beat the recall. Although the recall may be an uncommon event in urban politics, the initiative and referendum are now considered more routine.

In a growing number of communities across the nation, zoning and land-use regulations are sometimes being written not at city hall but by grass-roots citizen movements concerned about the quality of life in their neighborhoods. "No-growth" or "slow growth" advocates are behind many of these initiative drives. But "ballot-box planning" also involves efforts to slash property taxes and defeat school and highway bonds. Occasionally even the developers or a union will bypass normal legislative channels and put measures on the ballot. Residents in the suburbs are especially watchful in guarding against parking problems, high-density housing, traffic gridlock, and other woes they fled the city to escape.

An interest group confronts many different centers of power and decision making. Bargaining exists between interests, between interests and city leaders, and between interests and the bureaucracy. The interest-group arrangements of the central city are in many ways similar to those of the national electorate. Within many central cities the electorate is made up of the foreign born, blacks, Hispanics, and blue-collar workers. In national elections these groups generally support the Democratic party, and the same partisan ties usually hold for local politics. But to gain control of the central city, politicians must also appeal to the middle classes in the "outer wards," whose interests are much like those of suburbanites, and to upper-income apartment or townhouse dwellers.

"The City as a Growth Machine"[5]

Until recently everybody, or at least almost everybody in most cities, wanted to see their city grow bigger. Everybody was a city booster. The local newspaper, the television stations, the radio stations, the chamber of commerce, the union leaders, the business community, the developers, the teachers, and proud citizens worked together to attract new industries. Such industries would bring, they hoped, new jobs, more amenities, increased land values, and more opportunities for the young. The consensus was that a city with a growing population was a healthy one; one with a losing population a sick one.

There were quarrels about where the new airport should be built and through whose backyards the new freeways would be located, but the question of whether there should be a new airport or new freeways or a new convention center and a new community college was never an issue. Local politicians competed with one another to make the city grow. Federal dollars were eagerly sought to make it possible to build mass transit systems and new sewer systems. Cities competed with one another to attract new industries.

Local politicians found, and still find, it difficult to oppose the "growth machine." Those who do sometimes find it difficult to secure campaign funds. However, beginning in the early 1980s an anti-growth movement has developed. There

MILLARDSVILLE
POP. 509
WE ARE SMALL
BUT WE ARE
SOLVENT

SEN MAYO

*From The Wall Street Journal by permission of
Cartoon Features Syndicate.*

has always been one, centered primarily in the wealthy suburbs surrounding central cities. In fact many suburbs were created to escape the growth taking place in central cities. They adopted building and zoning codes and land-use regulations making it difficult, if not impossible, for any new industries to be located in their suburb and to keep out any persons except those who could afford large houses on large lots. They carefully planned their new suburbs to ensure they would not become too crowded. These zoning regulations were attacked in the courts as designed to keep the poor and the blacks out of the neighborhood, but as long as they were racially neutral on their face the courts left them undisturbed.

By the 1980s environmental concerns began to spread from a few suburbs into most suburbs, especially in the Sunbelt. Around the city, and in areas undergoing development, coalitions began forming to fight this growth. Individuals disturbed by noise, pollution, and traffic jams and fearful that developers would build too many houses too close together bringing too many people for the infrastructure of roads, and sewage disposal in the community, joined together. Toxic leakage at Love Canal in New York, dioxin-tainted soil at Times Beach, Missouri, and hazardous waste at the Rocky Flats nuclear plant near Denver sensitized the nation to the dangers from industrial plants. Environmentalism is now a major political force to counter growth.

The issue of growth, slow growth, or no growth, has come to the fore, and brought together new coalitions and new issues. The new battles now tend to take place over Environmental Impact Reports (EIRs). EIRs came into being in 1969 as a result of a requirement of the federal government that stipulated an Environmental Impact Report must be filed and approved for large projects funded by federal monies. These reports must specify all benefits and all costs of the projects and provide a process for public comments to be registered and to be heard.

The requirement for EIRs has now been adopted by most states. The reports are usually prepared by local consulting firms. During the 1960s and 1970s they tended to be neither as much trouble and costly as their opponents claimed nor as helpful as their proponents had hoped. But they have become a new part of the local political scene and are increasingly being used as legal documents to attack projects for their failure to provide adequate protections for health and safety of those close to the proposed projects. Developers can be required to provide "mitigation" and the process tends to focus debate on the pros and cons of projects so that they are no longer accepted without debate as an unqualified public good.

The Special Problems of the Central City

One persistent problem facing most core cities is the exodus of many businesses, taking with them important jobs and revenues while low-income groups remain in the city. At the same time the need for city services has greatly expanded. In the last century masses of new immigrants arrived from Europe. In this century migrants have come from the rural areas, especially from the South. More recently we have welcomed waves of newcomers from Puerto Rico, Cuba, Korea, Vietnam, the Philippines, Nicaragua, Haiti, and Mexico. The number of immigrants from other Latin American countries is also on the rise. The majority of migrants settle first in the inner cities—usually in the poorest, most decaying sections. Invariably, these new arrivals cause great stress for the schools and for community safety. Overcrowding and substandard housing in these areas increase health and fire hazards. And despite city-renewal efforts, central cities, in contrast to the middle and outer rings of suburbs, have:

1. More older persons
2. More substandard housing
3. More students from non-English speaking backgrounds
4. More unemployment
5. Older buildings
6. Higher crime rates
7. Higher population densities
8. Higher percentages of blacks and most other minorities
9. Higher costs for city services per resident.

Why do problems accumulate in the core city? The migration of persons lacking the job skills needed for an automated and complicated economy puts heavy demands on welfare agencies. Crowding in segregated districts accelerates the process of urban decay and slum conditions. To meet stepped-up housing needs of people who cannot pay high rents, the city provides public housing programs. But this creates tension both among those who are forced to move out of these areas and among those who are forced to move into the housing. People who live in congested areas require more police protection, but police problems grow when different racial groups live close together in slum areas. Also problematic are the movement of thousands of people into the core city in the morning and out to the suburbs in the evening, the congestion of the streets, and the pollution of the air. Faced with all these problems, big cities need money, and this is precisely the resource they usually lack.

Any picture of the central cities as composed exclusively of huddled starving, homeless, and unemployed masses, however, is misleading. Nor is it fair to say simply that central cities have all the problems and suburbs all the resources. Central cities do, to be sure, have more "high-cost-citizens" (truly needy, handicapped, and senior citizens). And most aging cities are losing population. Yet the decline in population is not a major cause of higher per capita costs in the old central cities. The spreading of costs among fewer taxpayers is not the sole cause of financial stress in the inner cities. Rather, higher operating costs in the cities "occur as a direct product of an aging physical plant, reduced proportions of middle-class homeowners, and increased proportions of populations requiring government services."[6] Then, too, land, rents, utilities, and taxes are less expensive in the outer suburbs, and service companies that can easily move are doing so to lower operating costs. Many workers in the inner cities are left as these companies flock to cheaper locations on the metro outskirts.

Central-city mayors find it difficult to increase revenues or to force suburbanites to pay a larger share of the bill for the city services they use. From the perspective of a mayor, the lack of politically available tax resources is an ever present reality. This is the economic problem. The legal problem is that the states have not permitted the cities to get at wealth in any meaningful way with a local income tax. One result has been the increased organization of cities to lobby for fiscal relief in state capitals and especially in Washington, D.C. In an effort to recapture part of the tax base that escapes to the suburbs in the evenings, some cities have imposed local payroll or other types of commuter taxes seeking to obtain revenue from people who work in the central cities and make frequent use of their facilities yet live in the suburbs. Some city officials say the payroll or commuter tax is an effective way to shift some of the burden to those who benefit from the city but live beyond its borders. But others say it is unlikely to provide significant long-term revenue growth, and they think it encourages even more businesses to leave the city.

Governing Central Cities— Mayors, Bosses, and Political Machines

Two hundred years ago the notion of a strong mayor providing vigorous leadership was nonexistent. The need for strong mayoral leadership developed a hundred years ago in the late nineteenth century. It was seen as a means to deal with the social revolution brought on by urbanization, massive waves of immigration, and mounting economic problems of growing cities. In the larger cities, gradually and often grudgingly, the office of mayor became a key position for political leadership. In 1899 the reform-minded National Municipal League adopted the "strong mayor system" as part of its first model city charter in an attempt to lead cities out of the "dark ages" of municipal government. Confidence in the strong mayor system has waxed and waned over time, and its adoption in cities varies considerably depending on both partisan and ideological considerations.[7]

MAYORS

The typical mayor is a college graduate, an experienced grass-roots politician, usually has a business or legal background, and is forty to fifty years old. Although most mayors are male, several of the largest cities now have women mayors, including Pittsburgh, Houston, Dallas, San Diego, and San Antonio. In fact, more than 1000 of the more than 19,000 municipal governments in the United States are headed by women, and the number is growing. Many of these women worked their way up through service on school boards and city councils and in the League of Women Voters. An increasing number of blacks also serve as mayors. Currently black mayors serve in about 300 cities, including Atlanta, Baltimore, Los Angeles, Philadelphia, Detroit, Seattle, New Haven, New York, and Washington, D.C.[8] Hispanic mayors can be found in Miami and Denver.

Today mayors head large urban bureaucracies. Most put in long hours and six-day weeks. They are frequently caught in the middle of public-employee strikes, tax controversies, and city-suburb clashes. They make endless trips "with hat in hand" to state and national legislatures. Central-city mayors in the largest cities earn $70,000 to $130,000, and in middle-sized cities between $40,000 and $80,000. City managers, chief city administrators, and the top appointees at city sometimes make more than the mayors.

Mayors of large cities have the same basic functions as any major executive. As chief of state they issue proclamations, receive important visitors, appear at endless breakfasts, luncheons, and dinners, and launch community and charity drives. As chief executives they appoint heads of agencies, draw up budgets, check up on administration, deal with sudden emergencies, mediate among warring department chiefs, and try to get rid of incompetents or misfits. Although partisan politics is becoming less a feature of city government, mayors as chief of their party still usually dominate the parties' city organizations. Mayors help recruit candidates for office, deal with revolts and opposition within their parties, and represent their parties in Washington or the state capitals. As chief legislator mayors draw up proposed legislation and also make many specific policies. As chief fundraiser mayors bargain for more money for their cities before state and national legislatures. Indeed, the only presidential powers metropolitan mayors do not hold at the city level are commander in chief and chief of foreign relations. Yet many mayors, such as those in New York, San Francisco, Atlanta, and Miami, often do have their own "foreign policies" as they travel abroad seeking foreign investments and singing the praises of the local exportable goods.

Mayors share legislative power with the city council. Typically, mayors have extensive power to recommend legislation and to participate in the legislative process; for example, most have a broad veto power over policy measures and appropriations. But the balance of power varies from city to city. Much depends on the basis on which the council is elected, for example, whether its members are elected by the same party organization that supports the mayor or by a personal organization of their own. A mayor's relations with the city's legislative branch are essentially political, much as they are for the president and governor. Sometimes the mayor must depend on control of the party organization to ensure support in the council, as in Chicago, for example, because the city council (called the Board of Aldermen there) consists of fifty members elected in relatively small districts or wards. Other cities may have more streamlined executive-legislative relationships, yet the mayor is likely to be a weak official unless his or her political and personal influence is able to encourage considerable council or board cooperation.[9]

MAYORS AS RENEWERS-IN-CHIEF

One of the mayor's roles in a major city is to help revitalize the economy and attract new investments, sports teams, conventions, and tourists. Sometimes it takes an almost missionary zeal to overcome the pessimism and despair that often beset inner cities in America. Recent mayors in Indianapolis, San Antonio, and Baltimore have won high praise for their leadership and renewal efforts. They have been model renewers.

It used to be said that Indianapolis was the city you drove through or flew over on your way to somewhere else. But in the past ten years Indianapolis has become the Cinderella city of the Snow- and Rustbelts. More than $1 billion in downtown developments changed the landscape of the inner city. A 61,000-seat Hoosier Dome was constructed; the Baltimore Colts were lured to town; countless major restaurants sprang up; a world-class zoo was opened in a 260-acre state park just west of the downtown area; and the old Union Station was renovated.

Indianapolis Mayor William H. Hudnut, III, has been reelected twice by landslide margins. "Cities are," he says, "the laboratory in which the experiment that is American democracy is being conducted." Preaching a bit, he says cities are the training ground for civilization. "If we do not succeed there, we will not succeed anywhere. If we can't make the city work, we can't make the country work—or the world either, for that matter. But we can." What did Hudnut do? He instilled a can-do, entrepreneurial attitude about what Indianapolis could become. He bucked the trend of suburban investment and urban disinvestment, emphasizing that you cannot be a suburb of nothing. He persuaded banks, local foundations, and universities, as well as state and federal officials, to join his downtown renewal programs. Realizing Indianapolis needed to diversify its economy, he worked to attract high-tech, mid-tech, low-tech, and some nontech companies—whatever would create jobs.

Mayor Hudnut claims five principles guided the leadership style he used to help Indianapolis gain population and revitalize its economy.

1. *The entrepreneurial city creates partnerships with the private sector.* Public- and private-sector joint ventures are key. "The for-profit and not-for-profit segments of the private sector get together with some government to make things happen. Sometimes one sector takes the initiative, sometimes another, but they are all involved in creative leveraging of each other; they cooperate, establish a consensus, and move ahead."[10]

2. *The entrepreneurial city takes risks.* Hudnut puts it bluntly: The really good local public officials are not afraid to share power, risks, and rewards with the private sector. Cities, he says, are investors too; in return for tangible support for a project, they earn a share of the profit by participating in revenues, rents, and cash flow.

3. *The entrepreneurial city looks for better methods of management.* When it makes sense, a city should contract operations out, for example, trash collection, snow removal, even parts of its transportation system. Although a city is not exactly the same as a business, it has distinctive social, moral, and civic responsibilities too. "The bottom line of all that we are doing," says Mayor Hudnut, is "to make the running of local government more like a business . . . reduce city costs, to improve city services, to increase investor confidence in the city, and to sharpen our competitive edge."[11]

4. *The entrepreneurial city treats amenities as economic assets.* Hudnut suggests there is a profitable connection between a commitment to culture, the arts, and preservation projects on the one hand, and job generation and economic-development opportunities on the other. He claims that many businesses are coming into Indianapolis because of the city's commitment to the arts as well as to the theme of fitness. These quality-of-life projects make the central core of the city more attractive, enhancing business growth and helping reverse the negative trend of a declining industrial base.

5. *The entrepreneurial city combats urban decline and attracts urban reinvestment, not by going to Washington and asking for more money but by creatively using nontraditional resources at home.* Hudnut, who is not only Mayor of Indianapolis but who also recently served as president of the National League of Cities, notes that venture capital funds are being set up in cities all around the nation. Business incubator programs for new and existing companies are being established. Home-grown economic-development projects are springing up and producing results, encouraging investment, creating new jobs, and expanding the revenues of the inner cities.

Hudnut, a Presbyterian minister, loves his job; he says that the mayorship is just "another form of ministry." According to Hudnut, being mayor is also like conducting an orchestra; he provides the direction and empowerment as Indianapolis continues to prosper.[12]

Four-term Mayor Henry Cisneros, who stepped down in 1989 as the chief executive of San Antonio, the tenth largest city in the country, was an effective leader-renewer. Born in a Hispanic barrio in the "across the tracks" west side of San Antonio, Cisneros earned degrees from Texas A & M, Harvard, and George Washington University. After serving on the city council for several years, he narrowly won election as mayor in 1981. He won reelection by landslides. Although San Antonio still has plenty of problems, Mayor Cisneros was able to attract scores of new companies and was partially responsible for helping launch a major biotech research park, a $125 million world amusement area, and a domed sports complex.

Cisneros says providing successful urban leadership requires working twelve- to fourteen-hour days, a strategy he followed. He maintained personal relationships with the plant managers and company leaders he lured to and involved in the life of San Antonio. The real answers, he observes, are not found in confrontation, obstruction, or denial of access, but rather in cooperation and inclusion in the fashioning of a common stake in the future.

What was his strategy for leadership? "I have a two-fisted strategy," he said. "One is to be better in delivering services, to be more financially responsible, to be leaner, tougher, better than anybody. But the other fist has to work with equal intensity to make the system work for those who have been outside the economic mainstream."[13]

Baltimore Mayor William Schaefer was another recent take-charge, entrepreneurial modern mayor who did so well as mayor that he became governor of Maryland. Along with business, civic, and architectural leaders, he capitalized on Baltimore's splendid harbor and transformed a bleak scene of deteriorating warehouses into a visually exciting center for retail, residential, cultural, and waterfront activity. Although he was called the best mayor in America, "the genius mayor," and the like, Schaefer had more than his share of problems in the city rated by the U.S. Census Bureau as the nation's eighth poorest. He (and Baltimore) also lost their football team to Indianapolis.

Undaunted, this several-term mayor set out to improve things. He rebuilt city hall. He built five interstate highways, got a solid subway system going, helped build one of the nation's foremost aquariums, and launched a world trade center. He fought for the Harborplace that has been an enormous boost to civic pride and economic revitalization. He provided the leadership for a new symphony hall and for a new stadium that helped keep Baltimore's major league baseball team in the city. The list goes on and on. He may not be a dashing, telegenic Clint Eastwood, but he is a tough, canny, cunning wheeler and dealer.[14]

MAYORS AS CHIEF EXECUTIVES

The main job of the mayor is administrative in the broadest sense of the term. Mayors supervise the big "line" agencies—police, fire, public safety, traffic, health, sanitation—as well as a host of special agencies, such as the board of elections, the city planning agency, and commissions that regulate particular occupations and professions. Big-city mayors usually have staffs that carry out typical executive office functions such as personnel, management, budgeting, scheduling, and public relations. In this respect mayors face the same tasks as executives: coordinating a variety of different activities, assigning responsibilities, checking that projects are carried out, finding the ablest people to take charge, and allotting money through control of budget.[15]

As already noted, many of the nation's better mayors are especially adept at forging economic partnerships with corporate and private-sector leaders. Together they have initiated some significant revitalization projects: The Quincy Market–Faneuil Hall in Boston, the Nicollet Mall area in downtown Minneapolis, the smoke control and Golden Triangle projects in Pittsburgh, and countless similar enterprises resulting from the joint efforts of creative mayors and civic entrepreneurs (often bankers, architects, and corporate officers) to beautify their cities.

Usually mayors become involved with the private sector in economic-development activities in an effort to help promote economic activity and economic opportunities. They try to secure additional jobs, increase a specific tax base, make the city more attractive to certain kinds of businesses, or coordinate future public-service expansion with private-sector requirements and projected uses. The private sector becomes involved in city economic-development projects because its economic success depends upon having a solid labor base with appropriate skills, a constant consumer population, stable communities as measured by housing and school indicators, and stable or increasing property values, which prevent erosion of private assets.[16]

Mayors also have to deal with public or special authorities. Essentially like such public corporations as the Tennessee Valley Authority, these authorities have been set up to undertake important yet specialized functions in the big cities. (Examples are Metropolitan Water District of Southern California and the Port Authority of New York.) These agencies oversee functions lying outside as well as inside the boundaries of the city. They have a legal mandate granted to them by the state (or states) to raise money, hire experts, and take over some city services, such as transportation, water, and housing. Why public authorities? In part because state legislatures are sometimes hostile to mayors and prefer to place important functions outside the reach of mayors and political "machines," and in part because the authorities have financial flexibility (for example, they might be able to incur debt outside the limits imposed on the city by the state). But most important, many problems are simply too big or cover too wide a geographic area to be handled properly by the city itself.

Public authorities pose a special problem for central-city mayors. Not only are many of the vital functions of metropolitan government placed beyond the mayor's direct control, but even worse, a mosaic of special authorities and special districts constantly comes into contact—and conflict—with "line" agencies dealing with the same problems in the city. It is hard enough for mayors to coordinate and mediate among their own agencies; it is infinitely harder to deal with independent authorities. But if public authorities are a problem for mayors, they are also a temptation. By helping to sponsor these independent agencies, mayors can sometimes cut down on their direct administrative loads. They can tap other sources of funds and keep their own cities' tax rates lower than they would otherwise be. If things go wrong, they can say they did not have authority over a certain function and hence cannot be held responsible. However, this may adversely affect the city's welfare and the capacity of its residents as a whole to govern themselves effectively.[17]

THE CITY MACHINE

At the turn of the century party bosses ruled many of our larger cities and some of our smaller ones. After touring the United States, a famous Populist era muckraker reported: "St. Louis exemplified boodle; Minneapolis, police graft; Pittsburgh, a political and industrial machine; and Philadelphia, general civic corruption."[18] Why were these big American cities boss-ridden? There were many reasons: lack of public interest and the refusal of leading citizens to take part in public affairs; the influx of immigrants who found that the ward leaders and precinct captains were their friends and that politics offered the main means of climbing the economic and social ladder; a government structure so weak that some political leader had to take charge; and finally, business interests that stood behind the bosses and used them to secure franchises, contracts, and protection from regulation.

Few strong citywide **political machines** exist today. The number and power of citywide party bosses has declined since the turn of the century, partly because of a steady drumbeat of criticism and opposition from reform groups. It is also due in part to shrinking patronage, as more and more city jobs come under the civil service. In addition, today there is stricter supervision of local spending by

---

Reflections of a Mayor

We hear more about politicians who are indicted or convicted of crime than we do about the thousands of good men and women who work hard, often for very little in return. One is reminded of the fellow who decided to visit an old college buddy in a small town in another state. He had heard his chum had become the town's mayor. It being Saturday afternoon, he asked at the local service station where he might find Mayor Jones and was told: "That no good so-and-so? He's probably off fishing, just like every other day." At the local drug store on Main Street, he heard: "That jerk? I wouldn't tell you if I knew."

After similar repeated attempts, he decided to go by City Hall on the chance someone there might be able to direct him to his friend's house. The building was almost deserted, but there in the mayor's office, hard at work, was his old friend. After a few pleasantries, the out-of-towner asked why his friend wanted a job that kept him working on a beautiful Saturday afternoon. Was it the high salary? "Oh no," the Mayor replied, "there is no pay at all." Well, then, was it for the bribes—contractors' graft and the like? No, the Mayor said, all city contracts were let by competitive bidding. Perhaps the Mayor controlled a lot of patronage jobs? No, all the jobs were now treated under a civil service system. "Why in the world, then," demanded the out-of-towner, "do you take a job like this?" Replied the Mayor "For the prestige, of course."

state and national governments and more affluence, which makes city dwellers less dependent on the machine. Then, too, increasing numbers of national welfare programs supply social security, unemployment insurance, medical assistance, and relief checks. And not without significance has been the growing reality in many big cities, especially in the Northeast, of polarizing ethnic politics.

To some extent the personal organizations of mayors, other powerful city officials, or organized public bureaucracies have taken the place of political ma-chines. Tom Bradley of Los Angeles, Raymond Flynn of Boston and David Dinkins of New York built their own coalitions. But more often the machine has been succeeded by a much less centralized system. Political influence may shift into the hands of many powerful and perhaps competing office holders, or into the hands of state and federal officials from the metropolitan area, or into the hands of such nonoffice holders as newspaper publishers, union heads, bankers, and leaders of ethnic groups.

Although the pattern of power varies widely from city to city, we again confront the problem that has occupied us throughout this book. Bossism, to be sure, brought problems, yet how much better off is a metropolis that has no central system of leadership—one that may be politically nothing more than a collection of warring factions or ethnic blocs? Among other things, bosses wanted to do things for the people, and at least they had the power to operate through the various units of government. A divided government might be more honest, yet it is generally less effective, especially in shaping and administering programs for lower-income groups and for the long-term improvement of the city.

Party weakness is intensified because most central cities tend to favor one party, usually the Democrats. The absence of real two-party politics has somewhat the same effect on the city as it has often had on the South: one party is so big, and wins with such little effort, that it fails to keep in fighting trim and disintegrates into factions. The minority party is too weak to have much hope of success and it fails to provide a strong opposition or meaningful alternatives.

More Reflections of a Mayor

"On balance, my generation of mayors—the Daleys, the Wagners, the Dilworths, the Dave Lawrences, the Charley Tafts, the Joe Clarks and Tuckers, the Hartsfields and Ivan Allens, the Henry Maiers—all felt the game was worth the candle, and that for every failure we recorded we had more than our share of successes, and by God, I am proud of that era. We would dream, and we did; we would try, and we did. When we failed, we failed magnificently, and when we succeeded, we succeeded beyond our fondest expectations, and, after all, what's wrong with a record like that?"

Source: Mayor Richard C. Lee of New Haven, Connecticut (1954 to 1969) speaking to the 1980 U.S. Conference of Mayors, Seattle, Washington.

Can the Mayor Lead? A Case Study

The mayor is usually the most important and visible political figure in a big city. Like presidents, mayors are supposed to spell out the city's goals, play the leading role in getting these goals accepted by the people and adopted by the city government, and carry out these goals. Yet like presidents, mayors are hemmed in on many sides. Big cities vary widely in their politics, and mayors vary in their power. Let's explore the problem of mayoral leadership by taking one example—the mayor of New York. This job is considered by some to be second in complexity to the national presidency, for not only is New York the nation's biggest city and one of the financial, cultural, intellectual and trading centers of the world, but the New York metropolitan area sprawls over parts of three states and hence continually faces city-state-federal problems.

ADMINISTRATIVE CHIEF?

The mayor of New York City is supposed to be (and in some respects is) the administrative head of the city government. The mayor appoints the heads of most departments, such as police or fire; members of city boards and commissions, such as the parole commissioner, and city magistrates and justices. Unlike a president and most governors, New York mayors do not share appointive power with legislative bodies, and their authority to remove subordinates, despite numerous restrictions, is also fairly sweeping. In short, with power to hire and fire, the mayor of New York is truly "the chief executive officer of the city," as the city charter says.

The mayor also has limited administrative power over the city's independent authorities. Some heads of authorities have won such wide recognition that they are politically effective in their own right. Most notable of these was Robert Moses, a charismatic adviser and administrator who might well have been called "Mr. Authority." Moses's jobs suggest the versatility of this brilliant, aggressive, and often controversial man. From the 1930s through the 1960s, Moses was chairperson of the Triborough Bridge and Tunnel Authority, commissioner of the Parks Department, a member of the City Planning Commission, chairperson of the Mayor's Committee on Slum Clearance, a member of the New York City Youth Board, and president of the Jones Beach State Parkway Authority, and many other jobs.[19]

In all these positions he attracted friends (and enemies) within the city's administration as well as among the public. Clearly, in dealing with Moses the mayor was dealing with an independent leader who had his own constituency. Relations between the two were often made more difficult because Moses was a lifelong Republican, and most New York mayors are Democrats.

LEGISLATIVE LEADER?

Mayors of New York, like other mayors, find policy-making power splintered and fragmented from the moment they take office. They are working within a system that divides power among the national, state, and local governments, and among many officials at each level. Practically speaking, a mayor must coordinate or at least clear major policies with the governor of New York, the state's two United States senators, several members of Congress, state legislators from the city, and other officials, such as the state attorney general, members of Congress from the adjoining states of New Jersey and Connecticut, and even the president and perhaps a cabinet member or two. A mayor's power is further fragmented within the city government.

The structure of the government of New York City is undergoing major revision. A Charter Revision Commission is writing a new charter for the city, and its work has been hastened by the U.S. Supreme Court's decision that the Board of Estimate (see below) violates the constitutional principle of one person one vote. The five borough presidents on that Board have one vote despite the fact they represent populations of widely varying size.

Whatever the new structure turns out to be, it is likely that in the future, as in the past, the mayor will have the formal responsibility of shaping and presenting the city's legislative program. Formally or informally, the mayor has been presenting it several times—to the council, to the governor and the state legislature, and to other official bodies. Formal law-making power has been vested in the thirty-five member city council; twenty-five members are elected by districts and ten are elected boroughwide, two from each borough. On paper the council appeared to be virtually a little Congress. Actually, it played a rather passive role, and allowed the mayor or other officials to take the leadership. The council generally failed to exercise the historic weapon of legislative bodies against executives—the appropriating power.

For some decades fiscal control of the city was exercised not by the mayor or the council but by the Board of Estimate, a rather curious institution. This Board's dominant role was called into question when the Supreme Court held in 1989 that its method of selection violates the equal protection clause requirement of one-person–one-vote.[20] It seems unlikely its role will be revived. Instead the Charter Commission is giving serious consideration to an expanded role for the City Council that would incorporate a role for the five borough presidents.[21] Until declared unconstitutional the Board's eight members had varying numbers of votes (two each for the mayor, president of the council and comptroller; one each for the five borough presidents).

The degree of cooperation a mayor can get from a council member depends primarily on how well the mayor can control political pressures on the legislators. And this often depends on the mayor's political coalition-building efforts or occasional direct appeals to the people.

PARTY LEADER?

A Democratic mayor of New York is usually the most powerful single party leader in the city. Still, party power must be shared with other officials and with party leaders. There is no single citywide political-party organization. Democrats are organized on the basis of county committees from the five boroughs, which in turn oversee vast hierarchies of precinct, ward, and assembly-district organizations. The mayor deals not with a unified party organization, but with five county leaders, about twenty members of the New York City delegation to the United States Congress, borough presidents, and some traditional party bosses who hold no major offices. Sometimes New York mayors benefit from the absence of unity, for they can "divide and conquer" county leaders. However, party divisions may handicap them in pushing through new programs.

What strong mayors must do is build their own campaign organization inside and outside the regular political party. This is a formidable task. Even though they have considerable patronage, handing out jobs is usually not enough to build a political machine. They must deal with party committee officials who may be much more interested in working for other candidates and office holders than for them. Usually the mayors find they must supplement their personal organizations by acquiring allies from among the other office holders and the heads of personal organizations.

More recently, ethnic and racial blocs have rivaled the party as strategic political interests in New York and other big cities. More and more the pattern is for cities to consist of blacks, Hispanics, and immigrant groups who enjoy increasing influence on political decisions. Yet as their influence has increased, they have often found the city with diminished financial resources and increased social and economic problems. Ethnic-group politics is alive and well but the problem of governing remains. We return to this issue in Chapter 10 when we discuss the taxing and spending problems of the big cities.

LEADER OR CHIEF BARGAINER?

Clearly, New York City mayors are restricted, no matter how great their ability. Most of the time they must piece together coalitions of various politicians and fragments of influence. They are less leaders who draw swords, point out the direction, and rally the battalions than horse traders who talk and swap and persuade and compromise. Their governmental roles tend to be more defensive than affirmative. They are continually involved in the process of building administrative, legislative, or party coalitions, and the price of such coalitions is usually weakened programs and policies. They are in the middle of the political marketplace because little of importance can be accomplished without their consent.

For a while in the 1980s, Mayor Ed Koch appeared to provide exactly the kind of mayoral leadership New York City needed. Gutsy, zestful, combative, vain, outspoken, and seemingly devoted to restoring confidence to New York, Koch presided over the city as it enjoyed economic recovery and a big increase in convention and tourist trade. Most important, under Koch's leadership the City was able to balance its books. Koch also wrote political books (one of which became a Broadway musical).[22] He declared he wanted to be mayor forever. Then in Koch's third term his leadership was dealt a major blow. Several of his political allies and top appointees were indicted for involvement in what was apparently a widespread system of bribes and kickbacks for doing business with the city. The city also was dogged by racial strife. New Yorkers lost confidence in the way the city was being run, and Koch was defeated in the primary election.

The Suburban Boom and Its Political Implications

In the recent past the suburbs, the areas around the cities, have been the fastest-growing places in the United States. About 45 percent of us now live in these communities. The suburbs grew because of a variety of factors: inexpensive land; lower taxes; better air; more open space for recreational purposes; better services; less crime; better highways; and the changing character of the inner cities. In the post-World War II years massive numbers of the poor and dispossessed—both black and white—migrated from rural areas to the central cities, especially in the northeast and north central regions. Three of every five blacks in the United States now live in the central city of a major metropolitan area. Middle- and upper-middle-income whites have fled from many of these metropolitan areas to the suburbs in search of more homogeneous communities.

Young families who could afford it left the crowded and blighted business areas and moved out of the cities in search of more pleasant living quarters. Industries also moved from the central cities in search of cheaper land, lower taxes, and escape from city building and health codes. Business followed both the people and the industries, and myriad shopping centers grew in outlying communities. Much of this exodus was encouraged by one or more federal policies concerning such issues as inner-city busing and the construction of public housing in the inner cities.[23]

About 125 million Americans are now suburbanites, that is, they live outside the central cities in the 280 regions designated by the Bureau of the Census as **Standard Metropolitan Statistical Areas. (SMSAs).** Demographers predict a 10 percent increase in the suburban population by the year 2000 and that most of the new jobs created in the United States will continue to be located in the suburbs. In short, suburbs clearly have been the most economically dynamic parts of the nation during the past thirty years. Governing these metropolitan areas, cities, and suburbs are dozens—in some cases even hundreds—of governments. For example, the four-county Pittsburgh metropolitan area contains 704 local governments, 441 of which can levy property taxes. One county—Allegheny—has eighty-four municipalities, forty-two townships, sixty-two school districts, and at least 129 school boards. Citizens of Whitehall, located in this metropolitan area, have sixteen layers of government between them and the state level:

Layers of Governance in Whitehall, Pennsylvania

17. United States of America

  16. Commonwealth of Pennsylvania

    15. Air Quality Control Region

      14. Southwestern Pennsylvania Regional Planning Commission

        13. Western Pennsylvania Water Company

          12. Allegheny County

            11. Allegheny County Port Authority

              10. Allegheny County Criminal Justice Commission

                9. Allegheny County Soil and Water Conservation District

                  8. Allegheny County Sanitary Authority

                    7. City of Pittsburgh

                      6. South Hills Area Council of Governments

                        5. South Hills Regional Planning Commission

                          4. Pleasant Hills Sanitary Authority

                            3. Baldwin-Whitehall Schools Authority

                              2. Baldwin-Whitehall School District

                                1. Borough of Whitehall

On average there are at least ninety governments per metropolitan area, fifty per metropolitan county. Many Clevelanders, that is, people who work in Cleveland, shop in Cleveland, and read Cleveland newspapers, do not live in Cleveland. By and large they tend to be white and wealthier than those who do live in Cleveland. Only about half the St. Louisans live in St. Louis. Less than half of the residents in the Philadelphia metro area live in the central city, and much less than half of the labor force works there. The sheer complexity and fragmentation of government administration in suburbia often creates confusion, if not frustration. Each suburban city has its own government, fire and police departments, school system, street-cleaning equipment, and building and health codes. Special-district governments piled on top of one another further complicate the situation. Also, all the major tasks of suburban government are bound together with those of the metropolis. Criminals do not stop at city boundaries. The central city usually maintains an elaborate police department with detective bureaus, crime-detection laboratories, and communications networks, but its jurisdiction stops at the city line. Suburbs have fewer police, and they are often untrained in criminology. Or consider traffic problems. Superhighways run through suburbia, and they all have a number of access roads. In matters of health, too, there are often wide differences in standards between parts of a metropolis. But germs, pollution, and smog do not notice city signposts.

15 Wealthiest Suburbs

SUBURB	PER CAPITA INCOME	SUBURB	PER CAPITA INCOME
Kenilworth, Ill. (Chicago)	$61,950	Oyster Bay Cove-Mill Neck (New York)	$51,650
Bloomfield Hills (Detroit)	$59,830	Cherry Hills (Denver)	$50,016
Hewlett-Woodburgh (New York)	$59,300	Franklin (Detroit)	$49,961
Ladue, Mo. (St. Louis)	$55,962	Frontenac (St. Louis)	$49,615
Mission Hills (Kansas City)	$55,136	Hunters Creek (Houston)	$48,727
Sands Point, N.Y. (Long Island)	$54,393	Bal Harbour (Miami)	$48,725
North Hills-Roslyn Estates (New York)	$52,150	Kings Point (New York)	$47,480
Harding Township, N.J. (New York)	$52,067		

Source: The Associated Press, June 1989, citing analysis of census data by urbanologist Pierre de Vise.

What of government and politics in the suburbs? It is dangerous to generalize, because individual suburbs vary so greatly. Some, like Paradise Valley, Arizona, Atherton, California, or Potomac, Maryland, are the exclusive residences of the rich, and are governed by an efficient cluster of specialists. Others are lower-middle-class neighborhoods of blue-collar workers. Some, like Compton and East Palo Alto, California, or Glen Arden and Seat Pleasant, Maryland, are predominantly black. Still others are populated with young professional families who are more interested in their next promotions than in their communities. Some suburbanites tend to consider local government a device to protect property, schools, and homes against "invasion" by minority groups. Occasionally suburban dwellers become aroused over major problems like educational policy or taxation, but in the absence of explosive issues, local suburban politics is often low key.

CITIES VERSUS SUBURBS: HOW MUCH OF A CONTRAST?

Many of us have grown up thinking that a suburb is a place where all the houses are alike, the husbands travel to the city to work, and the lifestyle is based on children, well-kept lawns, and single-family dwellings. Some of these stereotypes have a basis in reality, but these myths greatly distort the fast-changing character of our suburban areas. In fact, there are all kinds of housing patterns in suburbia, and an increasingly large number of the residents of both sexes work in their own communities or in other nearby suburbs. Many of the suburbs provide the services and economic opportunities once found only in the central cities. Older suburbs face growth and aging problems. And although tax levels and rates generally remain higher in central cities, suburbs have experienced increases in taxes and expenditures similar to those of the central cities. Moreover, as noted earlier, not all suburbs are the same, and many who live in the central cities have the same lifestyles and values as those in the suburbs. Still, many central cities find that their principal antagonists in the state legislature and in Congress are not the rural areas but the suburbs. The longstanding cleavage between city and suburbs persists as a major feature of political life in many metropolitan areas.

But we must not draw too sharp a contrast between suburban and central-city problems. Many suburbanites have discovered that lower prices for land and lower taxes are deceptive. They often have to pay higher fire insurance rates; they pay more for garbage collection; and they often have to build and maintain their own septic tanks. Moreover, as suburban real estate becomes improved, and as the suburb grows in size, many new facilities are needed. Suburbs are also beginning to suffer the nagging problems of crime, traffic congestion, pollution, troubled schools, and racial hostility. "There's no constituency for serious long term planning, and few localities put serious dollars into it," writes Neal R. Peirce, a veteran observer of local government in the United States. "Suburbanites often distrust their local councils—and not without reason, because developers contribute the biggest campaign dollars."[24]

Further, few of the fastest growing suburbs care about housing for their poor or even for the employees of the giant firms that relocate to them. To ask typical suburban government officials to think creatively or compassionately about housing for lower-income groups or minorities is simply unrealistic. Whether intentionally or not, and surely some of it is intentional, many of the zoning and related ordinances have the effect of excluding low- and moderate-income people. A resegregation of America is often the result.

BACK TO THE BIG CITY?

Partly because of the problems of the older suburbs and partly because of some dynamic revitalization efforts in many of our older cities, fewer people today are leaving the central cities; some are even heading back to the cities from the suburbs.[25] Impressive downtown renewal in Boston, Chicago, Baltimore, Detroit, and Philadelphia has led many people to once again see cities as alive and exciting. In Savannah, Charleston, Boston, San Francisco, and Washington, D.C., old "row houses" have been remodeled into fashionable "town houses." Neighborhoods that were "blighted" have been rebuilt. Young working couples, retired couples, and families who can afford to send their children to private schools have moved into the fashionable and now-expensive neighborhoods. Shopping centers, down-town malls, boutiques, and art galleries flourish. But the poor, often the blacks,

"We love the view. It helps to remind us that we're part of a larger community."

Drawing by Weber; © 1986 The New Yorker Magazine, Inc.

are moving out of these "gentrified" neighborhoods, and they must usually crowd into other areas of the city or into nearby urban suburbs.

Can We Govern Metro Regions Effectively?

The division between central city and suburbia; the existence of divided executive authority, fragmented legislative power, splintered and noncompetitive political parties; the absence of strong central governments for whole metropolitan regions; and the necessity that mayors and other city leaders bargain with so many national, state, local officials—all these factors seem to suggest that metro regions are shapeless giants with nobody in charge.

At the turn of the century reformers were afraid of boss domination. But in the modern metropolis the mayor of the central city lacks authority even over agencies within the city. Political machines don't run the central city, let alone the whole metropolis. Urban bureaucracies may wield a lot of power over a few areas but they do not offer metropolitan leadership. "Special interests" seldom really control the metropolis, nor usually does a "business elite," or any other kind of "they." And even if "they" did control politics, that is not the same as governing. Who, then governs the metropolis? Does anybody provide coherent leadership?

METROPOLITAN REFORM STRATEGIES

The growing fragmentation of governments in large metropolitan areas has brought about a variety of metropolitan reform movements and structural inventions aimed at improving performance and reducing corruption. Political scientists and public administration specialists have not been bashful about proposing remedies. We look here at some of the better-known ideas, all of which have been tried somewhere, but none of which has been generally adopted nationwide.

Annexation In the growing cities of the South, West, and Southwest, the large central cities have absorbed adjacent territories. Oklahoma City, for example, added almost 600 square miles. Houston, Phoenix, and Kansas City, Missouri, San Antonio, El Paso, and Colorado Springs have also expanded their boundaries. In these and several other cities, the now-extended city serves almost as a de facto regional government. Annexation has not proved helpful, however, to most cities in the Northeast and Midwest because the cities are ringed by entrenched suburban communities that do not want to be annexed, and state laws make it difficult for the central city to do so against the wishes of the suburbs. Even in such places as the Houston metropolitan area, the annexation option is plagued by legal obstacles, political jealousies, and additional complications.[26]

Agreements to Furnish Services The most common solution to the problems of overlapping and duplicating jurisdictions is for the units of government to contract services. This "reform" is applauded by many economists. They say it comes close to providing a market that operates according to laws of supply and demand. Most agreements involve just a few cities and a single activity. For example, a city may provide hospital services to its neighbors, or contract with the county for law enforcement. Especially popular in the Los Angeles area, the contract system is also used in other parts of the country.[27]

Regional Coordinating and Planning Councils Just about all metro regions have some kind of council of government (COGs). These began in the 1950s and were encouraged by the national government during the 1960s and 1970s. Congress, in fact, mandated that certain federal grants be reviewed by this kind of body. In essence councils are forums established to bring locally elected officials together. They have devoted most of their time and resources to physical planning and noncontroversial activities that do not touch the urban problems of race and poverty. Councils are set up, moreover, in such a way as to give suburbs a veto over any project that would threaten their autonomy. In a few regions the councils do assume operating responsibilities over such regional activities as garbage collection, transportation, and water supply. Yet the councils rarely provide for creative areawide governance.

City-County Consolidations One traditional means of overcoming the fragmentation of metro regions is to merge the central city with the larger county. This was a pet reform of business elites, the League of Women Voters, and chamber of commerce. It was viewed as a rational, efficient way to simplify administration, cut costs for taxpayers, and eliminate duplication.

At least twenty-five city-county mergers have taken place. They can usually be brought about only by a public referendum that the citizens of the region must approve. Although efforts have been made to consolidate cities with counties—

Boston, New York, Philadelphia, for example—few such efforts have been successful. In addition to St. Louis, Nashville, Jacksonville, and Indianapolis, consolidations have occurred in only a handful of smaller urban areas. What happened in Indianapolis is typical of these consolidations, most of which are in the South and West. In 1970 Indianapolis combined with Marion County to create UNIGOV. This required special permission by the legislature. UNIGOV provides many services, but the school systems remain separate, as do police and sheriff departments.

Although some scholars advocate total consolidation of all small units of government into one regional, usually county, system, such total mergers never take place in practice. In order to bring about modest consolidation, compromises have to be made. "What appears to casual observer to be complete consolidation," on closer inspection turns out to be a "multi-tiered structure . . . with the county as upper tier and the lower tier as a municipality or a special service district."[28]

Federated Government One strategy that attempts to take into account political realities advocates building on existing governments. Backers of this strategy conclude that it is both undesirable and impossible to create a single giant metropolitan government for a large area. To do so would be to eliminate all of the "us" governments and substitute a distant "them" government. Instead, they advocate keeping the units with which people identify but assigning some crucial functions to an areawide metro government.

One of the few attempts, and there are only a few, to create a federated government is the Twin Cities Metropolitan Council for the Minneapolis-St. Paul region. This regional organization, established by the legislature in 1967, consists of a seventeen-member council. Sixteen members are appointed by the governor to represent equal population districts, and the seventeenth is a full-time chairperson-executive who serves at the pleasure of the governor. A staff conducts research, planning, and coordination for the 140 cities, 7 counties, and about 36 special districts in the region. In matters defined as regional, this council can and does veto local actions or prevent actions by local governments. Prior to 1967 the Twin Cities region had been plagued for years by governmental fragmentation, tax inequities, and inconsistent provision of services. Because the central cities were tightly ringed by established suburban communities, the idea of a city-county merger was not appropriate. Today the Metropolitan Council, in essence a new layer of government superimposed on top of existing units, serves as a metropolitan planning and policy-making, as well as policy-coordinating, agency. It reviews applications for federal funds from the region. It guides regional planning and development and opposes local actions that would endanger the overall welfare of the region.[29] The Twin Cities model would appear to be a ready candidate for transfer elsewhere, yet this has not happened.

THE POLITICS OF METROPOLITAN REORGANIZATION

Nearly every metropolitan area today has or wants regional bodies that can integrate and coordinate the maze of governmental structures. There is already a degree of cooperation, although much of it is informal, voluntary, or contractual. Progress in designing areawide, multipurpose, integrated metropolitan governing bodies has been slow and will remain that way. Why? In part because different cities and jurisdictions have differing political needs. They depend on specific needs to arise and changes in the physical and political context. Reformers who proceed on the assumption that what is appropriate for Syracuse must also be best for San Antonio or Sacramento are not likely to meet with success. For example, city-county consolidation has been an effective solution for Nashville, but it could not get beyond the proposal stage in Pittsburgh or beyond the electorate in Memphis. Annexation has worked well in Phoenix and Oklahoma City but would be of little help in cities ringed by incorporated suburbs, such as Boston, Denver, or Miami. Similarly, although the urban county approach serves the Los Angeles area reasonably well, it would be less effective in New England's traditionally weak counties.

In most metropolitan regions, to combine city and suburbs would be to shift political power to the suburbs. In most northern centers this would give Republicans more control of city affairs. In other cases it would enable Democrats to threaten the present one-party Republican systems in the suburbs. Under these circumstances neither Democratic leaders in the central cities nor Republicans in control of the suburbs show much enthusiasm for metropolitan schemes. Blacks usually oppose area consolidation or similar reform proposals because they would dilute their political power, often rather severely.[30] In the Jacksonville consolidation with Duval County, the proportion of the black population to the total population was halved. Moreover, many of the larger metro-area cities now have black mayors. Most of the black residents in these cities and in cities that might soon elect black mayors fear that metropolitan political reorganization would (1) undermine the political opportunities that have only recently come to blacks, and (2) not result in structures that would be responsive to social and economic problems of the poor.

In general, although residents of the metropolis want better services, they hope to achieve them by negotiation and other traditional or innovative devices. Although there is no rebellion against the existing structure, a notable increase of interlocal and regional collaboration has occurred. It was generally done on an issue-by-issue basis and reflects an incremental pattern of evolution.[31] Through patchwork, piecemeal, and pragmatic arrangements, the public receives the services it wants—and is willing to pay for.

A SOLUTION OUTSIDE METROPOLIS?

Some people believe solutions to metropolitan problems are beyond the capacity of the metropolis itself. Some favor a strengthened role for the national government, with special emphasis on ensuring "equity" or on relating services directly to needs.[32] Some advocate reviving federal revenue sharing, yet they would give back revenue only on the condition that local governments rationalize the governmental machinery of the whole metropolis. Others believe the job must be done by the states, which hold the fundamental constitutional power. Still others put forward bold revised proposals to establish regional governments that would rule huge regions embracing many metropolitan areas.

Big-city mayors have made it clear that, in their judgment, the urban condition is acute, and that we must rearrange our national priorities and allocate billions of dollars for massive aid to large cities. The cities themselves lack the resources and political jurisdiction necessary to attack the basic causes of urban pathology. "We surrender," some mayors have been saying, in effect, to Washington. "Treat us like a conquered and occupied nation. Give us the kind of aid you gave Germany and Japan after the Second World War." Mayor Terry Goddard of Phoenix, who served recently as the president of the National League of Cities, shares this view. "We have the S&L bailout, the nuclear-waste bailout at $100 billion, and the treasury secretary (under George Bush) is talking about writing off the debt to foreign countries," Goddard notes. "We [as mayors] think the nation's cities would do better either to merge with an S&L or to become a foreign nation. We would be a lot better off in terms of the budget, and nobody would talk about the deficit [as an excuse not to help us]."[33]

In the matter of federal aid, however, the Reagan administration was seldom sympathetic to big-city mayors and the Bush Administration has shown little indication of giving these matters higher priority. Fiscal constraints are limiting federal programs. As we enter the 1990s most states have had to cut services and raise taxes. States are also unable to deal easily with the problem of giant cities that stretch over state lines. New regional governments? A bold idea, but one that appears beyond the capacity of the American people to engineer without destroying our basic constitutional structure and threatening local home-rule values.

The issue, however, goes deeper than all these considerations; it goes back to the heart of the question of government by the people. Can popular government best be realized through strong executive leaders like Mayors LaGuardia or Richard J. Daley—individuals who build political power and then try to pull the divided city government together behind their program? Many say yes; they contend progress can come only as result of strong personal leadership by elected officials, though such leaders should be willing to make concessions to particular groups and local areas. Just as the nation has needed Presidents Jackson, Lincoln, and the Roosevelts, so the cities need popular, visible, and purposeful leadership. Others disagree. Progress in our cities and metro regions, they hold, will come from piecemeal efforts, from bargaining among leaders of all types, from community action, from exerting pressure here and there, and from hammering out agreements or "treaties" among diverse groups.

There are positions between these extremes, of course, yet the extremes pose once again our crucial problem: choosing between centralized political control and a more open and decentralized form of governance.

Summary

1. We live in a metropolitan nation with most of us living in central cities or in outlying communities known as suburbs. There is considerable fragmentation of governmental units in our metropolitan areas, and this fragmentation tends to undermine citizen involvement in the problems of the metropolis.

2. The standard of living in the central cities of the United States may be much better than it was fifty years ago, but the inequalities between many central cities and their middle and outer rings of affluent suburbs are increasing. Central cities are often faced with economic hardships. Fragmentation and dispersal of political authority in the metro areas and even in many of the central cities themselves often make it difficult to govern the big cities.

3. The role of big-city mayors is crucial to the successful governance of cities. Several mayors in recent years have led impressive efforts to rebuild and renew downtown areas that have made inner-city living more attractive again.

4. The politics of who should govern and who actually governs metropolitan areas is complicated by the fragmented political jurisdictions within most metro areas. Compounding the difficulty is the existence of powerful public-employee unions and the decline of central-city political bosses and political-party machines. Power has become dispersed as the problems in many central cities have multiplied.

5. There is no typical suburb. Although many suburbs are homogeneous, suburban America is highly heterogeneous. Suburbs are confronting urban problems, and the inner rings of older suburbs often look very much like the central cities.

6. For a generation or more, reformers thought the answer to the problems of metropolitan government was to elect a strong central-city mayor or to establish a regional government for the whole area. Both solutions have been difficult to achieve and have some drawbacks. The structure of many of our largest cities, such as New York, seems designed to undermine effective, honest governance. Finally, resistance to regional government continues to be great.

Further Reading

DAVID AMMONS and CHARLDEAN NEWELL. *City Executives: Leadership Roles, Work Characteristics and Time Management* (SUNY, 1989).

JANET K. BOLES, ed. *The Egalitarian City: Rights, Distribution, Access and Power* (Praeger, 1986).

MATTHEW CRENSON. *Neighborhood Politics* (Harvard University Press, 1983).

BARBARA FERMAN. *Governing the Ungovernable City* (Temple University Press, 1985).

HARLAN HAHN and CHARLES LEVINE, eds. *Urban Politics: Past, Present and Future* 2d ed. (Longman, 1984).

JOHN J. HARRIGAN. *Political Change in the Metropolis*, 3d ed. (Little, Brown, 1985).

KENNETH T. JACKSON. *Crabgrass Frontier: The Suburbanization of the United States* (Oxford University Press, 1985).

DENNIS R. JUDD. *The Politics of American Cities*, 3d ed. (Scott Foresman, 1988).

CHARLES R. MORRIS. *The Cost of Good Intentions: New York City and the Liberal Experiment* (Norton, 1980).

PAUL PETERSON, ed. *The New Urban Reality* (The Brookings Institution 1985).

N otes

1. See, for example, Edward Banfield, *The Unheavenly City* (Little, Brown, 1968), pp. 3, 5, 12. For different views, see H. M. Hocham, ed., *The Urban Economy* (Norton, 1976); and Gerald L. Houseman, *State and Local Government: The New Battleground* (Prentice Hall, 1986).

2. See *Cities: The Forces That Shape Them* (Cooper-Hewitt Museum–Smithsonian Institution, 1982).

3. See the case studies in R. Scott Fosler and Renee A. Berger, eds., *Public-Private Partnership in American Cities* (Heath, 1982).

4. Neal R. Peirce, "Kellogg to Battle Creek: Merge Governments or We Leave Town," *Today* (November 16, 1982), p. 5.

5. Title of Chapter 3 in John R. Logan and Harvey L. Molotch, *Urban Fortunes: The Political Economy of Place* (University of California Press, 1987), pp. 50–98.

6. Thomas R. Dye, "Government Finances in Declining Central Cities," *Publius: The Journal of Federalism* (Spring 1984), p. 29. For a more general discussion, see the essays in Paul Peterson, ed., *The New Urban Reality* (The Brookings Institution, 1985).

7. See Russell D. Murphy, "The Mayoralty and the Democratic Creed: The Evolution of an Ideology and an Institution," *Urban Affairs Quarterly* (September 1986).

8. See William E. Nelson and Philip Meranto, *Electing Black Mayors: Political Action in the Black Community* (Ohio State University Press, 1977).

9. See John P. Kotter and Paul R. Lawrence, *Mayors in Action* (Wiley, 1974); and Douglas Yates, *The Ungovernable City* (MIT Press, 1978).

10. Mayor Hilliam H. Hudnut, III, Wilson Award Address, Princeton University, February 1986.

11. Ibid.

12. "A Rust-Belt Relic's New Shine," condensed from *Newsweek* (September 9, 1985), p. 26. © Copyright 1985.

13. Quoted in *US News & World Report* (April 7, 1986).

14. See Richard Ben Crammer, "Can the Best Mayor Win?" *Esquire* (October 1984), pp. 57–72.

15. See Jeffrey L. Pressman, "Preconditions of Mayoral Leadership," *American Political Science Review* (June 1972), pp. 511–24.

16. Pastora San Juan Cafferty and William C. McCready, "The Chicago Public-Private Partnership Experience," in Fosler and Berger, *Public-Private Partnership in American Cities*, p. 130.

17. For studies of how some independent authorities have abused their autonomy and contributed to the economic problems of the central city, see the analysis of Robert Moses's many roles in Robert A. Caro, *The Power Broker: Robert Moses and the Fall of New York* (Knopf, 1974). See also Annmarie Hauck Walsh, *The Public's Business: The Politics and Practices of Government Corporations* (MIT Press, 1978); and Diana B. Henriques, *The Machinery of Greed: Public Authorities Abuse and What to Do About It* (Lexington Books, 1986).

18. Lincoln Steffens, *The Shame of the Cities* (1904) (Peter Smith, 1948), p. 16. For a historical perspective on the beginnings of New York City's famed Tammany Hall machine, see Martin Shefter, "The Emergence of the Political Machine: An Alternative View," in Willis D. Hawley et al., *Theoretical Perspectives on Urban Politics* (Prentice Hall, 1976), pp. 14–44.

19. See Caro, *The Power Broker*.

20. *Board of Estimate of City of New York v. Morris*, 103 L ed 2d 717 (1989).

21. Todd S. Purdum, "Bid to Save Estimate Board in New York City Is Rejected," *The New York Times*, May 3, 1989, p. 14.

22. Mayor Koch is author with William Rauch, of *Politics* (Simon & Schuster, 1985). His first was *Mayor*, also with William Rauch (Simon & Schuster, 1984).

23. Kenneth T. Jackson, *Crabgrass Frontier: The Suburbanization of the United States* (Oxford University Press, 1985).

24. Neal R. Peirce, "The New Suburbia is Transforming Open Lands to Urban Village Ghettos," *Today Journal* (September 6, 1985), pp. 6–7. See also John J. Harrigan, *Political Change in the Metropolis*, 3d ed. (Little, Brown, 1985), chap. 10.

25. See, for example, Michael H. Lang, *Gentrification amid Urban Decline: Strategies for America's Older Cities* (Ballinger, 1982).

26. Robert D. Thomas, "Metropolitan Structural Development: The Territorial Imperative," *Publius: The Journal of Federalism* (Spring 1984), pp. 83–115.

27. Gary J. Miller, *Cities by Contract: The Politics of Municipal Incorporation* (MIT Press, 1981). See also C. J. Hein, "Contracting Municipal Services: Does It Really Cost Less?" *National Civic Review* (June 1983), pp. 321–26.

28. Vincent L. Marando, "City County Consolidation: Reform, Regionalism, Referenda and Requiem," *Western Political Science Quarterly* (December 1979), p. 416.

29. See William Johnson and John J. Harrigan, "Innovation by Increments: The Twin Cities as a Case Study in Metropolitan Reform," *Western Political Quarterly* (June 1978), pp. 206–18. For an analysis of the early years of the Twin Cities Council, see Stanley Baldinger, *Planning and Governing the Metropolis: The Twin Cities Experience* (Praeger, 1971).

30. John C. Teaford, *City and Suburb: The Political Fragmentation of Metropolitan America, 1850–1970* (The Johns Hopkins University Press, 1979), p. 181–82.

31. David B. Walker, "Snow White and the 17 Dwarfs: From Metro Cooperation to Governance," *National Civic Review* (January–February 1987), pp. 14–28.

32. See, for example, Michael Pagano and Richard Moore, *Cities and Fiscal Choices* (Duke University Press, 1985); and William Tabb and Larry Sawers, eds., *Marxism and the Metropolis*, 2d ed. (Oxford University Press, 1984).

33. Quoted in *USA Today* (March 14, 1989), p. 11a.

9

State and Local Policy Making

Since 1789, when the new Republic truly got under way, the national government has vastly increased the scope of its power over a whole range of public policy matters. This does not mean, however, that the state and local governments have reduced the services they perform. On the contrary, they have broadened their functions. As the national government has expanded, especially in the past fifty years, jointly run programs or federally financed but locally administered programs have enlarged the scope of state and local governments. In the 1980s the Reagan administration cutbacks in domestic spending forced state and local governments to pick up the costs of maintaining certain services to which their constituents had become accustomed.

State and local policy makers face constant challenges: crime, crack, AIDS, overcrowded prisons, teachers' strikes, too many hazardous waste sites, smog, timber industry and farm-belt depression, lowered prices for oil and gas, bridge and highway deterioration, water shortages in the Southwest, and many others. In summer, heat waves kill scores of people in the South and Southwest; in winter, snowstorms sometimes paralyze cities in the upper Midwest. Auto factory closings throw countless thousands off assembly lines and onto welfare lines. Disruptions, dissent, and a relentless stream of public wants pour in on statehouses and city halls.

If you listen to debates in state legislatures, attend city council meetings, or watch state and local candidates, you come face to face with people who plead for better schools, who insist on better crime-prevention programs, who demand the truly needy receive better care, who become irate about the potholes and decay of our highways and streets, and who are outraged by the hazardous waste

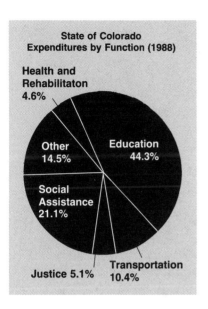

State of Colorado
Expenditures by Function (1988)

Health and
Rehabilitaton
4.6%

Other
14.5%

Education
44.3%

Social
Assistance
21.1%

Justice 5.1%

Transportation
10.4%

dumps near their neighborhoods. Should the city close another school? Where? Will the voters approve a bond issue to construct a new hospital? Should the state superintendent of schools be given authority to establish minimum standards or merit pay for teachers? Should the city or state adopt a comparable worth policy? How can our Western states best allocate their water? What can be done about the traffic jam on Main Street? Should commercial growth be encouraged because of the jobs it will bring, or discouraged because of the traffic and pollution it will generate? Hundreds of people—mayors, legislators, judges, ward bosses, civic commissions, unions, real estate and builders associations, chambers of commerce—participate in the process of determining what officials will do.

As it is impossible to explore each activity of every state, city, county, school district, and township, we will review a few highlights. In this chapter we examine the basic policy functions of the various levels of government. The accompanying figure indicates government priorities for expenditures at the state level in a typical state.

Education

In ancient Greece, Plato and Aristotle insisted that education was a vital task of government. To them, government itself was an educational institution. Thomas Jefferson, too, was convinced an educated citizenry was essential to democratic government. But only during the past century has the idea that government should provide tax-supported schools become generally accepted.

For a long time many groups opposed "free" education. They said it would lead to social unrest, undermine the family, give government control over the minds of the young, require a huge bureaucracy, and result in a fatal mixture of education and politics. And was it fair, they asked, to tax people who could afford to educate their own children in private schools in order to educate others?

Today compulsory public education is an established fact (although parents may, of course, send their children to approved private schools). A strong movement has developed to extend public education downward to kindergarten, nursery school, and day care, upward through college and adult education, outward to cover more subjects, and deeper to cover them more extensively. About 36 percent of all state and local government expenditures are for education—more than for any other function. Today our public schools spend an average of over $3,752 per pupil, per year for elementary and secondary schooling. On average, about 50 percent of the costs are borne by the states and almost 45 percent by local governments—yet there is great variation in how the states finance education. The richer states spend a larger proportion of their budgets on schools than do the poorer states, although the poor states make a greater tax effort. (Poorer

---

High School Graduation Rates by State

Alabama	65.8%	Montana	80.0
Alaska	82.5	Nebraska	75.5
Arizona	72.4	Nevada	75.5
Arkansas	73.2	New Hampshire	72.3
California	73.5	New Jersey	73.2
Colorado	78.6	New Mexico	68.9
Connecticut	79.3	New York	71.2
District of Columbia	67.1	North Carolina	64.3
Delaware	68.6	North Dakota	66.4
Florida	73.4	Ohio	71.5
Georgia	68.1	Oklahoma	73.8
Hawaii	73.8	Oregon	75.6
Idaho	80.5	Pennsylvania	72.9
Illinois	72.4	Rhode Island	61.1
Indiana	72.8	South Carolina	64.0
Iowa	71.5	South Dakota	67.9
Kansas	72.3	Tennessee	64.3
Kentucky	68.7	Texas	67.3
Louisiana	57.7	Utah	86.5
Maine	78.3	Vermont	71.0
Maryland	75.5	Virginia	68.1
Massachusetts	76.3	Washington	77.6
Michigan	71.7	West Virginia	72.0
Minnesota	73.1	Wisconsin	69.6
Mississippi	63.9	Wyoming	77.9
Missouri	74.8		
		United States	73.5

Source: *Educational Attainment* U.S. Bureau of Census, 1986.

The figures were calculated by dividing the number of graduates by the number of ninth-graders enrolled four years earlier, and were adjusted for moves between states.

states have to tax themselves at a higher rate because they have less wealth to tax.)

GOVERNING OF EDUCATION

The city, the county, the township, or the school district is chiefly responsible for providing public elementary and secondary education. The school district, of which there are almost 15,000 in the United States, is the basic unit. In each district the voters elect a board of education. This board sets the school tax rate, in most cases independently of the city or county; appoints a superintendent of schools and other personnel; hires teachers; and runs the schools from kindergarten or grade one through grade twelve.

Each state has a superintendent of public instruction or a commissioner of education. In about a third of the states these officials are popularly elected; in almost all states they share some authority with a state board of education. Although actual operation of the public schools is the responsibility of the local community, state officers have important supervisory powers and distribute financial assistance to the communities. State money is passed out according to many formulas, but the trend is toward giving more money to poorer communities. Critics charge that methods of financing public schools in most states are chaotic and unjust, and reformers are pressing for better formulas.

Controversy has recently risen in several states, especially in Arkansas and Texas, over the question of testing or assessing teachers who are currently in the system. More than thirty states test prospective teachers before granting certification, but only a few test certified teachers. Arkansas began such tests (sometimes called "no pass, no teach" rules) in 1985, and nearly 10 percent of its teachers failed to qualify. Georgia tests teachers in their particular subject areas. And in 1986 Texas required more than 200,000 teachers and school administrators to take a basic-skills quiz. About 3 percent of the Texas teachers failed the exam on their first attempt. The three-hour multiple-choice test consisted of eighty-five questions about grammar, job-related vocabulary, and other matters. An assessment was also mandated by the governor and the state legislature to restore confidence in public education. Texas Governor Mark White, who had been bitterly opposed on this issue by many teachers and teacher groups, claimed the exam was necessary to ensure quality education. He said he was pleased with the results.

Some educators and educational reformers say teacher testing will be a fact of life by the mid-1990s. State legislators in states requiring these tests decided to impose these new regulations after finding too many teachers inadequately prepared to teach. Many teachers and educational observers find mid-career competence tests offensive. Good teaching, they point out, is an art based more on a teacher's personality, character, and caring than on knowledge. Memorable teachers who make a difference are those who demonstrate that they care about and can inspire students. No paper-and-pencil test is likely to be able to measure these qualities. The rush to teacher testing will probably divert attention from the more important need to creatively supervise and evaluate teachers on the job. "The best way to judge the effectiveness of a teacher is to see how he or she performs in the classroom," notes the president of the Educational Testing Service.[1]

Others suggest that testing only a teacher's basic reading and writing skills is not a fair enough measure. "A meaningful test should include evaluation of classroom performance and mastery of subject matter," says an editorial in *The New York Times*. "That might be best accomplished through peer reviews, with counseling sessions by respected teachers and administrators. With that approach, teachers might find 'competence' tests less objectionable and the public would have a more accurate measure of their performance."[2] Other states are likely to adopt variations of the Arkansas, Georgia, and Texas plans, yet the debate over how to evaluate effective teaching will continue as long as we have schools and teachers.

The debate about teacher competency testing also involves the charge by some critics that such tests are biased against minorities. Defenders deny these charges. Minorities tend to do less well on the tests, yet it is said this reflects not the bias of the test but the fact that on the average minority teachers have had fewer opportunities to become prepared.

State officials are sometimes consulted by local authorities to ensure that new school buildings meet the minimum specifications set by the state. Some state officials have the authority to set the course of study and to determine what must be taught and what may not be taught. In the South and Southwest state authorities often determine which books will be used as well.

Until the 1950s most local school districts provided only for elementary and secondary education, although some of the larger cities also supported junior colleges and universities. Since the end of World War II, there has been a major expansion of community colleges. Students may attend the first two years of college or receive technical education within their own communities. The trend is to create separate college districts with their own boards to operate and raise funds for the local community colleges; in a few areas, however, the colleges are still part of the regular public school systems.

States support many kinds of universities and colleges, including land-grant universities created by the Morrill Act of 1862. These colleges and universities are governed by boards appointed by the governor in some states and elected by the voters in others. These boards are designed to give public higher-education institutions some independence, even though they depend on the legislatures and governors for funds. A few states have gone even further and have written provisions securing the independence of some universities into their constitutions.

With over 80 percent of our 13 million college students now attending publicly supported institutions, the control and support of higher education have become significant political questions. State after state has created either a super-board to take over the operation of all public universities or a coordinating board with varying degrees of control over operations and budgets. In addition, governors are trying to impose controls on universities and colleges that university administrators insist are inappropriate. No longer do public universities have the degree of independence they once had to decide teaching loads, implement internal procedures, and spend and account for funds.

What of the national government? For a long time the United States left the funding and control of education to states and local units of government, but this has changed somewhat in the past generation. The national government's share in financing local education rose from about 2 percent in 1940 to about 8 percent in the early 1980s; however, it is declining once again. The federal government, through the national Department of Education and other agencies, makes grants for facilities, equipment, scholarships, loans, research, and general aid at the elementary, secondary, and higher-education levels. Federal controls over how the money may be spent have come with these federal dollars. Today federal regulations cover school-lunch programs, employment practices, admissions, record keeping, care of experimental animals, and so on. Indeed, school authorities note there are often more regulations than dollars. Although the federal government may contribute 7 percent of local school funding, it imposes or accounts for more than 20 percent of the regulations found in our local schools.

EDUCATIONAL ISSUES

Educational politics have long been part of our policy-making process. What shall be taught and who shall teach it are often hotly contested questions. Schools are favorite targets for groups eager to have children taught the "right" things. Patriotic groups are concerned about "un-American doctrines" sneaking into the textbooks, classrooms, and school libraries. Labor leaders want students to get the right impressions about labor and its role in society. Business leaders are eager for children to see the free enterprise system in a favorable light. Minorities and women's groups want textbooks that avoid unfavorable stereotypes and present issues about which they are concerned and from the perspective they consider correct. Professional educators and civil libertarians, however, try to isolate schools from the pressures of outside groups. They say decisions regarding what textbooks

"It's one thing for the National Commission to comment on the quality of teaching in our schools. It's another thing entirely for you to stand up and call Mr. Costello a yo-yo."

Drawing by Stevenson; © *1983 The New Yorker Magazine, Inc.*

should be assigned, what books should be placed in school libraries, and how curriculums should be designed are best left to professionals.[3]

In recent years many cities have fought battles over how to integrate public schools to secure racial balance, and especially whether or not students should be bused from one neighborhood to another. The Constitution does not require public schools to be racially balanced. But if racial segregation is the result of deliberate activity by the authorities, then officials have the duty to take appropriate actions, including busing, to overcome the consequences of these unconstitutional violations. Further, proponents of busing argue that bringing minority pupils from depressed areas to schools attended by children from more advantaged families raises the achievement of those from the depressed parts of the city without impairing the accomplishment of other children. Opponents of busing stress the desirability of neighborhood schools and emphasize the negative consequences of busing, such as encouraging white flight to the suburbs.[4]

A whole series of important issues arise from the growing public concern about the quality of our schools, especially our high schools. The 1983 report of the National Commission on Excellence in Education, *A Nation at Risk*, became for a while a centerpiece of national debate.[5] The report, which came from respected people at the right time, received widespread public attention and reinforced public convictions that all is not right with our educational system. In stark language the Commission, among other things, called for a substantial raising of standards for both students and teachers, a core curriculum, more emphasis on science and mathematics, more homework, a longer school day, and merit systems of teacher pay. The Commission's findings were confirmed by other prestigious committees.[6]

The National Educational Association (NEA), the largest teachers' union, challenges the merit pay recommendations. Merit teaching, they say, is difficult, if not impossible to measure, and favoritism enters most merit pay evaluation programs. In addition, Democratic party leaders took issue with President Reagan's recommendations for tuition tax credits and George Bush's view that the national government's role in education is limited. They advocated an increase in salaries for teachers and substantial national programs to strengthen science, mathematics, and foreign-language instruction. They have been less clear about their stand on merit pay.

In 1986 another national commission called for the first nationwide system for certifying elementary and secondary teachers. This proposed National Board of Professional Teaching Standards won both praise and criticism. States don't want to yield their autonomy over education policies, yet the current absence of transferable standards is a major problem in our highly mobile society.

Nearly all the states have responded to these various reports with stepped-up efforts to strengthen their high school graduation requirements and to encourage longer school days, smaller classes, more student testing, and better financial rewards for good teaching. Plainly these reports are making a difference. Still, the educational reforms these days differ significantly from the reforms of the

1960s and 1970s. Their focus is more on excellence than on equity for the disadvantaged.[7]

EDUCATION AND GOVERNMENTS

Elaborate attempts have been made to isolate educational agencies from the rest of government. This isolation is strongly supported by well-organized groups: parent-teacher associations, the National Education Association, the American Federation of Teachers, the American Association of University Professors, the American Council on Education, and other university and educational groups. It is also supported by most citizens' general conviction that education should be kept out of the hands of politicians. However, education is of such concern to so many people, and there are so many different ideas about how schools should be run, that it cannot be divorced from the political system. Educational policies, like agricultural, law enforcement, or any other policies, are determined by the political processes available and accessible to the people.[8]

Social Services

WELFARE

The number of Americans on welfare has soared from about 2 million in 1950 to well over 11 million today. Why such growth? Some say it is because governments at the national and state levels finally recognized their obligation to care for the truly poor. Others point out that welfare systems enslave their participants: government "handouts" rob some recipients of the self-confidence needed to go to work and succeed. In this sense, they say, dependence on welfare has become a curse.

Welfare programs in the United States are among the most emotional and controversial public policies. Access to welfare benefits is based on the qualifications and specific needs of the recipients, who almost always have to prove they have no incomes or that their incomes are insufficient to meet their needs. Welfare policy, a complex web of federal, state, and local programs, often involves shared or matching financial responsibilities. Most of the administrative burden, however, falls on state and local governments.

The national government picks up the costs for aid to the aged, blind, and disabled. The national government also pays for Medicare and food stamp programs. Joint federal and state efforts pay for Aid to Families with Dependent Children (the well-publicized AFDC program), public housing, and Medicaid (a federally sponsored program under which states can obtain about 80 percent of the cost of providing medical care for the poor).

States themselves provide for and administer unemployment compensation; assistance supplementing federal aid to the aged, disabled, and the poor; specialized hospitals and institutions for the ill, handicapped, or destitute; and some general-assistance programs for those needy who somehow do not qualify for other welfare programs.

States commonly pick up about 25 percent or more of welfare and related social service costs, making welfare the second largest expenditure for most states. Every state has a department of human services or welfare that either directly administers welfare programs or supervises local officials who administer the benefit programs. County welfare departments determine who is entitled to assistance and deal directly with recipients.

Within the limits of federal guidelines, each state is somewhat free to determine the size and details of its own welfare programs. Variations in programs among the states are significant, with the wealthier states paying higher benefits (see Table 9–1). Federal policies in recent years have sought to diminish the variations among the states, yet notable disparities remain.[9] People on welfare acknowledge that higher benefits in certain states such as Wisconsin encouraged them to move there. This had led Wisconsin to consider a lower benefit schedule for newcomers in an effort to discourage "welfare migrants."

Some debate in recent years has focused on the possible federalization or nationalization of the whole welfare system, but this has not come to pass. Thus, states continue to perform some rather important policy and administrative functions in this policy area. States continue to crack down on welfare cheating, and

TABLE 9–1
Unequal Welfare Benefits in the States

Monthly welfare payment, as of 1989, for a family of three headed by a mother who has no other income.

Alabama	$118	Louisiana	$190	Oklahoma	$325
Alaska	740	Maine	416	Oregon	420
Arizona	293	Maryland	377	Pennsylvania	384
Arkansas	204	Massachusetts	579	Rhode Island	517
California	633	Michigan	459	South Carolina	206
Colorado	356	Minnesota	532	South Dakota	366
Connecticut	534	Mississippi	120	Tennessee	173
Delaware	333	Missouri	282	Texas	184
Dist. Columbia	393	Montana	359	Utah	376
Florida	275	Nebraska	364	Vermont	629
Georgia	270	Nevada	330	Virginia	291
Hawaii	557	New Hampshire	486	Washington	492
Idaho	304	New Jersey	424	West Virginia	249
Illinois	342	New Mexico	264	Wisconsin	517
Indiana	288	New York	539	Wyoming	360
Iowa	394	North Carolina	266	Guam	165
Kansas	401	North Dakota	371	Puerto Rico	80
Kentucky	218	Ohio	309	Virgin Islands	171

Source: Family Support Administration, Department of Health and Human Services. *The New York Times* (March 15, 1989), p. C19.

states and localities are under continued pressure to encourage able-bodied welfare recipients either to seek employment or to perform various public-works services.

About half of the states, including Massachusetts, New York, and California, have experimented with so-called workfare programs, designed to provide a transition that helps welfare recipients develop the self-confidence, skills, and habits necessary for regular employment. Despite criticism, especially by public-employees' unions, many states are adopting mandatory or voluntary workfare programs. (The mandatory programs are subject to the most criticism.) These programs provide able-bodied adults who do not have preschool aged children the opportunity to learn job skills that can lead to employment. Another proposal, advocated by conservatives, such as Secretary of Housing and Urban Development Jack Kemp, and liberals, such as New York Governor Mario Cuomo, is to create "opportunity zones" in our large cities by providing tax incentives to companies to invest in plants and provide job training for the unemployed.

PUBLIC HEALTH

During one hot summer in the 1780s, a yellow-fever epidemic struck Philadelphia. The streets were deserted. All who could afford to do so had taken their families and fled to the country. Every night the sounds of the death cart echoed through the empty city. Few families did not lose a child, father, or mother. Only when cool weather returned did the city resume normal activity.

Yellow fever, dysentery, malaria, and other diseases have periodically swept American cities. As late as 1879, yellow fever struck the South, and Memphis was nearly depopulated. State after state, following the lead of Louisiana and Massachusetts, established a board of health. Spurred by the medical discoveries of Pasteur and other scientists, authorities began programs for the protection of public health. Open sewers were covered and other hygienic measures instituted.

Today thousands of local governments—counties, cities, townships, and special health districts—have some kind of public-health program. Every state has an agency, usually called a Department of Health, that administers the state program and supervises local officials. The U.S. Public Health Service conducts research, assists state and local authorities, and administers federal grants to encourage these agencies to expand their programs. Every state also administers various federal medical-benefit programs for the needy, such as Medicaid. As usual, however, wealthier states tend to take advantage of or match these programs more liberally than poorer states, despite fixed federal incentives to the contrary.[10]

Prevention and disease control are still major public-health activities. Doctors are required to report cases of communicable disease. Health department officials then investigate to discover the source of the infection, isolate the afflicted persons, and take whatever action is called for. Most state health departments give doctors free vaccine and serum; many local departments give free vaccinations to those who cannot afford private physicians. Because the public is more enthusiastic about specific programs than about general disease control, some afflictions, like tuberculosis, venereal disease, and AIDS, have received special attention. Mobile X-ray units take free X-rays of schoolchildren, teachers, and the general public. Public-health officials try to protect water supplies and ensure the safe disposal of waste and sewage. They protect the community's food supply by inspecting hotels, restaurants, and food markets.

State and local governments have gradually moved onto the environmental health front, with several states leading the way. California, New York, and Pennsylvania began clean air programs before the federal government acted. Congress has followed the states' lead by gradually adopting more stringent federal regulations, yet the primary responsibility for building facilities and enforcing regulations still belongs to the states. Pollution-control, air, and water agencies have also been created in the states. Although pollution control accounts for only a small portion of total state spending, these allocations have risen in recent years.[11]

Unsafe Streets and Law Enforcement

In 1835 the famous Texas Rangers were organized as a small border patrol. In 1865 Massachusetts appointed a few state constables to suppress gambling, a job the local police had been unwilling or unable to do. But not until 1905, with the organization of the Pennsylvania State Constabulary, did a real state police system come into being. It was so successful that other states followed Pennsylvania's example.

THE STATE POLICE

State police became a part of our law-enforcement system for a variety of reasons. The breakdown of rural law enforcement, the coming of the automobile (and the resulting demand for greater protection on the highways and creation of a mobile force for catching fleeing criminals), and the need for a trained force to maintain order during strikes, fires, floods, and other emergencies all led to the creation of state police.

The establishment of the Pennsylvania State Constabulary marked a sharp break with traditional police methods. The force was a mounted and uniformed body organized on a military basis. Centralized control was given to a superintendent who was directly responsible to the governor. The pattern has been followed by other states, and these forces are now among the most respected police organizations in the world. They are well equipped, and they maintain high standards of conduct and discipline.

The military organization of state police forces shields them from temptation, builds morale, and helps officers develop a pride that contrasts sharply with the cynical attitude of some urban police. Because of their mobility and professional character, state police are less accessible to "the smaller fry of urban and rural politics." Moreover, they maintain rigorous systems of recruitment and training.

Other state police systems have developed out of the rather modest highway patrols of a few decades ago. During the 1930s traffic control in rural regions became an acute problem, and state after state organized highway patrols, usually as subordinate units of the highway or motor vehicle department. Gradually their authority was extended from enforcing the rules of the road to exercising the usual powers of the police. Generally speaking, the state police that have grown out of highway patrols are not as well trained nor are their standards as high as those who were trained under the Pennsylvania model.

OTHER POLICE FORCES

State police are not the only law-enforcement agencies maintained by state governments. There are liquor-law enforcement officials, fish and game wardens, fire wardens, independent detective bureaus, and special motor vehicle police. This dispersion of functions has been widely criticized, but each department insists it needs its own law-enforcement agency to handle its special problems.

At the local level almost every municipality maintains its own police force; the county has a sheriff and deputies; and some townships have their own police officers. In fact, over 40,000 separate law-enforcement agencies are composed of more than 500,000 men and women.

FEDERAL-STATE ACTION

The national government has gradually moved into this field traditionally reserved for state and local governments, although the main cost of local law enforcement is still borne by local governments. Today, for example, it is a federal offense to transport kidnapped individuals or stolen goods across state lines. Taking firearms, explosives, or even information across state lines for illegal purposes is also a federal offense.

Despite increased national and state expenditures, crime rates have not diminished. After heated feuds over how best to spend federal funds, and after considerable debate about whether past spending has made any difference, Congress cut almost all the block-grant assistance monies for state and local law-enforcement agencies out of the 1981 budget. These federal cutbacks, which amounted to almost 5 percent of the funds spent at the state and local levels, had the immediate effect of placing virtually all fiscal and administrative responsibility for law enforcement at the state and local level. Federal efforts to make our streets safe fell victim in part to anti-inflationary budget cutting, and in part to the fact that the causes and cures for crime still elude the experts at all levels of government.[12]

Students of crime in America now acknowledge that federal and state funds have not significantly reduced criminal activity. It may also be fair to conclude, writes one expert, "that crime cannot be effectively addressed by the customary local policies. If I am correct in concluding that change in the crime rate is a national phenomenon that is the product of macrosocial forces beyond the control of local government policy, local planning will be doomed to failure."[13]

In short, what most of us regard as a local problem may never be resolved solely by local initiatives—no matter how bold, innovative, or well funded. President Bush proposed a limited anti-crime program for the early 1990s, most of it aimed at hiring more federal marshals, building more federal prisons, and various anti-drug programs. Local law enforcement officials applaud President Bush's initiative, even though it won't have much effect on local crime fighting efforts.

Planning the Urban Community

Are our cities good places in which to live and work? Crime, pollution, garbage, crowded shopping areas, dented fenders, shattered nerves, slums and blighted areas, inadequate parks, impossible traffic patterns—are all these necessary?

For many decades American cities were allowed to grow unchecked. Industrialists were permitted to erect factories wherever they wished, developers were allowed to construct towering buildings that shut off sunlight from the streets below. Drivers were transformed into malevolent maniacs and pedestrians into traumatized wrecks by traffic conditions. Schools were sandwiched in where land was cheap or where the political organization could make a profit on the sale.

The most common method of assuring orderly growth is *zoning*—creating specific areas and limiting uses to which property may be put in each area. A community may be divided into areas for single-family, two-family, or multifamily dwellings, for commercial purposes, and for light and heavy industry. Other regulations restrict the height of buildings or require that buildings be located a certain distance apart or a certain distance from the boundaries of the lot.

Zoning regulations attempt to prevent garbage dumps from being located next to residential areas, stabilize property values, and enable the city or county government to coordinate services with land use. A zoning ordinance, however, is no better than its enforcement. This is usually the responsibility of a building inspector, who ensures that a projected building is consistent with building, zoning, fire, and sanitary regulations before granting a building permit. In most cases a zoning or planning commission or the city council can amend ordinances and make exceptions to regulations. These officials are often under tremendous pressure to grant exceptions, but if they go too far in permitting special cases, the whole purpose of zoning is defeated. Zoning can also be used as a means of keeping "undesirables" out of a community, usually an upper-income white suburb. This is done merely by manipulating zoning requirements; for example, by mandating that all new homes be built on lots of an acre or more and by prohibiting the building of multifamily homes and apartments.[14]

But zoning is only one kind of community planning. Until recently, planners were primarily concerned with streets and buildings. Today many city planners are concerned with the quality of life, and planning covers a broad range of activities, including methods to avoid pollution of the air and improving the quality of water. Planners collect all the information they can about a city and then prepare long-range plans. Can smaller-scale communities be devised within urban centers? Can downtown areas be revitalized, and, if so, how? Where should main highways or mass transit be constructed to meet future needs? Will the water supply be adequate for the population ten, twenty, or fifty years from now? Is a larger or new regional airport needed? Are hospitals and parks accessible to all? Does the design of public buildings encourage crime and energy waste?

Many communities attempt to make some order out of the chaos of random growth, and most have some kind of planning agency. Federal laws support state regulations for careful long-range planning and require environmental impact statements before any major changes can be made in the roadways or land usage. These regulations provide opportunities for all persons affected by these developments to be heard and for care to be taken to ensure that proper provisions are made to mitigate unavoidable adverse effects on the environment.

States have a vested interest in controlling the negative effects of population growth. Florida is a good case in point. Its economy rests largely on its beauty, tourism, and its ability to attract companies to relocate there. Thousands of people per day move into Sunbelt areas such as Florida. "People are loving Florida to death, literally."[15]

Floridians believe growth has caused several problems that cry out for state planning. Two-thirds or more say the state's population growth has contributed to increased crime, air pollution, declining water quality, and a loss of their natural areas. This same survey (see Table 9–2) found that about 50 percent (this figure rises in highly urban areas and decreases in rural counties) of the Florida public thinks government should do something about population growth. When asked what should be done, however, citizens voiced varying levels of support for planning programs, depending on what the programs might mean for their own self-interest.

TABLE 9–2
Population Control and Tradeoffs Involved

	AGREE	DISAGREE
The number of apartments and condominiums built should be strictly limited. Do you agree, disagree, . . . ?	71%	25%
Building in fragile natural areas, such as flood plains, beaches, scenic areas, or marshes, should be prohibited.	81	16
It is important to control population growth even if it results in fewer jobs in your community.	45	47
It is important to control population growth even if you must pay higher taxes or fees as a result of the regulations.	46	47

Source: Adapted from James E. Frank and Charles E. Connerly, "Florida's Growth Problems: Public Perceptions and State Policy Responses," Florida Public Opinion (Winter 1985), p. 6.

Critics of urban and state planning are skeptical whether governors, mayors, or state and local legislators can prevent what they sometimes call the "Los Angeleza-tion" of America. Unregulated market forces can cause severe harm to residents, and politics as usual—with governmental entities' continually adjusting to the prevailing political pressures—does not necessarily ensure sensible growth patterns and the protection of the air, water, and beauty of most states and communities. The most idealistic plan may be little more than a reflection of one or more private interests.

Seattle and San Francisco, in recent years, have voted to limit the height and bulk of downtown buildings. These steps to regulate both the size and the pace of urban development are an effort to protect cities like Seattle from excessively fast growth. The Seattle campaign pitted a host of community and neighborhood groups against the downtown business interests and most of the city's elected officials. Opponents of the "slow the growth" referendum, who outspent the proponents ten to one, predicted doomsday side-effects such as rising office rents, increased property taxes, declining investments and local revenues, but 62 percent of the local voters were apparently alarmed by the decline in the quality of life. Said one local resident: "There are things money can't buy that this area's got. You can't buy the slower pace. . . . A lot of people think this is the last outpost. They've escaped other cities that have been ruined and if they let Seattle be ruined, there'll be no place left to go."[16] The Seattle measure leaves somewhat unresolved how the buildings are to be approved, other than on a first-come, first-serve basis. In San Francisco, a design review committee of architectural experts selects the projects. Other cities are likely to consider the Seattle and San Francisco precedents, although those with sagging economies are the least likely candidates.

Obviously, planning and sensible growth must be built upon public support. No plan will be effective unless it reflects the interests and values of the major groups within the community. Planning is clearly a political activity. Different groups view the ends and means of planning differently, and agreements on tough policy options are often hard to reach. Moreover, one of the barriers to successful planning is the general fear of governmental power. Thus, effective planning will always be difficult to achieve, and when successful, it will require imaginative collaboration between planners and the popularly elected officials who must bear the responsibility for implementing the plans.[17]

Transportation

State and local governments build highways, public buildings, airports, parks, and recreational facilities. Because highways and bridges around the nation are aging, a federal tax on gasoline was levied to help rebuild these public facilities. State and local governments, in fact, spend more money on transportation than

"Infrastructure"

There is much talk these days, especially in state and national legislatures, about rebuilding or investing in our infrastructure. What does this term mean? In the old days people just talked about "public works," and generally the two terms mean the same thing. The Latin word "infra" means below or beneath. In general, infrastructure refers to our roads, highways, bridges, water tunnels and pipelines, and similar public works that we often take for granted. It is true that in many places these public facilities are wearing out or deteriorating and massive new investments are needed. The term will become more common as this debate intensifies and the costs become a topic of heated political discussion.

on anything else except education and welfare. Their major program is building and repairing roads.

Until the coming of the automobile, canals and railroads were the major method of long-distance travel. Local roads were built and repaired under the direction of city, township, and county officials. Able-bodied male citizens were required either to put in a certain number of days working on the public roads or to pay taxes for that purpose.

By the 1890s bicycle clubs began to urge the building of hard-surfaced roads, but it was not until the 1900s and the invention of the automobile that road building became a major industry. The function was gradually transferred from the township to larger units of government. But counties and townships still have important building and maintenance problems.

The national government has supported state highway construction since 1916, and through various federal highway laws over the past forty years, federal aid has increased. States do the planning, estimate the costs, and get the construction done even when they receive federal assistance. In order to receive support, however, states must submit their plans to, and have their work inspected by, the U.S. Department of Transportation. All federally backed highways must meet certain standards governing the engineering of the roadbed, employment conditions for construction workers, and weight and load conditions for trucks.

Under the Federal Highway Act of 1956, states have planned and built the National System of Interstate and Defense Highways. The Interstate consists of 43,000 miles of superhighways linking almost all cities with a population of 50,000 or more. The federal government paid 90 percent of the costs. Most of the money has come from user charges or fees (taxes on gasoline, tires, and trucks) that are placed in a trust fund designated for that purpose.

Few aspects of government are more enmeshed in patronage politics than highway building. The large sums of money spent and the army of workers needed offer many opportunities for graft and favoritism.[18] Powerful interest groups, such as the American Automobile Association, support highway development. Automobile and tire manufacturers, oil companies, motel and restaurant associations, automobile and tourist clubs, trucking associations, and others join hands to protect their common cause. In most states they have been strong enough to persuade legislatures to allocate gasoline taxes, automobile drivers' license fees, trucking fees, and other user taxes for road purposes. But there is always conflict over how money should be spent. Farmers want secondary roads developed; truckers and tourists favor the improvement of main highways; and merchants prefer that roads come their way.

Today not everyone is pleased by the heavy commitment of public funds to highways. These roads, they say, are in effect a massive subsidy for automobile users and makers; without highways, autos would not be so popular or so widely used. Some people, they point out, use highways far more than others, and yet for the most part everyone contributes to the general taxes that help pay for highway construction. Why not tax people in proportion to their actual use of the highways? Just like seat belts, a federally mandated meter could be installed in each vehicle at a cost of less than $20. Advocates of this view, few in number at this time, say such a policy would encourage energy conservation, spread the cost of construction in a fair manner, and promote car and van pooling and public transportation. Others question the practicality of administering a highway user tax and are skeptical about its political feasibility. Doubtless this idea is in advance of its day, yet it may get more of a hearing as a result of the higher costs of highway building and maintenance.

Recently some people have urged the federal government to spend a sizable percentage of the highway trust funds on developing public mass transit systems. Congress at various times and through a variety of programs has permitted the use of some highway trust funds to purchase buses and finance mass transit systems. But even though more attention is being paid to mass transit, bus systems, and transportation modes other than the auto, any expectations that the age of the automobile is over should be cast aside. Generally, urban mass transit programs have had a difficult time in recent years,[19] especially after the Reagan administration sharply slashed urban mass transit funds.

"Adulation of the auto, combined with a popular disdain for mass transit as a kind of publicly subsidized sop to the poor or aged, is too deeply ingrained. . . . Yet the need for clean air and energy conservation alone dictate that we keep trying—whether the current administration in Washington cares or not."[20]

Regulation at the Grass Roots

Regulation involves a government's restricting in some way the activities of individuals, groups, or corporations. State and local regulations are adopted on the assumption (sometimes mistakenly) that benefits to the public interest will outweigh the costs to the individuals and groups being regulated. An overriding public goal is typically viewed as a justification for imposing a regulation on an individual or industry. Thus, laws requiring drivers' licenses, compelling motorists to stop at red lights, mandating seat-belt use, or imposing severe penalties on those caught driving under the influence of alcohol or drugs are intended to protect the safety and freedom of innocent pedestrians or occupants of other motor vehicles. Most such laws are accepted as both necessary and legitimate. States have raised the drinking age and stiffened the punishments for drunk driving. Most states acted because the federal government forced them to; if they hadn't, they would have lost federal funds.

In all discussions of state and local regulations the following questions arise: How does one determine when a regulation is needed? How much regulation is needed? When do the costs of regulation outweigh the benefits? Are there side effects of the regulations that outweigh the expected benefits? How can we tell when regulations have outlived their purposes and need to be terminated (or when is the time to deregulate or sunset a set of regulations)?

As the federal government has retreated from its role as chief setter and enforcer of standards, these questions have taken on even greater importance to the states: "As federal pressure is removed, interstate variability in policy will increase. In areas such as environmental protection or occupational health and safety, the outcome of regulatory politics at the state level will largely determine the economic and physical well-being of most Americans."[21]

Corporations receive their charters from the states. Banks, insurance companies, securities dealers, doctors, lawyers, teachers, barbers, and various other businesses and professions are licensed, and their activities are supervised by state officials. Fears about nuclear waste, "acid rain," and hazardous wastes of all kinds have sparked extensive efforts at regulation within states, as well as court battles with nearby states over the export of unwanted byproducts of contemporary energy development. Both farmers and workers—especially union members—are regulated. But of all businesses, public utilities are the most closely monitored.

PUBLIC UTILITIES

It is easier to list than to define public utilities. They include (among others) water plants, electric power companies, telephone companies, railroads, and buses. Public utilities are distinguished from other businesses because government gives them certain special privileges, such as the power of eminent domain, the right to use public streets, and protection from competition. In return, utilities are required to give the public adequate services at reasonable rates. Public utilities are used to supply essential services in fields in which competition is not suitable.

In the United States, private enterprise subject to public regulation rather than public ownership has been the usual method of providing essential services. Nevertheless, more than two-thirds of our cities own their own waterworks, about a hundred operate their own gas utilities, and more and more are taking over the operation of their transit systems. But other services—intercity transportation, airplanes, telephone, and telegraph—are almost everywhere provided by private enterprise subject to governmental regulation.

Because public utilities are not subject to the restraint of competition, the way they are regulated is important. Every state has a utilities commission (usually called the Public Utilities Commission or PUC) to ensure utilities operate in the interest of the public they are supposed to serve. In about thirty-five states, commissioners are appointed by the governor with the consent of the state senate. In two states they are chosen by the legislatures, and in about a dozen more they are elected by the voters.

Formerly these commissioner posts were considered political plums, and commissioners used them as steppingstones to higher elective office. This is less common today. PUC commissioners raise or lower utility rates—perhaps the most visible part of their job—but they are also involved in such issues as toxic waste, nuclear power, and truck regulation, as well as telephone, cable television, and other energy related disputes. The average stay for commissioners is three and a half years, a statistic that suggests the burnout and fatigue involved.

Utility commissioners operate under the assumption that their decisions are not "political," yet nearly every decision they make comes under political attack or stirs political reaction. Several states have enacted laws prohibiting conflict of interest, limiting commissioners' affiliations with the utilities they regulate, and prohibiting them from becoming employed by any company that was under their regulation for at least a year after they resign from the PUC. Other states have established a separate office of state consumer advocates to encourage even greater responsiveness to consumer needs.

The politics of regulation, especially regulation of public utilities, is of growing interest to more and more citizens and consumers. In many areas, citizens' groups form to make their own presentations and to monitor or "watchdog" the operations of the public utilities boards or commissions. "The tremendous work load on these commissions," writes one observer, "finds commissioners constantly walking a tightrope between helping a regulated industry get a decent return on investment, and making sure consumers get good service at a fair price."[22]

EMPLOYERS AND EMPLOYEES

Despite the expanded role of the national government, state and local governments still have much to say about working conditions.

Health and Safety Legislation States require proper heating, lighting, ventilation, fire escapes, and sanitary facilities in work areas. Machinery must be equipped with safety guards. Some standards have also been established to reduce occupational diseases. Health, building, and labor inspectors tour industrial plants to ensure compliance with the laws.

Workers' Compensation Today all states have created worker-compensation programs based on the belief that employees should not have to assume the costs of accidents. Like depreciation of machinery and other items, the costs of accidents are borne by the employers and are part of the price consumers must ultimately pay. No longer do employees have to prove their employers were at fault. If they are injured or contract a disease in the ordinary course of employment, employees are entitled to compensation set by a prearranged schedule.

Child Labor All states forbid child labor, yet laws vary widely in their coverage and in their definition of child labor. Many states set the minimum age at 14. Higher age requirements are normal for employment in hazardous occupations and during school hours. Many of these regulations are now superseded by federal laws for most businesses.

Comparable Worth The idea of comparable worth is advocated by those who believe jobs traditionally dominated by women—nurses, secretaries, and elementary school teachers, for example—have lower wage rates compared to jobs traditionally dominated by men, for example, plumbers, electricians, and janitors, because of discrimination and role stereotyping. The comparable worth concept is not to be confused with equal pay for equal work.

Regulation of Unions and Collective Bargaining National regulation of collective bargaining applies only to industries in or affecting interstate commerce. Although national law takes precedence over state enactments, states can impose their own regulations in many important areas of labor-management relations.

Environmental Protection Citizens in many states are becoming more critical of the environmental havoc caused by industrial water and air pollution, chemical dumping, strip mining, and abandoned hazardous waste sites. Normally their complaints turn into requests that the states set up some kind of regulatory and monitoring agencies with stiff penalties for violations.

Consumer Protection Consumer groups are similarly restless and often relentless supporters of regulatory efforts. Consider the example of auto repairs, the biggest single headache for those who handle consumer complaints. Many consumer advocates believe auto mechanics should be licensed by the state to control incompetence and dishonest practices. But would this ensure that repairs are made competently or honestly? Regulation is nearly always controversial and is always shaped by political forces.

Can We Explain Policy Differences?

Political scientists have been attempting to learn why states do or do not enact various policies. Investigators visualize each state as producing certain policy "outputs," for example, expenditures for welfare, a public-housing program, or a civil rights law. They are trying to understand the dynamics of the political process and figure out why one state acts one way while another does something else.

Researchers have looked at such variables as levels of urbanization and industrialization, education, economic resources, and home ownership. They have studied structural variables such as types of party systems and innovation in state administration, and political variables such as citizen participation and voter interest in state politics.[23]

The results of earlier studies often suggested that factors such as urbanization, wealth of the state, and geographical region account for public policy differences much more than party system or governmental structure. Thus, the more urbanized and wealthy the state, the more likely it would be to invest in human resources; whether it was a one-party state or had competitive parties seemed irrelevant. More recent studies, however, suggest political and structural factors do count. One study concludes a state's policy outputs are partially determined by the attitudes and behavior of those who participate actively in state politics.[24]

Other scholars find creative leadership can make a difference. A governor who wants to encourage economic development can go abroad on trade missions,

States Ranked for Their Policy Liberalism

RANK	STATE	RANK	STATE
1	New York	25	Wyoming
2	Massachusetts	26	North Dakota
3	New Jersey	27	New Mexico
4	California	28	Nebraska
5	Connecticut	29	Kentucky
6	Oregon	30	Texas
7	Wisconsin	31	Florida
8	Minnesota	32	South Dakota
9	Colorado	33	Utah
10	Michigan	34	West Virginia
11	Pennsylvania	35	Indiana
12	Rhode Island	36	Louisiana
13	Washington	37	Virginia
14	Illinois	38	Oklahoma
15	Maryland	39	Missouri
16	New Hampshire	40	North Carolina
17	Vermont	41	Georgia
18	Iowa	42	Nevada
19	Kansas	43	Tennessee
20	Ohio	44	Alabama
21	Idaho	45	Arizona
22	Maine	46	South Carolina
23	Montana	47	Arkansas
24	Delaware	48	Mississippi

Source: David Klingman and William W. Lammers, "The 'General Policy Liberalism' Factor in American State Politics," *American Journal of Political Science* (August 1984), pp. 602–603.

This ranking is based on several state policy efforts in welfare, civil rights, consumer rights, and social service innovations. Alaska and Hawaii are omitted because of missing data.

open overseas offices, and spend time on promotion and development. Through determined leadership and skillful use of available resources, a governor or a group of state leaders can overcome the constraints that traditionally stifle change: "For instance, half a century after Huey Long's service as governor of Louisiana, that period is still termed Huey Long's Louisiana, with its combination of heavy taxation on mineral extraction and high expenditure for social services. In a similar way, LaFollette left his imprint on Wisconsin, Rockefeller on New York."[25]

Policy outputs are expenditures and laws. Policy outcomes are the actual changes these expenditures and laws make in the lives of citizens—"the bottom line" of politics. Today political scientists are asking how policy outcomes could be changed by altering some of the conditions over which we have some control. Most of us reject or want to reject the proposition that social and economic forces determine everything governments do. We like to believe the quality of our constitutions, leaders, and political participation can and do make a difference.

Summary

1. We ask our state and local governments to do countless things for us, and what we request in the areas of education, public welfare, health and hospitals, public safety, and transportation are the most costly. These account for more than three-fourths of state expenditures and almost two-thirds of local government spending.

2. In addition, we ask states and communities to keep our streets safe, protect our natural resources, provide parks and recreation, encourage job opportunities, and protect consumers. There are, of course, great differences in how states and communities set their priorities in these areas. Some communities, for example, are so concerned about environmental quality that they are seeking selective growth even at the expense of job opportunities. Other communities favor attracting jobs and industry despite pollution and the environmental costs.

3. Political scientists often conduct research on the differences among the states and cities and their policy outputs and outcomes. They are interested in why some states, for example, invest more in one policy function than in another, and why benefits are distributed in the way they are. There is also a growing interest in how citizens evaluate the way their governments provide and administer public services.

Further Reading

BLANCHE BERNSTEIN. *The Politics of Welfare: The New York City Experience* (Abt Books, 1982).

THAD L. BEYLE, ed. *State Government: CQ's Guide to Current Issues and Activities* (Congressional Quarterly Press, 1989).

THOMAS DYE. *Understanding Public Policy*, 5th ed. (Prentice Hall, 1987).

VIRGINIA GRAY, HERBERT JACOB, and KENNETH VINES, eds. *Politics in the American States*, 4th ed. (Harper Row, 1983).

BRYAN D. JONES. *Governing Urban America: A Policy Focus* (Little, Brown, 1983).

National Commission on Excellence in Education. *A Nation at Risk: The Imperative for Educational Reform* (U.S. Government Printing Office, 1983).

DAVID OSBORNE. *Laboratories of Democracy* (Harvard Business School Press, 1988).

PAUL PETERSON, ed. *The New Urban Reality* (Brookings Institution, 1985).

RICHARD C. RICH, ed. *The Politics of Urban Public Services* (Heath, 1982).

MARK S. ROSENTRAUB, ed. *Urban Policy Analysis: Problems, Theory and Prescription* (Praeger, 1986).

JACK TREADWAY. *Public Policymaking in the American States* (Praeger, 1985).

N otes

1. Gregory Anrig, "Tests Can't Solve Every Problem," *U.S. News and World Report* (May 19, 1986), p. 84.

2. "The Right Way to Test Teachers," *The New York Times* (March 19, 1986), section A, p. 26.

3. Harmon Zeigler and M. Kent Jennings, *Governing American Schools: Political Interaction in Local School Districts* (Duxbury Press, 1974). See also George Kaplan, *Who Runs Our Schools? The Changing Face of Educational Leadership* (Institute for Educational Leadership, 1989).

4. For a look at some of the consequences of busing in Boston and its impact on different families, see Anthony Lukas, *Common Ground* (Knopf, 1985).

5. The National Commission on Excellence in Education, *A Nation at Risk: The Imperative for Educational Reform, An Open Letter to the American People* (U.S. Government Printing Office, 1983).

6. Ernest L. Boyer, *High School: A Report on Secondary Education in America* (Harper Row, 1983), based on observations of high schools, contains a detailed series of recommendations. See also the National Science Board Commission on Precollege Education in Mathematics, Science, and Technology, *Educating Americans for the 21st Century* (U.S. Government Printing Office, 1983); and *A Nation Prepared: Teachers for the 21st Century*, a report from the Carnegie Forum on Education and the Economy (1986).

7. "School Reform Movement Requires Added State Support," *State Legislatures* (January 1985), p. 6; and Peggy M. Siegel, "School Reform Momentum Continues," *State Legislatures* (March 1985), pp. 11–15.

8. See Frederick Wirt and Michael Kirst, *The Political Web of American Education* (Little,

Brown, 1972); and Zeigler and Jennings, *Governing American Schools*.

9. Robert B. Albritton, "Subsidies: Welfare and Transportation," in Virginia Gray, Herbert Jacob, and Kenneth Vines, eds., *Politics in the American States* (Little, Brown, 1983), p. 378.

10. Russell L. Hanson, "Medicaid and the Politics of Redistribution," *American Journal of Political Science* (May 1984), p. 336.

11. For discussions of the problem nationwide, see Rochelle J. Stanfield, "Drowning in Waste," *National Journal* (May 10, 1986), pp. 1106–10.

12. For commentary on the embattled and frustrating national effort to make our streets safer in the 1970s, see James Q. Wilson, *Thinking about Crime* (Basic Books, 1975); and Thomas E. Cronin, Tania Cronin, and Michael E. Milakovich, *U.S. v. Crime in the Streets* (Indiana University Press, 1981).

13. Herbert Jacob, "Policy Response to Crime," in Paul E. Peterson, ed., *The New Urban Reality* (Brookings Institution, 1985), p. 251.

14. See Michael N. Danielson, "The Politics of Exclusionary Zoning in Suburbia," *Political Science Quarterly* (Spring 1976), pp. 1–18.

15. See Jane Carroll, "Florida Reins in Runaway Growth," *State Legislatures* (November/December 1985), pp. 21–23.

16. Quoted in Jane Gross, "Seattle Decides to Limit Construction" *The New York Times* (May 18, 1989), p. A10.

17. See Alan Altshuler, *The City Planning Process* (Cornell University Press, 1965); David R. Morgan, *Managing Urban America*, 2d ed. (Duxbury Press, 1983); and Michael Uasu, *Politics and Planning* (University of North Carolina Press, 1979).

18. See Albritton, "Subsidies: Welfare and Transportation."

19. See Glenn Yago, *The Decline in Transit* (Cambridge University Press, 1983); Comptroller General of the U.S., *Why Urban System Funds Are Seldom Used for Mass Transit* (U.S. Government Printing Office, 1977); and Victoria Irwin, "Urban Mass Transit Faces Declining Federal Funds," *Christian Science Monitor* (April 2, 1986), p. 6.

20. Neal Peirce, "Toronto's Transit System Works," *Philadelphia Inquirer* (January 25, 1982), editorial page opinion column.

21. Bruce A. Williams, "Bounding Behavior: Economic Regulation in the American States," in Gray, Jacob, and Vines, eds., *Politics in the American States*, p. 370.

22. Nancy M. Davis, "Politics and the Public Utilities Commissioner," *State Legislatures* (May 1985), p. 20. See also William T. Gormley, Jr., "Policy, Politics, and Public Utility Regulation," *American Journal of Political Science* (February 1983), pp. 86–105.

23. See, for examples, David Klingman and William W. Lammers, "The 'General Policy Liberalism' Factor in American State Politics," *American Journal of Political Science* (August 1984), pp. 598–610; Thomas R. Dye and Virginia Gray, *The Determinants of Public Policy* (D. C. Heath, 1980); and John C. Kincaid, *Political Culture, Public Policy and the American States* (Institute for the Study of Human Issues, 1982).

24. M. Kent Jennings and Harmon Zeigler, "The Salience of American State Politics," *American Political Science Review* (June 1970), p. 535.

25. Herbert Jacob, "Public Policy in the American States," in Gray, Jacob, and Vines, eds., *Politics in the American States*, pp. 282–83. See also David Osborne, *Laboratories of Democracy: A New Breed of Governor Creates Models for National Growth* (Harvard Business School Press, 1988).

10

Staffing and Financing State and Local Governments

A few years ago, the only police car on the streets of Mansfield, Ohio, for several days was driven by Richard A. Porter. With a badge in his pocket and a deputized assistant at his side, Porter, who was also the city's mayor, filled in for a police force that was on strike. The town's eighty-five police officers believed they deserved a substantial wage increase. "It was the type of face-off that has become exasperatingly familiar in American cities, where public employees are striving to better their lot while municipal governments are striving to solve expanding problems with declining revenues."[1]

Government is very much a matter of people and money. People must be elected and hired, salaries must be negotiated and paid, and materials must be purchased. About 13.5 million people work in state and local governments in the United States. The cost and quality of government depend partly on the ability of these people, and their ability in turn depends on how well they are paid and an adequate public funding. The success of our public office holders also depends on their ability to recruit, motivate, and reward able career public servants. In a sense, personnel power is perhaps the greatest resource of those who govern.

Where Do the People Come From?

When we talk about the state, the city, or the county, we are simply using shorthand symbols for groups of people. When we say the government builds the roads or runs the schools, we really mean that a group of public officials or public employees performs these functions. In a sense, the people who work for our state and local governments *are* the state and local governments. How are these people chosen?

A few of them are elected. The rest are generally appointed through some kind of merit system in which selection or promotion depends on demonstrated performance (or merit) rather than on political patronage. The patronage system has not disappeared, and in many jurisdictions it still helps to know the right people and belong to the right party. But these practices are no longer so prevalent. Many jurisdictions now administer competency or "knowledge" tests to prospects and employees before hiring or promoting them. Moreover, the Supreme Court has declared it unconstitutional for most public employees to be dismissed for political reasons; affirmative action requirements call for recruitment through open procedures; and the effects of unionization are being felt as well.[2]

STATE AND LOCAL MERIT SYSTEMS

Almost all states now use merit systems to choose public servants. Merit systems are generally administered by a civil service commission, typically composed of three members appointed by the governor, with the consent of the senate, for six-year overlapping terms. The commission prepares and administers examinations, provides "eligible" registers for various jobs from which appointments may be made, establishes job classifications, and prepares salary schedules. It also serves as a board of appeal for persons who are discharged. Commissions are increasingly concerned with in-service training, collective bargaining, administering affirmative action programs, and filling top-level executive positions.

How well do the commissions do their job? Their many critics complain they are too slow and overly wrapped up in red tape and clumsy rules. Because eligible lists are not kept up-to-date, it also takes weeks to fill vacancies. But a more serious charge is that civil service commissions have deprived responsible officials of authority over subordinates. There is too much emphasis, it is argued, on insulating public servants from political coercion. As a result, employees enjoy so much job security that administrators cannot get rid of incompetents. It has been known to take months and several elaborate hearings to dismiss secretaries who could not type or librarians who could not read. Although merit systems reputedly emphasize ability and minimize political favoritism, they sometimes discourage people from seeking public-sector jobs.

PUBLIC-EMPLOYEE UNIONS

Public-worker unions have grown rapidly over the past generation; they have, in fact, become militant in demanding better wages, hours, working conditions, and pensions. They wield considerable political clout in most states and in many cities. Indeed, in places such as New York City they are viewed as one of the two or three most powerful forces in political life. State and local governments, thrust into the position of employer, have found themselves involved in collective bargaining and voluntary or binding arbitration processes.

More than half of all state and local public employees are organized. The American Federation of State, County, and Municipal Employees (AFSCME), which represents over 1.1 million members, has been the fastest-growing union in the country. Other public-employee unions are the International Association of Fire Fighters, which represents over 175,000 fire personnel, the National Education Association, which represents about 1.6 million teachers, and the American Federation of Teachers, which represents another 580,000 teachers. The firefighters union, often considered one of the most effective political organizations among the public-employee unions, sometimes engages in door-to-door and telephone campaigning to elect city officials. Unions raise funds for candidates and sponsor letter-writing campaigns to influence city officials. Union pressures in recent decades are a major reason the average pay of public employees has gone up about 25 percent faster than the wages of those in private industry. Today public employees in many areas of the country are reasonably well paid. According to some taxpayers, they are too well paid.

The failure of the civil service system to meet many of the needs of public employees encouraged the growth of public-sector unions. They were also spurred on by the success of unions and collective bargaining in the private sector. But much of the success of public-employee unions has come about because government workers learned how they could become a political force within cities and states. Most public employees are educated, intelligent people who can provide hard-pressed candidates with research, mailing help, and the always much-needed campaign contributions. The public-employee unions succeed in part because they can deliver two of the most valuable components of campaigns—money and labor (not to mention the votes of their members, members' families, and friends).

With success, however, has come a growing backlash in the form of public criticism. Surveys show the general public thinks public workers not only have more job security, but that they also have as good or better wages and fringe benefits than those working in the private sector. On the one hand, public employees retain civil service job protection. On the other, they have gained most of the bargaining power of a labor union. In addition, in some cities they are so well organized as special-interest groups that they can also help elect the very officials who must bargain with them. Even though collective bargaining and unionization have long been accepted in the private sector, these rights are not so widely accepted in the public sector. One reason for this is that the government generally operates as a monopoly with respect to the services it provides:

> There are still distinctions to be drawn between the private and public sectors in terms of the effects of labor problems. The public can afford to stand more or less aloof from even major private industrial labor disputes. If a widget plant is on strike or if the cost of a settlement pushes widget

prices too high, the consumer can generally get his supply elsewhere or substitute another product. Competition from marketplace alternatives pressures both labor and management to be reasonable.[3]

Because the public sector provides services everyone needs, demand is "inelastic"; it remains relatively constant. So when public-employee unions organize as an effective political force, they can influence crucial decisions that affect levels of taxation and the allocation of revenue. Some believe this may lead to unfair influence that results in a redistribution of income, with the beneficiaries being those who belong to public-employee unions. The awareness of this distortion effect and the rising clout of the unions have stiffened the spines of some city and state officials. It is not uncommon today for mayors in New York, Atlanta, and New Orleans to fight the unions and win support from taxpayer and business groups who think the unions have overstepped proper bounds.

ARE PEOPLE ON THE PUBLIC PAYROLL ENTITLED TO STRIKE?

Deeply embedded in our civic ethic is the idea that civil servants, especially those like police and firefighters on whom the public depends for vital services, should not strike. Many state and local elected officials, and certainly many ordinary citizens believe it is wrong and dangerous for police, firefighters, and hospital workers to strike. In 1919, Massachusetts Governor, Calvin Coolidge, became famous when he opposed the Boston police strike by saying: "There is no right to strike against the public safety by anybody, anywhere, anytime." And at the national level Ronald Reagan's firing of all air traffic controllers for engaging in an illegal strike was supported by the public.

Strikes by public unions are illegal in most states, yet even states permitting them prohibit strikes for those who provide "vital and essential services." But strikes do occur, and in most instances local and state officials become more concerned with getting people back to work than with sending them to jail for violating the law; amnesty to the strikers has usually been the rule. Union organizers refuse to consider their strikes as defying the law; instead, they accept the strike as a legitimate and useful weapon in a labor dispute. Still, the strike is generally viewed as a weapon of last resort, to be used only under intolerable conditions.

The strike, moreover, has political risks for the public-worker unions. Adverse public reaction sometimes sets in; in some cities, such as San Francisco and Seattle, public backlash in the wake of strikes strengthened the hand of the mayors, who won recall votes or referendums and were then able to force the unions to back down on their demands. Strikes in Chicago and in New York have also met with strong public and city hall resistance. Many union leaders now say they favor **compulsory arbitration,** and more than twenty states have enacted laws that permit some form of arbitration. These union leaders hope that through arbitration they will get something they might not get at a bargaining table without arousing the public backlash that usually comes with strikes. **Binding arbitration** is used in several states, mostly in the public-safety areas of police and fire protection. A neutral third party or mediating board hears the arguments of both sides and devises what it considers a fair settlement. The verdict is final.

An alternative to binding arbitration is *last-best-offer arbitration*. This requires an arbitrator to consider the final offers of both sides and to select one. The alleged advantage of this method is that it encourages realistic offers and voluntary settlement. Fearing that the other side's proposal may be chosen, both parties will make their offers more realistic. Although binding arbitration does not guarantee there will be no public-employee strikes, the number of such strikes has been reduced in states where it is practiced.

Settlements as a result of binding arbitration are often expensive. Each decision in a binding arbitration case has a ripple effect on the rest of a city or state administration. A pay raise to one group sets the standard for other public workers. In cities, for example, the police or firefighters are usually the pacesetters in the politics of winning higher pay. The director of labor-management relations for the U.S. Conference of Mayors complains that binding arbitration "is a lot like leading the mayor and the city council into a large closet, locking the door and turning the key over to a stranger who came to town to clear up a personnel problem in one department and wound up preparing a plan for fiscal chaos."[4]

PUBLIC-EMPLOYEE UNIONS: FUTURE DEVELOPMENTS

Here are some likely developments in the near future:

1. Public employees will continue to unionize. The teachers' associations, for example, have grown rapidly as teachers protected their jobs in the face of dwindling classroom enrollments.
2. Unions will continue to push for compulsory binding arbitration to settle disputes.
3. The debate over the right of public employees to strike will continue, yet it will probably not be resolved.
4. State and local officials will become more skilled in collective bargaining and arbitration.
5. State and local politicians will continue to court public-worker unions in campaigns, but they will appeal to the public for support in showdowns with the unions, especially when governments face severe financial troubles.
6. Public-worker unions will continue to play an important role in state and local politics above and beyond issues of pay and working conditions. They will influence who is elected, and they will certainly have a say on a whole range of public-policy issues, most especially on whether public services should be contracted out to private-sector enterprises.

PROVIDING PUBLIC SERVICES FOR A PROFIT?

In an effort to make government more efficient and perhaps also to curb the growing influence of public-employee unions, many communities have contracted out certain "public services" to those in the private sector who can provide the services at lower costs and still make a profit. Today, virtually every single city service is being contracted out somewhere in the United States, and this trend is expected to continue.

Gary Jensen's American Emergency Services is an example. This business employs nonunion workers to put out fires in Elk Grove Township, Illinois, and has been turning a profit. The township would have to spend about $200,000 more than it pays Jensen if it ran its own fire department. Jensen's principal saving comes from his lower labor costs. Although similar efforts are being tried in cities and states across the country, the idea of the **privatization** of fire and ambulance services, and even of the operation of city and state prisons, is relatively new. Bay County Jail, in Panama City, Florida, one of the few privately operated jails in the country, is being watched carefully by other public officials.

As cities and states have become hard pressed for cash, efforts to encourage entrepreneurs to provide public services at a profit have increased. Delegation of emergency and police powers to profit-making corporations, however, raises questions of liability and guarantees of individual rights; it also raises fears that private contractors will hire transient help at less pay, which will undermine merit systems and public-employee morale.

Philosophical differences among city and state officials about privatization of various public services have been hotly debated. Advocates, including many of those who bid on contracts, some academics, some city managers, and city- and state-elected officials, say privatization keeps taxes down and increases public sector productivity. Opponents, including public-employee unions, other academics, and other city and state officials, contend privatization raises serious issues of accountability, quality, flexibility, and integrity. Public employee groups such as AFSCME say privatization:

> Masks hidden costs to government, including the expenses of contract preparation and monitoring contractor performances
>
> Emphasizes the profit motive, making contracted services neither cheaper than publicly provided services nor of comparable quality
>
> Locks public officials into inflexible contracts that prevent responses to unforeseen circumstances
>
> Increases opportunities for corruption
>
> Diminishes government accountability to citizens[5]

Fiscal stringencies during the 1980s forced public-employee unions to make sacrifices and cooperate with elected officials to improve efficiency or even to reduce work forces. During the recession of the early and mid-1980s, Michigan Governor James J. Blanchard sliced his state work force by 20 percent and put a freeze on hiring until that state's economy rebounded. Elected officials in Dayton, Ohio, convinced municipal unions to approve a work-force attrition that included moving from four-person to one-person trash-collection crews. However, Dayton's mayor pledged in return a policy of no layoffs and no large-scale contracting out.

Where Does the Money Come From?

State and local governments get most of their money from taxes. Yet, unlike the national government, they do not control the monetary machinery and often have to secure voter consent through referendums before they can levy taxes. Still, state and local leaders have generally done a prudent job in raising revenue. Our state and local revenue system is now more diversified than it once was; it relies less on property taxes, and more on state income taxes. Federal aid, which greatly increased in the 1960s and 1970s, declined about 25 percent in real dollars by the 1990s.[6]

The overlapping layers of government by which the American people regulate their lives complicate the tax picture. Tax policies often conflict. While the national government is reducing taxes to encourage spending, states may be raising them.[7] Indeed when the federal government cuts taxes and cuts federal grants to states and local units, state and local governments may have no choice but to raise taxes. This is precisely what happened. Congress reduced federal taxes. Because taxes have been reduced, federal aid is soon also reduced. Reduction in federal aid to states and local governments forced many states to raise taxes to get the funds that provide essential services. Taxpayers' federal taxes were slightly reduced, but their state and local taxes, and the costs for local services, went up.

Until recently each level of government paid little attention to the tax policies of the others. The number of taxing authorities also makes tax gathering an expensive operation. For example, national officials, state officials, and some local officials collect taxes on gasoline. Sometimes gasoline taxes are increased simultaneously by the national and many state governments, which not only confuses matters but has a greater impact than either level of government had anticipated.

Each government maintains its own tax-collecting organization. Taxpayers are allowed to deduct certain business expenses and state taxes from their federal but not from their state income tax. Thus, changes in state laws can affect the amount of federal tax a person must pay. If a state increases its taxes, for example, the national government receives less money.

No matter who collects the taxes, however, all the money comes out of a single national economy. Although each government has a different tax base and each tax hits particular groups, all taxes rest on the productivity of the American people. And that productivity is increased by many of the activities of government.

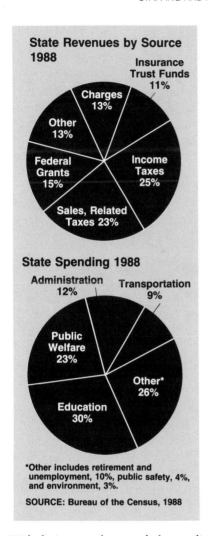

State Revenues by Source 1988

- Insurance Trust Funds 11%
- Charges 13%
- Other 13%
- Federal Grants 15%
- Income Taxes 25%
- Sales, Related Taxes 23%

State Spending 1988

- Administration 12%
- Transportation 9%
- Public Welfare 23%
- Other* 26%
- Education 30%

*Other includes retirement and unemployment, 10%, public safety, 4%, and environment, 3%.

SOURCE: Bureau of the Census, 1988

With their taxes the people buy police protection, parks and educational programs, highways, and other things they consider desirable.

WHO SHALL PAY THE TAXES?

A good tax might be defined as one somebody else has to pay; a bad tax, as one you have to pay. Who bears the cost of state and local services is decided in the United States by politics. The people of any state are free to extract whatever taxes they wish from whomever (in that state) they wish, subject only to the restrictions imposed by the federal Constitution.

The Constitution forbids states to tax exports or imports, or to levy tonnage duties without the consent of Congress; to use their taxing power to interfere with federal operations; to discriminate against interstate commerce or unduly burden it, or directly tax it, or to use their taxing power to deprive persons of equal protection of the law or to deprive them of their property without due process. Constitutional lawyers and judges spend much of their time applying these principles to concrete situations. Out of hundreds of disputes, courts have decided—among other things—that states may collect sales taxes from interstate sales and income taxes from persons and corporations within the states, even if the income was earned from interstate business, but states may not tax the privilege of engaging in interstate commerce or the unapportioned gross receipts from interstate transactions.

State constitutions also restrict state taxing power. Certain kinds of property are exempt from taxation; property used for educational, charitable, or religious purposes, for example. State constitutions frequently list the taxes that may be collected; those not mentioned are forbidden. They often also stipulate the amount of tax that may be collected from various sources.

The ability of people in a city, county, or other local unit to tax themselves is even more restricted. Their officials can collect only those taxes, in the amount, by the procedures, and for the purposes that the state constitution or state legislature authorizes. What kinds of taxes can they collect? Let's look more closely at the major types.

THE GENERAL PROPERTY TAX

Widely criticized as "one of the worst taxes known to the civilized world," the **general property tax** is still a chief revenue source for local governments. It used to be the major state tax, too, but in most states it is now of minor importance. The tax is difficult to administer, leads to favoritism and inequities, and takes little account of ability to pay.[8]

A hundred years ago wealth was primarily *real* property—land and buildings—that was relatively easy to value. Assessors could guess the value of the property a person owned, and this was a good test of his or her ability to help pay for government. Today wealth takes many forms. People own large amounts of *personal* property—both *tangible* (such as furniture, jewels, washing machines, rugs, and paintings) and *intangible* (such as stocks, bonds, and money in the bank). A person can concentrate a large amount of wealth, difficult to value and easy to conceal, in a small rented apartment. Real property has also changed. It no longer consists mainly of barns, houses, and land, but rather of large industrial plants, great retail stores, and office buildings, whose values are hard to measure. In addition, property ownership is less likely these days to correspond to ability to pay. An elderly couple with a large house valued at $200,000 may be living on social security payments and a small allowance provided by their children. They have to pay higher local taxes than a young, two-income couple who live in a rented apartment.

Although many communities stipulate that the general property tax be imposed on all property, this is not what actually happens. Over 20 percent of real property in cities is exempt. For example, about half of the actual property in Boston is tax-exempt, nearly 35 percent in New York City, and 25 percent in Baltimore. Intangible personal property is seldom taxed. Some communities place a lower rate on intangible property in order to induce owners to announce ownership. In addition, tangible personal property, such as watches, rings, and so on, often escapes taxation or is grossly undervalued. In most cities an unwritten understanding develops concerning the kind of property the honest taxpayer should list. The good citizen who attempts to follow the law exactly is kindly advised by the assessor that it is not necessary.

The general property tax is almost inflexible. During times of rising prices assessed values move up much more slowly than does the general price level. Thus, when governments need more money, the lagging tax bases fail to provide it. When prices fall, valuations do not drop at the same rate. When people cannot pay taxes, property is thrown on the market for tax delinquency. During the 1930s, for example, the general property tax only added to the miseries of many homeowners. In some areas property taxes are at such levels that to increase them may force businesses and middle-income families out. The general property tax rate is also difficult to compare from community to community. Property is assessed (assigned a precise value for tax purposes) by an assessor or board of assessors of the city or municipality in which the property is located. A property owner typically pays only one tax bite, yet the bite may include taxes earned for three, four, or more bodies, such as the city, county, or school board and special districts. The rate in one city may be only $10 per thousand; in another, $40 per thousand. But in the second city valuation may be computed at only a tenth of "real" value. Local politicians' claims that they have kept down the tax rate must be carefully scrutinized.

In recent years considerable controversy has been stirred up by heavy local reliance on the property tax to support public schools. As a result, the amount of money actually available to finance education varies tremendously from area to area; rich suburban areas with high property valuation per pupil are able to spend much more than poor areas, such as central cities, which need the most money. Reformers urge states to take over the financing of public education, or assume a greater share of the burden, in order to equalize differences from community to community. Although this is not a popular idea, most states do distribute funds to local districts and attempt to ensure more equitable expenditures.

Those hoping for greater state support for schools have often turned to the courts, alleging that reliance on the property tax results in a denial of equal protection and violates the Constitution. Several state courts have ruled that wide differences between school districts in per pupil expenditures are inconsistent with the equal protection clause of the Fourteenth Amendment. The California Supreme Court, for example, agreed (*Serrano* v. *Priest*, 1971); but the U.S. Supreme Court held (*San Antonio Independent School District* v. *Rodrigez*, 1973) there is no constitutional requirement that the amount spent per pupil in each district be the same.[9]

The Supreme Court's 1973 decision temporarily slowed the push toward intrastate equalization of school expenditures, but the controversy and the issues raised remain. Several other state courts have now handed down rulings similar to the *Serrano* ruling. New York and Wyoming, for example, have held that the state constitution requires the states to finance education in such a way as to avoid differences in funding because of the differences in wealth in local school districts.

The relationship between local property taxes and equitable public school financing will remain controversial, yet the steps already taken point in the direction of compromise solutions. And despite its weaknesses, the general property tax will remain an important source of revenue for local government. Supporters of the tax say it is a practical and suitable tax. After all, they say, real rather than personal property is the chief beneficiary of many local services, such as fire protection. Alternative taxes are few, and each has its own disadvantages. Moreover, some of the bad features of the general property tax can be and are being corrected by improving property tax assessing and administration methods.

One recent effort to reform the general property tax is the so-called circuit-breaker exemption (sometimes called a negative income tax) by which most states and certain cities give a form of tax relief to lower-income families and the elderly. A circuit breaker is a property tax credit, the value of which depends on a household's property tax bill and its income. The idea is to protect family income from property tax overload the same way an electrical circuit breaker protects a family home from an electrical current overload. "That is, when the property tax burden of an individual exceeds a predetermined percentage of personal income, the circuit breaker goes into effect to relieve the excess financial pressure."[10] The circuit-breaker property tax exemption seems to be most popular in the Great Lakes and Plains states. It is least popular in the Southeast where property tax burdens are low. Economists and tax authorities have debated the merits and problems created by this reform. Until a comprehensive negative income tax or some other income-maintenance plan is established to provide cash payments to the poor, circuit-breaker exemptions will probably be part of the tax structure in many states.

Then there is California's rather famous Proposition 13. As described by Chief Justice Rehnquist, this proposition is "grounded on the belief that taxes should be based on the original cost of property, and should not [be taxed on] unrealized paper gains in the value of the property." This means that anyone buying property in recent years must pay a much higher tax than those who have owned property of equal value that was purchased at an earlier date. Although specifically noting that it was not deciding whether a state constitutional amendment such as Proposition 13 is constitutional, the Supreme Court declared a similar provision adopted by a West Virginia county to be in conflict with the Equal Protection Clause (*Allegheny Pitt* v. *Webster County*, 102 L Ed 2d 688, 1989).

"It was just a sapling when we moved in."

Reprinted with permission from The Minneapolis Star and Tribune.

Even with improved tax administration, the general property tax is not supplying local units of government with the money they need to render the services their citizens want. Moreover, states have tended to leave the property tax to local units, and thus need other sources for their funds. What other taxes do states and cities collect?

OTHER TAXES

Sales Taxes Born during the Great Depression, the **sales tax** is now one of the most important sources of money for many states. Almost all states impose some kind of general sales tax, normally on retail sales. Local sales taxes were uncommon until after World War II, but now many larger communities also impose a general sales tax. City sales taxes are unpopular with local merchants, who fear they drive business away.

Sales taxes, especially those levied by the state, are usually easy to administer, and they produce large amounts of revenue. Despite their tendency to bear down hardest on lower-income groups, their popularity is increasing. Many consumers consider sales taxes relatively painless because they can thus avoid paying a large tax bill at one time. But labor groups and low-income consumers remain opposed to sales taxes; they favor wider use of the more progressive income tax instead. These groups argue that persons with small incomes spend larger percentages of their budgets for food and clothing than do the wealthy, so sales taxes fall heaviest on those least able to pay. Many states exempt food and drugs from the sales tax.

Several states tax various services as well as goods, but a broad-based tax on services recently backfired in Florida. A few months after approving this sales tax on services, a frustrated legislature bowed to vigorous opposition and repealed it, replacing it with a one-cent increase in the tax on goods. Television, radio, and advertising agencies led the opposition to this Florida service tax. "The media campaign against the tax took a variety of forms, including not merely editorials but also heavy TV and radio advertising against the tax. Some radio call-in shows devoted hours to discussion of the tax, mostly from a negative point of view and often distorting its nature with false information."[11] Floridians were led to believe, wrongly as it turns out, that they would have to pay this service tax on medical care and on barber and beauty shop bills. "Many retirees believed the tax would hurt them more than younger people, because older people hire workers to perform household chores younger people do themselves."[12] Retirees were told the tax on services would cost the average household about $75 less than the penny hike in the existing sales tax, but retirees didn't believe it. The repeal of this new tax in Florida has sent a signal of caution to other states who were hoping that Florida had discovered an expanding revenue source.

States and localities have long yearned for a way to collect tax revenues from yet another elusive source—the ever expanding mail-order catalog business. An estimated $3 billion in revenues may be lost to states and localities who are largely unable to put the arm on out-of-state mail order merchants.[13] As a result, Congress is being pressured to pass legislation forcing catalog merchants to collect sales taxes and return them to the appropriate states and communities. States plainly want this money. There is also a question of fairness, because local merchants have to collect sales taxes while competing against these huge mail order firms that do not collect them. Moreover, many of us are increasingly making catalog purchases and are likely to increase such purchasing in the future by phone, computers, and other high tech devices that save us from traditional shopping. The mail order merchants and their direct marketing association lobbyists claim it would be an administrative nightmare to collect and reimburse all the sales taxes and, rather lamely, they add they are not obligated to collect taxes for a state in which they do not have a presence. Sooner or later, however, the sales tax is likely to catch up with them. A few of the larger mail-order corporations are beginning to comply, either voluntarily or because courts have ordered them to do so.

Income Taxes This has been the fastest growing major revenue source for most states (it trails behind only the general sales tax). All but a handful of states impose a tax on personal income, and income tax revenue is higher than general sales tax revenue in nearly twenty states. Income taxes are generally **progressive** or graduated; that is, the rate goes up with the size of the income. State income tax rates, however, do not rise as sharply as the federal tax and seldom go over 10 percent. In some states exemptions are generous. Corporation incomes are frequently taxed at a flat rate. Because of the importance and burden of the federal income tax, many citizens feel that states should exercise restraint in this area.

States generally do not allow local governments to levy income taxes. However, some cities—following the lead of Philadelphia and Toledo—now collect a payroll tax. Philadelphia imposes a relatively small flat tax on salaries of all persons and net profits of unincorporated businesses and professions. The Toledo tax applies also to corporate profits. The municipal income tax enables hard-pressed cities to collect money from "daytime" citizens who use city facilities but live in the suburbs. This tax is especially popular among cities in Ohio and Pennsylvania, but it is also being collected by New York City, Detroit, and Louisville.

Special Excise Taxes Almost all states tax gasoline, alcohol, and cigarettes. Because many cities also tax these items, the local, state, and federal levies often double the cost of these "luxury" items to the consumer. Taxes on such items are known as **excise taxes.** Gasoline taxes are sometimes combined with the funds collected from automobile and drivers' licenses and are earmarked for highway purposes. Liquor taxes often consist of licenses to manufacture or sell alcoholic beverages and levies on their sale or consumption; they are used for general government spending. Some states own their own liquor dispensaries, and the profits go to the state treasury. High taxation of liquor is justified on the grounds that it reduces the amount consumed, falls on an item that is not considered a necessity of life, and eases the task of law enforcement. Some states, like North Carolina, set aside some alcohol taxes for mental health programs and the rehabilitation of alcoholics. If the tax is raised too high, however, liquor tends to be diverted into illegal channels, and tax revenues fall off. Minnesota has the highest excise tax on cigarettes—38 cents per pack. High tobacco taxes in states like New Jersey, Connecticut, and Maine, compared with low tobacco taxes in states like the Carolinas, have led to interstate smuggling up and down the East Coast.

Severance Taxes In several states the **severance tax** has been a key source of revenue. The severance tax is a tax on the privilege of "severing" such natural resources as coal, oil, timber, and gas from the land. In the early 1980s the severance tax accounted for more than 20 percent of tax collections in eight states: Alaska, Louisiana, Montana, New Mexico, North Dakota, Oklahoma, Texas, and Wyoming. Although more than thirty states rely on some type of severance tax, it is highly concentrated and most states cannot tap it. California is the only major oil-producing state that does not have a significant severance tax.

Most of the oil- and gas-producing states were hurt financially in the mid-1980s when oil prices dropped from $28 a barrel to less than half that. Texas, Oklahoma, and Louisiana, for example, which relied on severance and sales tax receipts, had to cut spending on education, libraries, and human services. They also postponed various public-works projects until oil prices might rebound.

This list does not begin to exhaust the kinds of taxes collected by state and local governments. Admission taxes, stock transfer taxes, inheritance taxes, parimutuel taxes, corporate franchise taxes, license fees, and other levies are common.

NONTAX REVENUES

In addition to taxation, states derive some revenue from fees and special service charges. In fact, at least 10 percent of the money collected by state and local governments comes from these sources. Fees are charged for inspecting buildings, recording titles, operating courts, licensing professions, disposing of garbage, and other special services. Parking meters have become an important revenue source for some cities. Municipal governments frequently operate water-supply and local transit systems. City-operated liquor stores are administered by, and turn a profit in, certain cities in Alaska, Minnesota, North Carolina, and South Dakota. Some states and cities run other business enterprises from which they make money (and sometimes lose it, too). North Dakota, for example, operates a state-owned bank. Municipally owned gas and light companies often contribute to city treasuries. In some cases utility profits are large enough to make other city taxes unnecessary.

About thirty states and the District of Columbia operate **lotteries** to generate more revenue without raising taxes. Lotteries are not entirely new: The Continental Congress ran a lottery to help finance the Revolutionary War. Indeed, all thirteen colonies used lotteries as a form of voluntary taxation in the 1780s. Lotteries were also employed to help establish some of the nation's earliest colleges, notably Princeton, Harvard, and Yale. In 1964, New Hampshire was the first state to revive the practice, in order to help balance its budget.

Most politicians like lotteries because they raise revenue without raising taxes. Yet because they take money from many people and return it to only a few, many economists say lotteries are a form of tax and an inequitable one at that. Further, critics contend that through lotteries the government makes poor people poorer. "You're seven times more likely to be killed by lightning than to win a million in the state lottery."[14] The lottery operations are also criticized as inefficient revenue producers; prizes and administrative costs sometimes take up to 60 percent of the money collected.

Americans now spend well over $12 billion each year buying lottery tickets from state governments. This is plainly a welcome revenue source now that federal aid has been sharply reduced. States use lottery funds for various purposes. Massachusetts sends its lottery money back to local governments; California sends most of its lottery windfall to local school boards for educational purposes; Pennsylvania gives it to programs for the elderly; Colorado uses the bulk of it for capital construction projects. Other states also allocate these monies to education, and the rest (for example, Oregon and Iowa) channel it into their general funds to be used for any purpose. The lottery may be an oversold and misguided innovation in state taxation, yet it is spreading to more states as elected officials transform everyone's dream of a pot of gold into much needed cold cash for their states.

Opposition to the lottery often comes from church groups who contend that state lotteries are immoral because they are a form of legalized stealing. Proponents counter that churches themselves often raise funds through raffles, bingo, and other games of chance. Opponents say lotteries are a bad investment because they yield a poor rate of return; proponents respond that tickets are purchased more for their entertainment value than as an investment. "When all is said and done," and everyone has had a say in this debate, "there are two inescapable facts about state lotteries: (1) they are capable of generating significant amounts of absolute revenue which can be used for public purposes, and (2) they are attractive to a willing public which is ready to play."[15]

USER FEES OR CHARGES

State and local collection of **user charges**—charges or fees paid directly by individuals who use certain public services—has grown rapidly in recent years. We are all familiar with certain applications of user fees: Those who pay tolls on the Massachusetts Turnpike or on the San Francisco Golden Gate Bridge are paying user fees. Not every suggestion for expanding such fees meets with success, however. Consider, for example, the city or town that provides public tennis courts. Because only tennis players actually use this service, supporters of user fees say, why shouldn't the tennis players pay for it? Perhaps they should deposit 50 cents into a box (at which time the tennis net might go up for play) in order to play for two hours. That way, people would pay for what they receive, and those who do not play tennis are not taxed for this particular local service.

It is not always easy to distinguish between individual and community benefits. Public schools obviously benefit the individual families who use them more than the families who do not. Yet education is generally thought to yield such considerable benefits to the community at large that taxes rather than user fees are used to support it. Similarly, we wouldn't want to pay for a fire department just by charging people whose homes or businesses experienced fires in a given year. Objections are also raised to user fees when they are a means of depriving persons of limited means of a service.

GRANTS

Grants from one level of government to another have become increasingly important during the last several decades. As we have noted, the national government has, until recently, allocated large sums to the states and cities through grants-in-aid. States gave over $140 billion to local government in 1989 alone. In the latter case, state officials return to local governments revenues collected from certain taxes, often without specifying the purposes for which the money should be used.

When all the taxes and fees are added together, state and local governments collect large sums. But often these funds are still not enough to pay for garbage collection, or to provide public assistance to the elderly, or to finance the other functions that voters demand. Thus governments often have to borrow money.

Borrowing Money

During the early years of the nineteenth century, states and cities often subsidized railroad and canal builders. The money for this, as well as for financing other public improvements, came from bonds issued by the cities or states and purchased by investors. Bribery and favoritism were common. Provision for payment of debts was inadequate; at times the citizenry were burdened with old debts long after the improvements had lost their value. As a result, default on obligations was frequent, and the city and state credit fell.

Aroused by the legislatures' abuse of their powers, voters insisted on constitutional amendments reducing legislative discretion to borrow money. Over the years state constitutions put elaborate restrictions on the power of state and local legislatures to borrow money or pledge credit. More recently the National Tax Reform Act of 1986 also added restrictions on the ability of states and localities to issue tax-exempt debt. The power to borrow money for a long term has been transferred from the legislatures and city councils to the voters as yet an added check on borrowing.

Fiscal planning to ensure that taxes are collected in time to cover necessary operating expenses has reduced the amount of short-term borrowing. Even so, officials sometimes need to borrow money for a short time. This **floating debt,** which consists of bank loans, tax-anticipation warrants, and other notes, is paid out of current revenues.

States and cities sometimes need to borrow money for longer periods— fifteen or twenty years. The cost of building schools and roads and clearing slums is so large that it is not feasible to pay for them out of current revenue. Moreover, these improvements have long lives and add to the wealth of the community, so it is reasonable to pay for them by spreading the cost. For this purpose governments issue bonds.

Government bonds are the equivalent of loans from private individuals to governments. Private individuals purchase government bonds at a fixed price. After a period of time the bond "matures," and the government that issued it pays back to purchasers the price they initially paid. Before the bonds mature, bondholders collect a usually predetermined rate of interest. The best practice, now required by many state constitutions, is to issue serial bonds, a portion of which come due each year and are retired out of current annual revenues. A bond is retired when the government that issued it buys it back.

State and local bonds are attractive to well-to-do investors because the interest is exempt from federal income tax. For this reason, these governments can borrow money at a lower interest rate than can private businesses. Although credit ratings do differ sharply according to jurisdiction and economic health, the credit of most cities and states is good, so they can easily find buyers for their bonds. *General obligation bonds* are backed by the credit of the issuing governments.

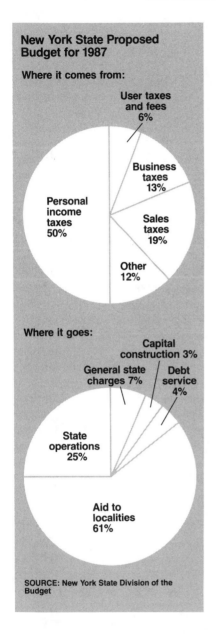

New York State Proposed Budget for 1987

Where it comes from:

- User taxes and fees 6%
- Business taxes 13%
- Personal income taxes 50%
- Sales taxes 19%
- Other 12%

Where it goes:

- Capital construction 3%
- General state charges 7%
- Debt service 4%
- State operations 25%
- Aid to localities 61%

SOURCE: New York State Division of the Budget

Revenue bonds are backed only by the income from the particular project in which the money is invested. Because governments are often permitted to issue revenue bonds beyond the limitations on their general indebtedness, they use them whenever possible.

TABLE 10–1
State Reliance on Tax Revenue Sources, 1985

	GENERAL SALES TAX	SELECTIVE SALES, EXCISE, AND LICENSE TAXES	INDIVIDUAL INCOME	CORPORATE INCOME
Alabama	28%	35%	24%	7%
Alaska	—	9	—	11
Arizona	46	22	21	7
Arkansas	40	24	27	8
California	33	12	37	13
Colorado	33	20	40	4
Connecticut	44	29	8	14
Delaware	—	41	45	9
Florida	54	30	—	6
Georgia	34	18	38	9
Hawaii	50	13	31	4
Idaho	33	26	35	6
Illinois	34	27	28	8
Indiana	49	16	30	4
Iowa	33	22	36	7
Kansas	29	23	33	8
Kentucky	27	23	26	7
Louisiana	31	28	14	8
Maine	35	28	30	5
Maryland	25	24	41	6
Massachusetts	22	15	48	13
Michigan	29	16	35	16
Minnesota	26	22	43	7
Mississippi	52	23	14	6
Missouri	42	23	31	5
Montana	—	31	28	10
Nebraska	33	31	31	5
Nevada	49	48	—	—
New Hampshire	—	61	6	22
New Jersey	29	30	25	12
New Mexico	42	20	6	4
New York	20	17	50	9
North Carolina	22	26	40	9
North Dakota	27	26	11	12
Ohio	33	29	32	5
Oklahoma	21	26	24	4
Oregon	—	21	66	8
Pennsylvania	30	30	26	9
Rhode Island	32	25	31	8
South Carolina	37	23	31	7
South Dakota	52	39	—	5
Tennessee	58	29	2	9
Texas	37	43	—	—
Utah	42	18	32	4
Vermont	19	40	32	8
Virginia	21	26	44	6
Washington	58	22	—	—
West Virginia	43	23	27	5
Wisconsin	29	19	40	8
Wyoming	22	14	—	—

Source: Calculated from U.S. Bureau of the Census, *State Government Finance in 1985* (1986), p. 6.

THE TAXPAYER REVOLT AND ITS CONSEQUENCES

Following the successful passage of Proposition 13 in California (June 1978), a wave of taxpayer-revolt proposals swept the country, ultimately affecting the tax rates in forty-five states. Proposition 13, the California initiative petition spearheaded by Howard Jarvis, specifically dealt with a reduction in and future limitations on local property taxes in California. Proposition 13 itself was not a spending limit on government, but it had these main effects: (1) it rolled back property assessments to 1975–76 levels; (2) it limited property tax increases to 1 percent of the assessed value; (3) it imposed a 2 percent ceiling on increases in annual property tax assessments. If not exactly a spending limit in a formal sense, Proposition 13 had the effect of decreasing the resources available to the California government for running schools, providing services, and paying public employees. Its effects were not immediately drastic, yet its impact has unquestionably been felt in more recent years. California's revenues from property taxes fell by as much as 20 percent. Public parks are mowed less often, libraries are open fewer hours, school enrichment programs and summer sessions have been cut back, and streets are repaired less frequently.

Years later Californians both praise and criticize the effects of Proposition 13. Supporters say it forced cities to become more efficient and created a more favorable business climate in California. Supporters also claim it has saved the average California homeowner $1000 a year. Critics of Proposition 13 point to diminished services and deteriorating public works.

In the late 1970s and early 1980s states were generally responsive to "tax revolts" when taxpayers indicated they opposed waste in state governments and wanted more accountability and efficiency. Taxing and spending limits, sometimes adopted as amendments to state constitutions, became popular in the 1980s. About twenty states enacted some form of taxation or spending limitation, although these differed widely in intent and impact; a few states have since allowed them to lapse. Arizona, Colorado, Hawaii, New Jersey, Tennessee, and Texas were among the states that adopted statutory or constitutional limits on state expenditures. Proponents of spending limitations contend this is a good way to fight inflation, weed out needless public programs, and curb the alarming growth in the number of public employees. Returning money to individuals and businesses who can make better and more productive use of the funds helps stimulate the economy. Advocates point to the generally healthy economies in New Jersey, Massachusetts, and California for support of their claims. Critics counter that public spending and growth are not inherently bad. Government produces essential goods and services, and the problems we face are more complex than ever. Critics point out too that state spending is not really a major factor in inflation. What we need, they say, is responsible state legislators, not rigid restrictions on state officials. If people lack faith in state officials, they can express their lack of confidence by voting them out.

In response to taxpayer discontent, thirty-six states cut effective income tax

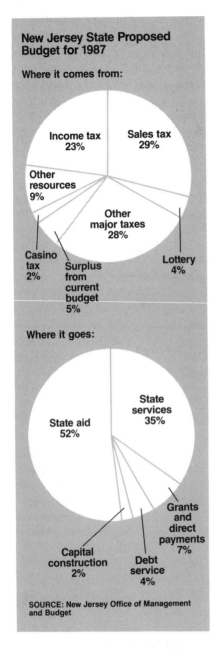

New Jersey State Proposed Budget for 1987

Where it comes from:

Income tax 23%

Sales tax 29%

Other resources 9%

Other major taxes 28%

Casino tax 2%

Surplus from current budget 5%

Lottery 4%

Where it goes:

State aid 52%

State services 35%

Capital construction 2%

Debt service 4%

Grants and direct payments 7%

SOURCE: New Jersey Office of Management and Budget

rates; twenty-two reduced state sales taxes; and several others introduced the indexing of income taxes so that "bracket creep" due to inflation would no longer generate automatic revenue increases. Still other states adopted legislation or constitutional provisions requiring referenda or extraordinary legislative majorities in order to pass new taxes or increase indebtedness.

In more recent years states and localities have had to raise taxes of one form or another for a variety of reasons. Such taxes are more often for maintaining existing services than for expanding state services, as in the "go-go" days before Proposition 13. Most states have raised or introduced new user fees; many have raised gasoline or fuel taxes; and others have raised sales, income, or related taxes to meet the fiscal stress of the 1990s.

Nonetheless, it would be wrong to conclude that the tax revolt is entirely dead. A whole generation of public officials became educated about the public's disillusionment with an overly activist government. Officials in Louisiana, Pennsylvania, and Wisconsin learned this lesson again in 1989 when "tax reform" packages were defeated by voters in all these states.

The impact of the tax revolt lingers on, and few officials in state and local government approve new taxes today without reluctance—and often trepidation. Nonetheless, taxpayers are occasionally willing to pay higher taxes, if they are persuaded they will receive improved services. But they need to be persuaded, and that is a continual challenge for elected officials.

RETRENCHMENT

The shift of jobs and economic power from the Northeast and upper Middlewest to the Sunbelt region, once thought to be permanent, appears to have been at least temporarily reversed. Oil- and gas-producing states in the South, Southwest, and Rocky Mountain states are going through the belt-tightening and reexamination of their taxing and spending processes that New York, Michigan, and Massachusetts did a decade earlier. Meanwhile, states such as Massachusetts and New Jersey enjoyed economic revivals, while states such as Louisiana and Oklahoma have fallen on hard economic times, either because of declining oil prices or farm recessions or both. Of course, there are variations even within these states. Newark, New Jersey, and New Bedford, Massachusetts, for example, are not enjoying the economic booms recently experienced by their neighboring suburbs.

Still, the most important development in recent years is that the federal government is pulling out of more and more federal assistance programs to states and localities. Every state must search for ways to make ends meet and also live within its revenue projections. Here are a few ways states are attempting to put their economic houses in order:

1. Several states have imposed freezes on any new state jobs. Some have even implemented public-employee layoffs to reduce expenditures.
2. States are searching for means to improve tax collection methods. They are using more sophisticated computer systems, and they are designing programs that deny state and local licenses and contracts to tax avoiders.
3. Several states have successfully held "tax amnesty" periods similar to local library-book amnesty weeks. A grace period is announced at which time tax avoiders can make their payments free of interest penalties. Immediately

after the amnesty period, prosecution and fines or penalties for unpaid taxes are stepped up and vigorously enforced.

4. Some states have adopted a controversial new form of taxing the profits of corporations: the **unitary tax.** A state's unitary tax takes into account a corporation's worldwide receipts and taxes the portion presumably earned in that state. But it is often difficult to determine how much was earned in a particular state. Whether they call it a unitary tax or not, most states employ a formula to determine the proportion of a company's profits that are taxable. Typically, a state "averages three factors: the percentage of total payroll in the state, the percentage of total property in the state, and the percentage of total sales in the state. This average is then multiplied by total profits to determine the amount of profits taxable in the state."[16] Corporations dislike this tax and several state legislatures have repealed it in the hope of inducing companies, including foreign investors, to relocate to their state. Meanwhile other states are using or considering adoption of this additional source of revenue.

Most states still rely on traditional sources of revenue as they try to balance their budgets. In addition to some reliance on the just-described strategies, states are likely to try slight increases in personal, corporate, sales, and excise taxes, and slightly greater reliance on lotteries. And, whenever the public resists such tax increases, we are likely to see further cutbacks in services. Indeed, we are likely to see cutbacks in services in any event. As every governor and state legislator learns, one of the grand paradoxes of government is that citizens simultaneously want improved and increased services *and* lowered taxes. The sharp federal cutbacks of the late 1980s, combined with depressed oil and farm prices, will force many states in the next few years to confront and weigh these stark economic and political realities more than at any time in the past generation.

New York City's Money Problems: A Case Study

In late 1975 New York City Mayor Abraham Beame admitted his city was on the verge of having to default on its financial obligations. New York had been running its budget in deficit for several years and had been making up the deficit by short-term borrowing. In addition, New York, like most other cities, was having to borrow money for its capital projects. When there was a danger that New York could no longer honor its financial obligations, its credit in the borrowing market dried up. No one wanted to invest in a city about to go bankrupt.

What caused the New York financial crisis? Most experts say New York's costly social services and welfare system and its public-employee salaries and benefits, the highest in the nation, were a major part of the problem. Moreover, one out of every eight people in New York was on welfare. As discussed in Chapter 8, New York City leaders make decisions through compromise and exten-

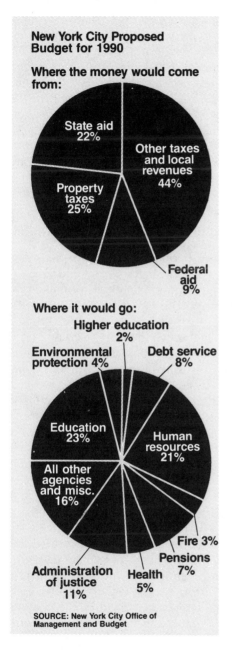

New York City Proposed Budget for 1990

Where the money would come from:

- State aid 22%
- Other taxes and local revenues 44%
- Property taxes 25%
- Federal aid 9%

Where it would go:

- Higher education 2%
- Environmental protection 4%
- Debt service 8%
- Education 23%
- Human resources 21%
- All other agencies and misc. 16%
- Fire 3%
- Pensions 7%
- Administration of justice 11%
- Health 5%

SOURCE: New York City Office of Management and Budget

sive bargaining. The mayor must nearly always form temporary coalitions in order to exert any influence on policy matters. Further, the mayor operates in a government that attempts to represent urban and suburban interests, the needs of the poor, the middle class, and corporate executives. Conflict is a way of life.

Many believe fragmented governmental structure led to the sharp escalation in the cost of running New York. They point to the growth of the political power of the city's municipal worker unions. In 1903 New York City employed 33,000 persons; by 1953 the number had risen to over 225,000. In the 1960s the number of city employees passed the 350,000 mark. By 1972 the number had peaked at approximately 400,000. As their power to force the city to yield to their demands grew with their numbers, the city's public-worker unions won major economic gains. The massive municipal unions gained their goals from a fragmented political structure that lacked the strength to fight the united employees. Through the late 1960s and into the 1970s, New York faced crippling strikes and work actions by teachers, sanitation workers, transit personnel, and others. Many claim the resulting settlements bankrupted the city and forced it into future obligations in the form of generous pension benefits.

Borrowing was the only way to make ends meet; New York began to borrow heavily to meet current operating expenses. The city sold short-term bonds characterized by high interest rates and short payback periods. When these notes came due, the city paid for them by issuing more bonds. The crisis surfaced in early 1975 when the big banks became unwilling to lend the hundreds of millions it took to run the city each month.[17] By June 30, 1975, New York City owed over $5.7 billion in short-term notes.

After some of the unions helped the city through the first of several bond-payment crises, New York Governor Hugh Carey devised a plan. New York state imposed a $200 million tax increase on the city. City officials agreed to require increased contributions to pension plans for city employees. Officials also pledged that they would continue to pare the city budget and would eliminate even more public jobs. (The mayor had already ordered a 22 percent cut in the city workforce.) The state levied added taxes on the estates of city residents, with proceeds to revert to the city. Union officials agreed to purchase $2.5 billion in city securities. They also agreed to defer payment of $1.2 billion soon to come due. Several banks agreed to hold on to $1.6 billion of soon-to-mature notes and accept reduced interest payments. In addition, investors in city bonds were asked to swap $1.6 billion of maturing notes for ten-year Municipal Assistance Corporation bonds.

In response to these pledges and the city's commitment to an austerity program that would help it achieve a balanced budget within three years, the federal government agreed to provide short-term loans of up to $2.3 billion annually for three years. More precisely, the national government would lend up to $2.3 billion a year to New York state to permit it to meet the city's short-term cash needs through mid-1978. These loans would have to be repaid by the close of each fiscal year and at an interest rate that would actually make the U.S. Treasury a small profit.

Did this plan work? Yes. With massive aid from New York state and the federal government, and with valiant efforts by city officials, New York avoided financial collapse. The city even boasted a balanced budget by 1981. But it was a hard time for New York City. Services were reduced, and streets and sidewalks were noticeably messier. Municipal unions had to settle for wage increases that lagged noticeably behind the pace of inflation. Mayor Edward Koch, elected in 1977 and reelected in 1981 and again in 1985, was a factor in the city's recovery. He made fewer promises to city employees and stressed instead the theme of sacrifice.

Events in New York and around the nation suggest these trends: taxpayers will continue to favor tax reductions yet also oppose any drastic reduction in services; federal aid to states and localities will continue to decrease during the next few years; states will increase state personal income and sales taxes, and both state and local governments will turn increasingly to selective user charges and fees.

Summary

1. State and local governments have been the fastest-growing part of government for the past twenty-five years. But the tax burdens on the middle-income family, although also increased, are not much greater in relative terms than they were twenty-five years ago, even though state and local governments provide more services than before.

2. One of the most controversial aspects of state and local government in recent years has been the unionization of over 50 percent of public employees at the state and local levels. Unions have been increasingly successful in recruiting new members and helping to bargain for better wages, hours, working conditions, and pensions. The success of the unions has caused some public backlash.

3. Many of the older industrial cities still have serious problems. Yet state and local governments have made considerable progress in the past several years. Several states and communities have modernized their constitutions or charters, upgraded their personnel systems, professionalized their legislative processes, reorganized and strengthened their executives, passed ethics codes, instituted improved budgeting procedures, and invested in urban redevelopment or what might be called "city recovery." A new psychology of hope is breeding fresh investment and confidence in most of our cities and states.

Further Reading

Advisory Commission on Intergovernmental Relations. *Significant Features of Fiscal Federalism*, 1989 Edition (U.S. Govt. Printing Office 1989).

TERRY N. CLARK and LORNA C. FERGUSON. *City Money: Political Processes, Fiscal Strain and Retrenchment* (Columbia University Press, 1983).

CHARLES T. GOODSELL. *The Case for Bureaucracy*, 2d ed. (Chatham House, 1985).

CHARLES H. LEVINE, ed. *Managing Fiscal Stress: The Crisis in the Public Sector* (Chatham House, 1980).

MICHAEL LIPSKY. *Street-Level Bureaucracy* (Russell Sage, 1980).

JAMES A. MAXWELL and J. RICHARD ARONSON. *Financing State and Local Governments*, 4th ed. (Brookings Institution, 1986).

RICHARD A. MUSGRAVE and PEGGY B. MUSGRAVE. *Public Finance in Theory and Practice*, 4th ed. (McGraw-Hill, 1984).

National Conference on State Legislatures. *Legislative Budget Procedures in the 50 States* (NCSL, 1988).

MICHAEL PAGANO and RICHARD MOORE. *Cities and Fiscal Choices* (Duke University Press, 1985).

PAUL E. PETERSON, ed. *The New Urban Reality* (Brookings Institution, 1985).

E. S. SAVAS. *Privatizing the Public Sector*, 2d ed. (Chatham House, 1987).

ALBERTA M. SBRAGIA. *Municipal Money Chase: The Politics of Local Government Finance* (Westview Press, 1983).

RICHARD SCHICK and JEAN C. COUTURIER. *The Public Interest in Government Labor Relations* (Ballinger, 1977).

DAVID O. SEARS and JACK CITRIN. *Tax Revolt: Something for Nothing in California* (Harvard University Press, 1982).

MARTIN SHEFTER. *Political Crisis/Fiscal Crisis: The Collapse and Revival of New York City* (Basic Books, 1985).

GROVER STERLING. *Managing the Public Sector*, 3d ed. (Dorsey Press, 1986).

Also, the U.S. Bureau of the Census regularly publishes reports on state and municipal finances.

N otes

1. Roger M. Williams, "The Clamor over Municipal Unions," *Saturday Review* (March 5, 1977), p. 12.

2. *Elrod* v. *Burns*, 427 U.S. 347 (1976).

3. James Ring Adams, "The New Labor Monopoly," *The New Republic* (May 10, 1980), p. 20. See also Kenneth M. Jennings et al., *Labor Relations in a Public Service Industry: Unions, Management and the Public Interest in Mass Transit* (Praeger, 1978).

4. "Compulsory Binding Arbitration," *State Legislatures* (April–May 1977), p. 15. For additional views see Nolan J. Argly, "The Impact of Collective Bargaining on Public School Governance," *Public Policy* (Winter 1980), pp. 115–41; and Robert E. Campbell, "Collective Bargaining: One Experience," *Public Management* (March 1980), pp. 9–11.

5. Thomas B. Darr, "Pondering Privatization May Be Good for Your Government," *Governing* (November, 1987) p. 47. A provocative and controversial book advocating this option is E. S. Savas, *Privatizing the Public Sector*, 2d ed. (Chatham House, 1987).

6. Steven D. Gold and Mark Seklecki: "The Federal Budget: What's (Not) in It for the States?" *State Legislatures* (April 1986), pp. 18–20. See also Steven D. Gold, *The Unfinished Agenda for State Tax Reform* (National Conference of State Legislatures, 1988).

7. Norman Walzer and Glenn W. Fisher, *Cities, Suburbs and Property Taxes* (Oelgeschlager, Gunn and Hain, 1981). See also C. Lowell Harriss, ed., *The Property Tax and Local Finance* (Academy of Political Science, 1983).

8. For a brief history of the property tax, see Dennis Hale, "The Evolution of the Property Tax: A Study of the Relation between Public Finance and Political Theory," *Journal of Politics* (May 1985), pp. 382–404. See also Harriss, ed., *The Property Tax and Local Finance.*

9. 411 U.S. 1 (1973).

10. James A. Maxwell and J. Richard Aronson, *Financing State and Local Governments*, 3d ed. (Brookings Institution, 1977), p. 158. See also U.S. Advisory Commission on Intergovernmental Relations, *Property Tax Circuit-Breakers: Current Status and Policy Issues* (U.S. Government Printing Office, 1975); and Steven D. Gold, "Circuit Breakers and Other Relief Measures," in Harriss, ed., *The Property Tax and Local Finance.*

11. Steven D. Gold, "Florida's Sales Tax on Services," *State Legislatures* (January 1988), pp. 12–13.

12. Marilyn Marks, "Florida Ends Tax on Services, Raises Sales Tax," *Governing* (January 1988), p. 57.

13. Dick Kirschten, "Division in Mail-Order Tax

Collection," *National Journal* (May 13, 1989), p. 1195.

14. Curt Suplee, "Lotto Baloney," *Harper's* (July 1983), p. 15. See also Elder Witt, "States Place Their Bets on a Game of Diminishing Returns," *Governing* (November 1987), pp. 52–57.

15. Marcia L. Whicker et al., "Lotteries as a Source of Revenue for State Government," *Public Affairs Bulletin*, Bureau of Governmental Research and Service, University of South Carolina, no. 29 (July 1985).

16. Steven Gold, "Unitary Tax: Wave of the Future?" *State Legislatures* (January 1984), p. 14. See also Martin Tolchin, "With Lobbies in Full Cry, California Debates Repealing Multinational Tax," *The New York Times* (February 18, 1986), section B, p. 12.

17. For an account of why New York City's financial situation worsened, and of the role the big banks and bankers played in causing part of the problem and then alleviating it, see Jack Newfield and Paul DeBrul, *The Abuse of Power: The Permanent Government and the Fall of New York* (Viking, 1977). For a study that has fewer villains and places New York's financial crisis in a broader historical context, see Martin Shefter, *Political Crisis/Fiscal Crisis: The Collapse and Revival of New York City* (Basic Books, 1985).

Glossary
of Key Terms

Advisory Commission on Intergovernmental Relations A permanent national bipartisan board created by Congress in 1959 to monitor the operation of and to recommend improvements for the U.S. federal system. ACIR is composed of representatives from the executive and legislative branches of the federal, state, and local governments, as well as members from the general public.

Assigned counsel system. Arrangement whereby attorneys are provided for persons accused of crime who are unable to hire their own lawyers. The judge assigns a member of the bar to provide counsel to a particular defendant.

Baker v. Carr A 1962 Supreme Court ruling that legislative apportionment could be challenged and reviewed by federal courts.

Bicameral legislature Two-house legislature; form for forty-nine of the states, as well as for the U.S. Congress.

Block grant Broad grant of funds made by one level of government to another for specific program areas—for example, health programs or crime prevention.

Categorical formula grant Grant of funds made by one level of government to another, to be used for specified purposes and in specified ways.

Centralists Those who favor national rather than state or local action.

City-manager plan Same as council-manager plan. A city hires a professional manager to administer city departments and agencies. In most cities, the city manager reports directly to the city council.

Commission charter Form of city government in which a group of commissioners (usually five) serve as the city council and act as heads of departments in the municipal administration.

Comparable worth The idea that jobs should be paid at the same rate if they require comparable skills and contributions, even if market considerations make it possible to secure employees for one job at a lower rate than for another. The notion of comparable worth is advocated by those who believe jobs traditionally dominated by women—as nurses, secretaries, and elementary school teachers, for example—are held down in wage rates compared to equivalent type jobs traditionally dominated by men—as plumbers and janitors, for example—because of discrimination and role stereotyping.

Compulsory (and binding) arbitration   Process whereby a dispute between management and a union is settled by an impartial third party. When the law dictates that a stalemated labor dispute must be turned over to an outside arbitrator, the process is called *compulsory arbitration*. When union and management are required by law to accept the decision of the arbitrator, it is called *binding arbitration*.

Concurrent powers   Powers the Constitution gives to both the national and state governments.

Confederation   Government created when nation-states, by compact, create a new government and delegate certain powers to it. In contrast to a federation, a confederation does not have power to regulate the conduct of individuals directly.

Constitutional home rule   State constitutional authorization for local governmental units to conduct their own affairs.

Council-manager plan   Form of city government in which the city council hires a professional administrator to manage city affairs; also known as the city-manager plan.

Decentralists   Those who favor state or local action rather than national.

Direct primary   Election, open to all members of the party, in which voters choose the persons who will be the party's nominees in the general election.

Doctrine of dual federalism   View that national and state governments are equal sovereigns, each granted certain powers by the Constitution with the Supreme Court to serve as arbitrator in case of conflicts between them.

Excise tax   Consumer tax on a specific kind of merchandise, such as tobacco.

Express powers   Powers specifically granted to one of the branches of the national government by the Constitution.

Floating debt   Short-term government loans, in the form of bank notes or tax-anticipation warrants, that are paid out of current revenues.

Full faith and credit clause   Clause in the Constitution requiring each state to recognize the civil judgments rendered by the courts of the other states.

General property tax   Tax levied by local (and some state) governments on real or personal, tangible property—the major portion of which is on the estimated value of one's home and land.

Gerrymandering   Drawing an election district in such a way that one party or group has a distinct advantage. The strategy is to provide a close but safe margin in numerous districts while concentrating (and hence wasting) the opposition's vote in a few districts.

Great Society   President Lyndon Johnson's vision of this country in which federal money was granted to states and localities to improve housing, mass transportation, and education.

Habeas corpus   See *Writ of habeas corpus*.

Implied powers   Powers given to Congress, by the Constitution, that allow Congress to do whatever is necessary and proper in order to carry out one of the express powers or department such as the National Aeronautics and Space Administration.

Indiana ballot   See *Party column ballot*.

Information affidavit   Certification by a public prosecutor that there is evidence to justify bringing named individuals to trial.

Inherent powers   Those powers of the national government in the field of foreign affairs that the Supreme Court has declared do not depend upon constitutional grants but rather grow out of the very existence of the national government.

Initiative petition   Procedure whereby a certain number of voters may, by petition, propose a law and get it submitted to the people for a vote. Initiative may be direct (if the proposed law is voted on directly by the people) or indirect (if the proposal is submitted first to the legislature and then to the people, if the legislature rejects it).

Interstate compacts   Agreements among the states. The Constitution requires that most such agreements be approved by Congress.

Item veto   Authority of the executive (usually the governor of a state) to veto parts of a legislative bill without having to veto the entire bill. Presidents do not have the power of the item veto.

Joint committee   Committee composed of members of both houses of a legislature. Such committees are intended to speed up legislative action.

Legislative home rule   Power given by the legislature to local governments that eliminates the need for local governments to go back to the legislature for additional grants of power. However, state law still takes precedence over local ordinances, and powers given to the local governments by the legislature may be rescinded.

Lobby/lobbying   To conduct activities aimed at influencing public officials and the policies they enact. This is, of course, part of the citizen's right to petition the government.

Long ballot   Ballot that came into general use in the late 1820s. Based on the belief that voters should elect all, or nearly all, the people who governed them. It is criticized as being unwieldy and confusing because it contains too many offices and candidates.

Lottery   A form of voluntary taxation used by more than half of the states and the District of Columbia; it involves distributing prizes by lot or random chance to the buyers of winning tickets. State income from lotteries typically amounts to less than 3 or 4 percent of state revenue; lotteries do, however, generate income without raising taxes. They are also sometimes defended as means of reducing the amount of illegal gambling and of minimizing the influence of organized crime.

Massachusetts ballot   See *Office group ballot.*

Mayor-council charter   The oldest and most common form of city government, consisting of either a weak mayor and city council or a strong mayor and council.

McCulloch **v.** *Maryland* **(1819)**   Celebrated Supreme Court decision that established the doctrine of national supremacy and the principle that the implied powers of the national government are to be generously interpreted.

Missouri Plan   System for selecting judges that combines features of the appointive and elective methods. The governor makes an initial appointment from a list of persons—usually three—presented by a panel of lawyers and laypersons (the panel is usually appointed by the chief judge of the state court of last resort). After the judge has served for a year, the electorate is asked at the next general election whether or not the judge should be retained in office. If a majority vote yes, the judge serves the rest of the term. At the end of the term, if a judge wishes to serve again, his or her name is once again presented to the electorate.

National supremacy   Constitutional doctrine that whenever conflict occurs between the constitutionally authorized actions of the national government and those of a state or local government, the actions of the national government take priority.

Necessary and proper clause   Clause of the Constitution setting forth the implied powers of Congress. It states that Congress, in addition to its enumerated powers, has the power to make all laws necessary and proper for carrying out all powers vested by the Constitution in the national government.

New judicial federalism   The practice of some state courts of using the bill of rights in their state constitution to provide more protection for some rights than is provided by Supreme Court interpretation of the Bill of Rights in the Constitution.

Office group ballot   Method of voting in which all candidates are listed under the office for which they are running. Sometimes called the Massachusetts ballot or the office-block ballot.

Ombudsman   Office in Sweden and elsewhere that handles citizen complaints against the government.

Party column ballot   Method of voting in which all candidates are listed under their party designations, which makes it easy for the voters to cast votes for all the candidates of one party. Sometimes called the Indiana ballot.

Party convention   A meeting of party delegates to pass on matters of policy and in some cases to select party candidates for public office. Conventions are held on county, state, and national levels.

Party primary   Election for choosing party nominees that is open to members and supporters of the party making the nomination.

Plea bargaining   Negotiations between prosecutor and defendant aimed at getting the defendant to plead guilty in return for prosecutor's agreeing to reduce the seriousness of the crime for which the defendant will be convicted.

Pluralistic power structure   The notion that even though some people do have more influence than others, that influence is shared among many people and tends to be limited to particular issues and policy areas.

Political machine   Organized subgroup within a party, consisting of a political boss and supporting ward and precinct workers who get out the vote and perform a variety of "services" for local constituents between elections.

Populists   Adherents of a movement and political party of the 1880s and 1890s. Their geographical base was rural—in the Midwest, South, and Southwest especially. Waging "reformist" efforts against the banks, railroads, and other establishments, Populists raised issues that influenced the Progressive movement and the Democratic party after 1892.

Power elite   Term originally used by sociologist C. Wright Mills to describe the small group of people he believed rule the country because of their socioeconomic status.

Privatization   The contracting out to the "for profit" private sector "public services" that are typically provided by public organizations. Trash collection, ambulance, and fire protection services have been the most common privatizations of public services. The objectives are to obtain the public services at lower costs, and sometimes to shrink the public bureaucracy to encourage additional efficiencies.

Pro bono   Term used to refer to the work lawyers (or other professionals) do to serve the public good and for which they either receive no fees or decline fees.

Progressives   Adherents of a "good government" movement in the first two decades of this century that advocated measures that would open up the system and weaken party bosses. They favored nonpartisan elections, participatory primaries, and direct elections of senators. The Progressive party, especially active from 1912 through the mid-1920s, emerged as a visible part of the Progressive movement.

Progressive tax   A tax whereby upper-income citizens pay a higher proportion of their incomes in tax revenues than do lower-income citizens.

Project grant   Federal funds given for specified purposes and based on the merits of applications.

Public defender   Public officer whose job is to provide legal assistance to those persons accused of crimes who are unable to hire their own attorneys.

Reapportionment   Redrawing of legislative district lines to recognize the existing population distribution.

Recall   Election held to determine whether or not an official should be removed from office before the end of his or her term. A certain number of voters must petition to hold a recall election.

Recidivists   One who habitually relapses into crime.

Redistributive policy   Governmental policy that seeks to use tax revenues in such a way as to help those who have less. In effect, tax monies from the upper and middle classes are channeled into programs that assist lower income or truly needy people by redistributing some of society's wealth.

Reduction veto   The power of a governor in a few states to reduce a particular money-providing measure approved by the state legislature.

Referendum   Practice of submitting to popular vote measures passed by the legislature or proposed by initiative. Use of the referendum may be required or optional.

Republic   Form of government that derives its powers directly or indirectly from the people. Those chosen to govern are accountable, directly or indirectly, to those whom they govern. In contrast to a direct democracy, in which the people make rules directly, in a republic the people select representatives who make the rules.

Republican form of government   See *Republic.*

Revenue sharing   Program whereby federal funds are provided to state and local governments to be spent largely at the discretion of the receiving governments.

Severance tax   Tax on the privilege of "severing" natural resources such as coal, oil, and timber, charged to the companies doing the extracting or severing.

Social stratification   Sociological theory suggesting that the upper class, or the wealthy, wield extensive influence over the decisions and policies made by governments at all levels.

Standard Metropolitan Statistical Area (SMSA)   A central city—or twin cities—of at least 50,000 people, along with those surrounding counties that are economically and socially dependent on the city.

Strong mayor-council   Form of local government in which the public directly elects the mayor as well as the city council. However, the mayor appoints the department heads, with the approval of the council, and in effect serves as the chief executive officer for the city and its administration.

Suburbs   Residential areas or communities in the outlying regions around a city.

Sunset process   Legislative review process that calls for the termination of a program after a certain number of years, often six or seven, unless it is carefully examined, certified to be doing what it was intended to do, and repassed by the legislature. Many states have adopted this practice. The word comes from the expression that "the sun should set" on programs that have outlived their usefulness.

Ticket splitting   Practice of voting for candidates at the ballot box with little or no regard to their parties, with the result that one voter may vote for a Democrat for governor and a Republican for Congress, or vice versa.

Tort law   Law, primarily judge made, dealing with damages to compensate people for legal wrongs done to them.

Unicameral legislature   One-house legislature, Nebraska and almost all cities use this form.

Unitary system   Government with power concentrated by the constitution in the central government.

Unitary tax   A state tax on a company's worldwide profits, typically based on a formula that takes into account payroll, property, and sales in the state as well as some percentage of out-of-state or worldwide receipts and profits. It is a controversial tax that is heatedly debated around the country: Some states view it as a legitimate means to secure added revenue, whereas other states avoid or repeal it as a means of luring companies to relocate into their states.

User charges   Fees charged directly to individuals who use certain public services on the basis of service consumed. Sometimes called a user fee or user tax.

Weak mayor-council   Form of local government in which the mayor must share most of the executive powers of a city with other elected or appointed boards and commissions. The mayor in weak-mayor cities is often mainly a ceremonial leader.

Writ of habeas corpus   Court order requiring jailers to explain to a judge why they are holding a prisoner in custody.

Zoning   The use of city laws to classify land uses and assign land to certain uses—for example, residential, commercial, or industrial.

Index